TWO NATIONS

BLACK AND WHITE,
SEPARATE, HOSTILE, UNEQUAL

ANDREW HACKER

SCRIBNER

NEW YORK LONDON TORONTO SYDNEY

SCRIBNER
1230 Avenue of the Americas
New York, NY 10020

First Scribner trade paperback edition 2003

SCRIBNER and design are trademarks of Macmillan Library Reference USA, Inc.,
used under license by Simon & Schuster, the publisher of this work.

For information regarding special discounts for bulk purchases,
please contact Simon & Schuster Special Sales at 1-800-456-6798
or business@simonandschuster.com

Manufactured in the United States of America

5   7   9   10   8   6

Library of Congress Cataloging-in-Publication Data

Hacker, Andrew.
Two nations : black and white, separate hostile, unequal / Andrew Hacker.—
1st Scribner trade pbk. ed.
p. cm.
Includes bibliographical references (p.) and index.
1. United States—Race relations. 2. Racism—United States.
3. African Americans—Social conditions—1975– I. Title.
E185.615.H23 2003
305.8'00973—dc21
2003042565

ISBN 0-7432-3824-9

For My Students and Colleagues,
Cornell University and Queens College

CONTENTS

PREFACE

Every one of us could write a book about race. The text is already imprinted in our minds and reflects our moral character. Dividing people into races started as creating some convenient categories. However, those divisions have taken on lives of their own, dominating our culture and consciousness, coloring passions and opinions, contorting facts and fomenting fantasies.

So race is more than simply a subject to be studied or an issue for debate. Given these conditions, objectivity is hardly possible. Which brings us back to the book that each of us might write. The volume in your hand offers one author's understanding of the role and meaning of race in the contemporary United States. Its title borrows from Benjamin Disraeli's remarks on the rich and poor of his Victorian England, and applies them to the two major races in America today: "Two nations, between whom there is no intercourse and no sympathy; who are as ignorant of each other's habits, thoughts, and feelings, as if they were dwellers in different zones, or inhabitants of different planets."

The subtitle, "Separate, Hostile, Unequal," has several sources. First, there has been the continuing debate in our courts and conversations over whether racially separated facilities can ever be equivalent in status and social worth. Another issue is whether the separation springs from choice, or is imposed by one race upon the other. Hence the conclusion of the National Advisory Commission on Civil Disorders back in 1968: "Our nation is moving toward two societies, one black, one back white, separate and unequal." Yet these two nations, these two separate societies, have existed from the start. And, to be utterly frank, their relations have never been amiable. Alexis de Tocqueville noted this hostility a

century and a half ago. "The most formidable of all the ills that
threaten the future of the Union arises from the presence of a black
population upon its territory," he observed during his visit to the
United States. If he wrote these words during the days of slavery,
they describe our racial reality today. Indeed, he could have been
in our midst when he saw how "the danger of a conflict between
the white and the black inhabitants perpetually haunts the imagination of the Americans, like a painful dream." We can benefit by
returning to Tocqueville's analysis in the concluding chapter.

My early training was in philosophy, where I soon discovered that
we should not expect a consensus on social and moral issues. Not
the least reason is that we frequently disagree on what we feel are
the facts. While research can be useful, past a certain point we must
bring intuition and imagination to bear. On this premise, the first
part of this book will expand on some personal impressions concerning race in our time. These chapters will include observations
on how we define and divide people into races; on what it is like
to be black in the United States; and why white Americans react
as they do to people of African ancestry. So the reader should be
forewarned: this section will rely on subjective interpretations,
since statements about how we behave in the realm of race are seldom amenable to evidence, let alone conclusive proof.

At the same time, in treating these and other topics, I have tried
to provide enough plausibility to keep the conversation going.
While the reader will not be asked to agree at every stage, it may be
hoped that he or she may say, "You could have a point; I'm still
willing to listen." Some of what will be said may seem overly gen-
eralized or unwilling to admit of exceptions. Here, too, indulgence
is asked. Race is a tense terrain, where we often try to hide crucial
truths from ourselves. One way to bring these premises to the surface is by making them as vivid as possible.

Part II of *Two Nations* will focus more precisely on the role race
plays in such spheres as education and family life, as well as the

economy, politics, and crime. This section, too, reflects the author's outlook and interests. Much of my career has been spent as a social scientist, which carries a commitment to revealing how the world really works. One way to array information is in statistical form. While numbers in and of themselves cannot pronounce final truths, they can offer insights and illumination if they are collated with care.

It is revealing that so much information about ourselves is classified according to race. We publish separate black and white breakdowns on whether mothers breast-feed their babies and on persons who have been arrested for embezzlement. The census even has separate racial columns for people who bicycle to work. But it would be a mistake to view such tabulations as depersonalized data. On the contrary, they can tell a very human story. And, as will be seen, statistics often surprise us with unexpected findings.

Nor will Part II rely entirely on tables. It will also offer a broader analysis of conditions impinging upon race. Thus the rise in fatherless households may emerge not as just one race's problem but as having larger social causes. In the same way, what we call crime can be explained in terms of class as well as race. Or, by exploring forces that run deeper, we may come closer to realizing why so many men commit the crime of rape. Also, any discussion of unequal education should be conjoined with at least a few comments on what we want our offspring to learn and why we place so much emphasis on multiple-choice tests. These chapters will also seek to explain why some conditions related to race have changed over time, while others manage to persist, and still others have become more painful and pronounced. Given the breadth of these issues, the reader should not be surprised if more than a few impressions find their way into these analytical chapters.

One or two more remarks should suffice. No one could possibly tally all the books and articles that have been written about race in America. A host of scholars, journalists, and commentators have produced an impressive literature. Prominent among these are authors who have actually lived on the nation's racial frontiers. J. Anthony Lukas's *Common Ground* about Boston, Elijah Anderson's *Streetwise* on Philadelphia, as well as Chicago as depicted in Nicholas Lemann's *The Promised Land* and Alex Kotlowitz's *There Are No Children Here* have all added dimensions to our understanding that statistics can never satisfy. For this reason, each book on race should be seen as part of a collective enterprise. If each of us focuses on certain aspects and issues, and explains them in our own way, we are all dependent on what others have discovered and said.

So separate mention should be made of America's most notable book on race. It was a over half century ago, in 1944, that Gunnar Myrdal published his classic study, *An American Dilemma: The Negro Problem and Modern Democracy.* By every measure, it was a masterful enterprise and one that can never be rivaled. If few people read him today, many of Myrdal's insights remain relevant and applicable. For example, he stressed the idea that race in America is essentially a caste condition, so that for all basic purposes, black people never escape their birth. And as his title made clear, Myrdal's central theme was that the United States was and is beset by an apparent paradox: the nation's commitments to universal justice and equality are contradicted by the way it treats its principal minority race. Myrdal, an eminent Swedish scholar, took seriously Americans' declarations about justice and equality. Perhaps, as a good guest, he did not want to accuse his hosts of hypocrisy.

As it happens, the pages that follow will contain relatively few citations or references. This should not be taken as suggesting that what others have written lacks significance. Rather, it is that too many allusions to fellow authors can end up as a book devoted to other books. Real issues like employment and welfare can become deflected into a debate over Charles Murray's formulations versus those of William Julius Wilson. Or questions of education and culture may become a battle of competing quotations from Diane Ravitch and Molefi Kete Asante. While this can often be a fruitful approach, especially for academic audiences, it has not been the one chosen here. References, listing source materials, have been gathered in a separate section.

The book's title might seem to intimate that a full portrait of America can be rendered in black and white. Obviously this is not the case. While persons we classify as black or white still comprise America's major races, they currently account for a smaller share of the population than at any time in our history. Since we want a full perspective, Asians and Hispanics and other ethnic groups will obviously appear on these pages. Still, *Two Nations* will adhere to its title by giving central attention to black and white Americans, and the reasons for this emphasis will be made evident. In many respects, other groups find themselves sitting as spectators, while the two prominent players try to work out how or whether they can coexist with one another.

Two Nations will also seek to explain why so much behavior regarding race remains so obdurate and ingrained. Not the least of its conclusions will be that racial tensions serve too many important purposes to be easily ameliorated, let alone eliminated or replaced. The reader should also be advised not to expect this book to end on an optimistic note. Nor should he or she look for a closing chapter with proposals for reducing discrimination and ending prejudice. *Two Nations* is not that kind of book. I leave it to others to propose measures they feel can break down racial barriers and bring more amity and equity to the racial sphere.

Of course, there are things that should be done, and some may be within the realm of possibility. At the same time, there is scant evidence that the majority of white Americans are ready to invest in redistributive programs, let alone give of themselves in more exacting ways. As will be shown, not only is the taxpaying electorate overwhelmingly white, but it is also middle-class, middle-aged, and—increasingly—ensconced in insulated suburbs. In short, our time is not one receptive to racial remedies. One aim of this book will be to show why this is the case.

Given the tempo of our times, a book on race must be kept up-to-date. This is all the more necessary for the classroom, where *Two Nations* is frequently used, not least because it encourages debate and discussion. Hence this new edition, in which every chapter has been revised. In particular, new or expanded material has been added in the following areas.

- Affirmative action has moved from being a series of varied programs to a serious constitutional issue. By the end of 2002, courts in different parts of the country had made conflicting rulings. One set of opinions allowed colleges to consider race in making admission decisions if their aim was to have a more diverse student body. Other courts asserted that race cannot be a factor, since giving preference to one group discriminates against others. By the time this edition of *Two Nations* is in your hands, parties to the cases will have asked the Supreme Court to choose between these principles and positions.

- This book focuses on America's two major races. This in turn calls for comments when behavior can be said to have racial associations. Where white Americans are concerned, recent years have seen some new developments that cast light on being white. One is that white parents are showing less of the commitment to family life on which they once prided themselves. Another is that white students—and most notably young men— no longer rank at the top in grades and scores and admission to selective colleges.

- The chapter on employment now has a balance sheet showing the records of corporations in choosing black candidates as their CEOs. Several firms have made such breakthroughs; so it remains to ask how many others will receive similar promotions. In the chapter on crime, the question is raised whether race plays a role, since the last few years have seen growing groups of white executives charged with illegally using their powers.

- The year 2001 found a Republican in the White House. While George W. Bush did not achieve a popular plurality nation-wide, he won the support of 55 percent of white voters, and he viewed them as his core constituency. Yet he has placed more black officials in visible positions than his party ordinarily does. This raises the question of whether the Republicans want to remake themselves into a racially integrated party.

- Back in 1960, individuals who had identities other than black or white constituted less than one percent of the population. By 2000, members of those groups had grown to 18.6 percent of the national total. In fact, persons of Hispanic origin now outnum-ber black Americans, and there has been a substantial rise in Asian-Americans. So it may be wondered if it is still valid to depict the United States as "two nations." The response, which will be elaborated in the opening chapter, is that race remains the country's principal division, and this is likely to continue in the coming century, even if not all Americans are included in that bifurcation.

ANDREW HACKER
January 2003

PART I

CHAPTER ONE

DIVIDING
AMERICAN SOCIETY

RACE HAS BEEN an American obsession since the first Europeans sighted "savages" on these shores. In time, those original inhabitants would be subdued or slaughtered and finally sequestered out of view. But race in America took on a deeper and more disturbing meaning with the importation of Africans as slaves. Bondage would later be condemned as an awful injustice and the nation's shame, even as we have come to acknowledge the stamina and skill it took to survive in a system where humans could be bought and sold and punished like animals. Nor are these antecedents buried away in the past. That Americans of African origin once wore the chains of chattels remains alive in the memory of both races and continues to separate them.

Black Americans are Americans, yet they still subsist as aliens in the only land they know. Other groups may remain outside the mainstream—some religious sects, for example—but they do so voluntarily. In contrast, blacks must endure a segregation that is far from freely chosen. So America may be seen as two separate nations. Of course, there are places where the races mingle. Yet in most significant respects, the separation is pervasive and pene-

3

trating. As a social and human division, it surpasses all others—
even gender—in intensity and subordination.

If white Americans regard the United States as their nation, they
also see it beset with racial problems they feel are not of their making. Some contrast current conditions with earlier times, when
blacks appeared more willing to accept a subordinate status. Most
whites will protest that they bear neither responsibility nor blame
for the conditions black Americans face. Neither they nor their
forebears ever owned slaves, nor can they see themselves as having
held anyone back or down. Most white Americans believe that for
at least the last generation, blacks have been given more than a fair
chance and at least equal opportunity, if not outright advantages.
Moreover, few white Americans feel obliged to ponder how membership in the major race gives them powers and privileges.

America is inherently a "white" country: in character, in structure, in culture. Needless to say, black Americans create lives of
their own. Yet, as a people, they face boundaries and constrictions
set by the white majority. America's version of apartheid, while
lacking overt legal sanction, comes closest to the system even now
overturned in the land of its invention.

That racial tensions cast a pall upon this country can hardly be
denied. People now vent feelings of hostility and anger that in the
past they repressed. Race has become a national staple for private
conversation and public controversy. So it becomes necessary to
ask what in recent decades has brought the issue and reality of
race to the center of the stage.

THE INVENTION OF RACE

The idea of "race" is a human creation. People have given names
to their varied strains since physical differences first began to
appear. Nor are there signs that racial lines have grown dimmer in
modern times. On the contrary, race continues to preoccupy the
public mind, a reminder of a past that cannot be willed away.

Since race is part of common parlance, people have used the term in many ways. Little will be gained by asking for clear-cut definitions or, for that matter, by trying to decide exactly how many different races occupy this planet. Anthropologists have their lists, but even they disagree on criteria and classifications. Still, some major groupings recur: Negroid, Mongoloid, Australoid, Caucasoid, and Indic, with American Indians and Pacific Islanders added as two encompassing categories. But there are also finer racial divisions, such as Aryans and Semites and Dravidians. Tribes like the Watusi and the Navajo have also been given racial designations. Indeed, since there is no consensus when it comes to defining "race," the term has been applied to a diversity of groups. The Irish have been called a race in their own right, as have Jews and Hindus. Many find these ambiguities unsettling, but then so is much of life. In the United States, what people mean by "race" is usually straightforward and clear, given the principal division into black and white. Yet, as it happens, not all Americans fit into "racial" designations.

In theory, Native Americans taken together belong to what most anthropologists would call a basic race. Yet, on the whole, they tend to be a loose residue of tribes rather than a racial entity. A single primal consciousness cannot be said to bind the aspirations and interests of Chippewas and Seminoles and Aleuts. As it happens, the Native American population has undergone an unusual increase. Between 1970 and 2000, the number of persons claiming tribal antecedents rose from 827,268 to 2,475,956, which works out to more than three times the growth rate for the nation as a whole. The chief reason is that a lot of people who had concealed their native origins are now reclaiming them as their primary identity.

Until a decade or so ago, Americans spoke of "Orientals," and the individuals so described are members of what the anthropologists call the "Mongoloid" race. However, these terms—along with "yellow"—are now hardly ever heard. For one thing, many of those subsumed under the "Oriental" rubric never liked that designation. After all, it was invented and imposed by Europeans, who saw their own continent as the center of civilization and relegated the "Orient" to Europe's eastern horizon.

Today, we have the generic term "Asian," which includes not only Japanese and Chinese and Koreans, but also Indonesians and Indians along with Burmese and Thais, plus Filipinos and Pakistanis. Geographically speaking, Asia extends from the Kuril Islands to Istanbul and Israel. In fact, "Asian-Americans" did not choose this title for themselves. Rather, the larger society has found it convenient to collect them into a single category that mingles racial and national origins. For this reason, obviously, "Asian" itself cannot be a race, since it embraces not only persons once described as "Mongoloid," but also Indics and Dravidians and Caucasians. Even the Koreans and Chinese and Japanese, who belong to the common "Mongoloid" race, seldom mix with one another and have few activities or interests in common. Rather than racial, their images of their identities are almost wholly national. So, although in textbook terms most Americans of Asian origin have specific racial origins, in social and political terms those identities have only a residual significance. In 1970, the census counted 1,438,544 people in what is now the Asian category. By 2000, due mainly to immigration, that group had grown sevenfold, to 10,242,998. (See the table on page 21.)

Nor can it be contended that Americans of Hispanic—or Chicano or Latino—heritage comprise a race. On the contrary, among their numbers can be found persons of almost pure European ancestry, as well as some of partial but visible African origin, along with individuals of unblemished Indian descent. One has only to recall that the founder of modern Chile was named Bernardo O'Higgins, while a recent president of Peru, Alberto Fujimori, is of Japanese ancestry. But far outnumbering these individuals and groups are people of such varied parentages as to render any talk of race impossible. Since 1970, the Hispanic group has increased from 9,072,602 to 35,305,818, three times the rate for the population as a whole.

In fact, the "nonracial" character of Hispanics has been reflected in recent census reports, where individuals are allowed to describe themselves as they choose. Accordingly, in one census question, individuals may indicate that they are Latin or Hispanic. In another place, they may also fill in a race. As the table on this page shows, they vary in their choices. In California, where Mexican-Americans predominate, only 39.7 percent say they are also white, while 51.2 percent said they had no "race" at all. For them, to be Hispanic is a sole and sufficient identity. However, in Florida, with a strong Cuban community, close to three-quarters—74.8 percent—took the white option, and only 16.7 percent identified themselves as Hispanic and nothing else. New York shows another variation, since many of its Puerto Ricans and Dominicans add a black designation. These figures should make clear that Latino or Hispanic is not a racial identity, but an ethnicity which can stand alone or combine with other attributions. (The same eschewal of "race" may be observed among immigrants from the Middle East.)

So it would seem that the country's fastest growing groups

RACIAL CHOICES OF HISPANIC-AMERICANS

	U.S.A.	California	New York	Florida
White	47.9%	39.7%	39.5%	74.8%
Black	2.0%	0.7%	7.0%	2.7%
Other*	7.9%	8.4%	9.3%	5.8%
No Race	42.3%	51.2%	44.2%	16.7%
	100.1%	100.0%	100.0%	100.0%

*American Indian, Alaskan Native, Asian, Hawaiian, or some combination of racial or other designations.

prefer to emphasize their cultural and national identities rather than traits associated with race. However, the same cannot be said for the rest of the nation, which remains either black or white.

To give the names "black" and "white" to races might seem, on its face, quite ludicrous. Clearly, no human beings have skins of either color. Indeed, very few come even close to those tones. But then "white" and "black" stand for much more than the shades of epidermal coverings. To start, they refer to the "Caucasian" and "Negroid" races, whose facial appearances can differ as prominently as their colors.

But more is involved than color or facial features or skeletal structure. The terms also carry cultural connotations. In its basic meaning, "white" denotes European antecedents, while "black" stands for Africa. Since the human species began in Africa, we can say that black people are those whose ancestors remained on that continent, while whites descend from those who embarked on migrations to cooler climates. This has led some to the presumption that the races are at different levels of evolutionary development. For at least half a dozen centuries, and possibly longer, "white" has implied a higher civilization based on a superior inheritance.

Europeans who colonized the Western Hemisphere sought to re-create it in their image and to transform North and South America into "white" continents. With conquest comes the power to impose your ways on territories you have subdued. The treatment of the Native Americans simply ratified that view. (In some places, the native populations remained large enough to exert a reciprocal influence, as in India and most of Africa. This was not to be the case in the United States.) Still, something can be learned by looking at how "white" was originally conceived, and the changes it has undergone.

BECOMING "WHITE"

From the colonial period through the Jacksonian era, most white Americans were of English ancestry. Alexis de Tocqueville, during his visit in the 1830s, felt he could characterize the country and its free citizens as "Anglo-Americans."

Given the changes in the population, this epithet could not last. Even so, the Anglo-American model has remained remarkably durable, with most subsequent immigrants adapting to its canons. They not only learned English, the single national language, but also adjusted their lives to the economy and technology associated with that prototype. This does not mean that the majority of white Americans regard themselves as "English" in a literal sense. They can and do identify with other origins. Even so, it could be argued that most contemporary citizens associate themselves to a greater degree with Anglo-American culture than with their ancestors' country of origin.

To say this would seem to resurrect the conception of the melting pot, which argued that immigrants would shed their older identities and assimilate to the new culture they encountered. That view has been challenged in many quarters. Rather than as a cauldron, many commentators today prefer to see America as a mosaic or even a lumpy stew. At best, the pot still contains plenty of unmelted pieces. Hence the renewed emphasis on "ethnicity," with its focus on the country's racial and national and religious diversity.

Even so, assimilation has taken place, and it continues apace. One of the earliest examples was the Germans, who in terms of sheer numbers once made up the nation's largest immigrant group. Yet for at least a generation, it has been hard to find many people who qualify as "German-Americans" in any serious sense. Soon after their arrival, which gained momentum after 1848, Germans quickly learned English and studied the customs of their new land. Many were merchants or farmers, familiar with the rules of a market economy. In addition, it became evident that they were not particularly committed to the country they had left behind. (In fact, there was no unified Germany at that time.) Each generation saw more intermarriage, accompanied by moves to mixed neighborhoods. Service in the Union army during the Civil War speeded the assimilation process, which was effectively completed during the First World War. With the suburbanization of Milwaukee and Cincinnati, there are no longer any neighborhoods with a German flavor.

What also eased acceptance of German immigrants was the realization by Americans of English origin that they needed an ally. For one thing, their own stock was not being renewed by immigration. And, as often happens with groups that arrive early, the offspring they produced began to feel they should no longer have to do society's less pleasant chores. German-Americans could see why they were being co-opted, and they welcomed the chance to show their ambitions and skills. The English had a further motive: encouraging the Germans, who were mainly Protestant, helped to hold the Catholic Irish at bay.

It took the Irish longer to shed an alien identity. Although they arrived already knowing English, rural folkways slowed their adjustment to an urban world. Furthermore, at the time of their arrival, Catholics were not regarded as altogether "white." (Thomas Nast's political cartoons gave Irish immigrants subhuman features.) Italians may have been less fervently Catholic than the Irish, but their acceptance was hampered by peasant habits. Many decided to return to Italy after brief sojourns here; and some of those who chose to stay took their time learning the new language.

Jews, who arrived in large numbers at the turn of the century, were at first kept at the margin of "white" America simply because they were not Christians. Still, by a generation after their arrival, they had set themselves to mastering the tests for college admission, civil service posts, and many professions. The Second World

War speeded the process of assimilation. At its end, people from every corner of Europe were considered fully "white." Two Americans of Irish extraction have been elected president, and being a Catholic was seldom a bar to promotion or preferment. The Chrysler Corporation had a Lee (from Lido) Iacocca for its chairman, while an Irving Shapiro headed Du Pont, and Ivy League universities have routinely appointed Jewish presidents.

By this time, it should be clear that the question is not "Who *is* white?" It might be more appropriate to ask, "Who *may* be considered white?" since this suggests that something akin to permission is needed. In a sense, those who have already received the "white" designation can be seen as belonging to a club, from whose sanctum they ponder whether they want or need new members, as well as the proper pace of new admissions.

Despite—or perhaps because of—their race's dominance, the two hundred million Americans who carry the majority pigmentation seldom think of themselves as "white." (Indeed, about the only times they do are the infrequent occasions when they find themselves in or driving through a black neighborhood.) While they have no objection to checking the "white" box on a form, they say they give more thought to specific aspects of their identity, such as their Italian or Scottish or Jewish origins, than they do to their whiteness. The white designation, they add, may fit egregious exceptions like neo-Nazis and the Ku Klux Klan. But they would be quite unhappy if, say, a group of stations sought to bill themselves as "White Entertainment Television." And they would also object were it proposed that "white" be added to the way we describe Yale University or General Motors.

Indeed, CBS would certainly reply that its *60 Minutes* gives Ed Bradley equal billing with Mike Wallace, or cite Bryant Gumbel's popularity with preponderantly white audiences. Given the nation's mosaic, it would be odd indeed if we encountered an outright refusal to hire a Connie Chung or a Geraldo Rivera.

Moreover, those who see the world through white eyes assert that they are unable to think of any traits or attributes that all Caucasians have in common. Where there is still some agreement that the nation's dominant antecedents are European, as is its reliance on Western literature and learning, this is seen as a cultural, not a racial heritage. Just as most white Americans protest that the charge of racism does not apply to them, so they also deny the centrality of their race. Nor does it occur to them that there might be a connection between these two disavowals.

REDEFINING WHO IS WHITE

Recent immigration from Asia and Latin America complicates any discussion of race. To start, we might ask if persons arriving from countries like Korea or Pakistan might somehow "become white." (This is not to say that they are requesting this designation.) As was noted earlier, Koreans and others who were once portrayed as belonging to the "yellow" race now reject that description. Their membership in the "Asian" category conjoins them with people as far west as Istanbul. Armenians are now considered "white," as are most Lebanese and Iranians. While in theory, some Asian Indians might be thought too dark to be "white," the appellation has shown itself to possess remarkable elasticity.

In many respects, therefore, color is becoming less important. Most Asian immigrants arrive in this country ready to compete for middle-class careers. Many come with a level of educational preparation at least as good as our own. Schools in Seoul and Bombay now offer course work as sophisticated as any in Seattle or Baltimore. As hardly needs repeating, Asia has been catapulting itself into the modern world; so if most Asians are not literally "white," they have the technical and organizational skills expected by any "Western" or European-based culture.

How Asians are currently being viewed has much in common with the ways earlier generations co-opted new talents and energies as their own were winding down. To cite a single example, which will be amplified in a later chapter, studies show that white students today spend less time on homework than their Asian classmates. At college, white undergraduates tend to select easier majors and are opting for comfortable careers in the more sociable professions. Right now, it is in science and technology where Asian talents are being co-opted. But a glance at the enrollment figures for law and business schools suggests that they are destined for broader representation in the professions and management.

As Asians find places in the economy, they are allowed to move upward on social and occupational ladders. Middle-class whites do not object if Asian children attend their local schools or populate their neighborhoods. Even now, we are beginning to see an increasing incidence of intermarriage, although it is revealing that current pairings usually involve an Asian woman and a white man. The grandchildren will undoubtedly be regarded as a new variant of white.*

Much the same process can be observed among Hispanics. Of course, large numbers are already quite "white." This is clearly the case with Cubans, a prominent example being Roberto Goizueta, the longtime chairman of the Coca-Cola Company. Many Central and South Americans can claim a strong European heritage, which eases their absorption into the "white" middle class. While skin color and features still figure in social grading, they are less obstacles to mobility than was once the case. More at issue is the divide between unskilled laborers, who will continue pouring across the border for the foreseeable future, and others with the skills and schooling that allow them to enter legally.

With the absorption of increasing numbers of Hispanics and Asians, along with Middle Eastern immigrants, being "white" will cease to carry many of the connotations it did in the past. The future population will reflect a more varied array of national

---

*Nor should all Asians be categorized as immigrants. Americans of Chinese and Japanese ancestry have been in this country for many generations, particularly in California and Hawaii. Indeed, in Hawaii, these citizens hold many of the state's prominent positions.

origins rather than races, since—as has been stressed—the new groups cannot be easily assigned to racial classifications.

Even so, we should not be too quick to proclaim that America will become "multicultural" as well. True, one can point to exotic neighborhoods, with their parades and festivals, to foreign-language newspapers and television channels, along with calls for new kinds of courses in colleges and schools. It would be more accurate to say that the United States will continue to have a single dominant culture. It doesn't really matter whether it is called "white" or "Western" or "Anglo-American" or "Eurocentric" or another title. It would be better simply to describe it as a structure of opportunities and institutions that has been willing to use the energies and talents of people of various origins. The reception given to recent immigrants is essentially similar to that accorded to successive waves of Europeans. In no case have the newcomers been given a very cordial welcome. Indeed, they have often met with mistrust, not to mention violence and hostility. Despite the felicitous words on the Statue of Liberty, immigrants are allowed entry on the condition that they serve as cheap labor and live unobtrusively. Many will tell you that now, as in the past, they find their religions scorned, their customs ridiculed, and their features caricatured.

Throughout this nation's history, the expectation has been that newcomers will adapt to the models they encounter on their arrival. If that means relinquishing old-country customs, there are signs that many are prepared to do just that, or at least watch as their children assimilate. Perhaps the first instance of the expanded purview of "white" was when the English founders sought the services of two talented men of Scottish ancestry—James Madison and Alexander Hamilton—to help found this nation. The process is still going on.

As with "white," being "black" is less one's particular shade of color than physical features and continent of ancestry. Of course, very few Americans are entirely African in origin. As is well known, slave owners and other whites felt free to force themselves on black women. Still, no matter how light their skin tones, if they retained any vestige of African features, they and their descendants continue to be delineated as "black."

The United States, unlike other countries and cultures, no longer uses terms specifying finer gradations. Hence "mestizo" and "mulatto" have disappeared from our parlance, as have "creole" and "quadroon." Nor has this country retained the generic term "colored" for people whose ancestries are obviously mixed. (The last use of an intermediate term was in the 1910 census, in which interviewers identified about 20 percent of the "Negro" group as "Mulattoes.") It has been far from accidental that this country has chosen to reject the idea of a graduated spectrum and has instead fashioned a rigid bifurcation.

Even more instructive, children who are born of white and black parents almost invariably think of themselves as black. Or, more accurately, they are regarded as black by the outer world and so have little choice but to accept that designation. Some of these offspring look white and could pass if they so chose. But that would entail cutting off all connections with their parents, something not many want to do. So it is necessary to ask, Why is it that white America, in particular, wants children of mixed matings to be added to the black population?

At bottom, there seems to be the worry that if an intermediate category is created, then some of those who are now deemed to be "pure" white might find it being wondered whether they belong in an in-between group. More than that, defining interracial offspring as black makes it less likely that they will become involved with the daughters and sons of white households. Were that to happen, while their children would remain white, although only marginally so, their grandchildren would not.★

★According to a 2000 census count, the country's 56.5 million married couples include 307,000 with black and white spouses. In proportionate terms, this is almost four times the figure for 1970, when there were 65,000 such couples in a 44.6 million total.

These fears suggest that even in a presumably enlightened time, there is still a strong concern with preventing any degrading of the white race.

THE STIGMA OF SLAVERY

So for all practical purposes, "whites" of all classes and ethnicities now prefer to present a common front. Unlike in the past, there are no pronounced distinctions of "purer" versus "lesser" whites or of those with older claims as compared with the claims of the newer arrivals. While immigrants from Colombia and Cyprus may have to work their way up the social ladder, they are still allowed as valid a claim to being "white" as persons of Puritan or Pilgrim stock.

Americans of African ancestry were never given that indulgence. The reason is not that their coloration was too "dark" to allow for absorption into the "white" classification. After all, the swarthiness of some Europeans did not become a barrier to their admission. Had white America really believed in its egalitarian declarations, it would have welcomed former slaves into its midst at the close of the Civil War. Indeed, had that happened, America would not be two racial nations today. This is not to suggest how far blacks themselves would have assimilated, since a lot depends on how much members of a group want to preserve their special heritage. The point is that white America has always had the power to expand its domain. However, in the past and even now, it has shown a particular reluctance to absorb people of African descent.

How do blacks feel about this bifurcation? Today, most express pride in their African origins, especially those who make a point of calling themselves African-Americans. While, like it or not, a lighter color remains an advantage for women, social advantage is no longer gained by alluding to white components in one's ancestry. Black Americans are aware that much in the "black" designation represents how whites have defined the term. Still, despite attempts by whites to describe and define them, black Americans have always sought to create their own lives and sustain their sentiments and interests. It started when the first slaves created a culture of their own. Similarly, the drive to replace "colored" with "negro" and the following moves to "Negro" and then on to "black" and "African-American" have all reflected a desire to maintain an autonomous identity.

For most black Americans, to be an African-American means literally that in that continent lies the primal origin of your people. The experiences of capture and transportation, of slavery and segregation, never diminished or erased the basic culture and character of tribal ancestries. Yet it is also instructive that blacks from the West Indies and other islands of the Caribbean seek to retain an independent history. Their forebears also originate in Africa and served as slaves, but blacks born in Barbados and Jamaica, or Haiti and Martinique, make clear the British or French connections that distinguish them from others of their race. This emphasis is not intended to render Haitians or Jamaicans "less black" in terms of color. Rather, they wish it known that their antecedents are not exclusively African, but also bear a European imprint.

Black Americans came from the least-known continent, the most exotic, the one remotest from American experience. Among the burdens blacks bear is the stigma of "the savage," the proximity to lesser primates. Hence the question in many minds: Can citizens of African origin find acceptance in a society that is dominantly white, Western, and European?

Even at a time when Americans of European backgrounds are giving less emphasis to their ancestries, it is not as easy for black men and women to assimilate to the American mainstream. Even those who aspire to careers in white institutions and emulate white demeanor and diction find that white America lets them only partly past the door.

Arguably, this is because the "Africa" in African-American

contrasts with much of the European structure of technology and science, of administrative systems based on linear modes of reasoning. Today, Africa is the least developed and most sorrow-ridden of continents. It has more than its share of malnutrition and debilitating diseases and at least its share of tribal rancor and bloodshed. It seems always to be petitioning the rest of the world for aid. Since the close of the colonial era, over a generation ago, there have not been many African success stories.

Yet the actual Africa of today is not really the model black Americans have in mind. Of much greater significance is how the continent is construed as a symbol: what it says about human spirit, what it connotes as a way of life. It is more the Africa of history, before the imperial powers arrived. It is also an Africa of the imagination, of music and dance and stories. This Africa speaks for an ancestral humanity, for an awareness of the self, the bonds of tribe and family and community. If the European heritage imposes the regimens of standardized tests, the African dream inspires discursive storytelling celebrating the spirit and the soul.

But as much as anything, being "black" in America bears the mark of slavery. Even after emancipation, citizens who had been slaves still found themselves consigned to a subordinate status. Put most simply, the ideology that had provided the rationale for slavery did not disappear. Blacks continued to be seen as an inferior species, not only unsuited for equality but not even meriting a chance to show their worth. Immigrants only hours off the boat, while often subjected to scorn, were—and still are—allowed to assert their superiority to black Americans.

And in our own time, must it be admitted at the start of the twenty-first century that residues of slavery continue to exist? The answer is obviously yes. The fact that blacks are separated more severely than any other group certainly conveys that message. Indeed, the fear persists that if allowed to come closer, they will somehow contaminate the rest of society.

What other Americans know and remember is that blacks alone were brought as chattels to be bought and sold like livestock.

As has been noted, textbooks now point out that surviving slavery took a skill and stamina that no other race has been called upon to demonstrate. Yet this is not what is usually recalled. Rather, there remains an unarticulated suspicion: might there be something about the black race that suited them for slavery? This is not to say anyone argues that human bondage was justified. Still, the fact that slavery existed for so long and was so taken for granted cannot be erased from American minds. This is not the least reason why other Americans—again, without openly saying so—find it not improper that blacks still serve as maids and janitors, occupations seen as involving physical skills rather than mental aptitudes. However, many will reply that slavery came to an end well over a century ago. While our history books remind us of its ravages, we ask, How can an abolished institution continue to influence the way whites regard blacks?

One way the legacy of slavery remains alive may be found in an interchange that occurred in a college classroom:

> The professor calls on a white student and asks him to imagine that he is a judge presiding at a South Carolina courtroom in the year 1850. A trial has just ended, and the jury has convicted a particularly sadistic murderer for the wanton slayings of at least a dozen people. It is now the judge's responsibility to decide on a sentence. It is also noted that the murderer is white.
>
> The professor adds that the defendant has been deemed sane and shows no signs of remorse. Also, due to a legal technicality, the death penalty cannot be used. So what sentence would the judge impose?
>
> The student ponders for a while and then says that the severest punishment he can think of is a life sentence with no possibility of parole. But why not, the professor suggests, do something even harsher, which would also save the taxpayers some money? Why not sentence the murderer to slavery, selling him to the cruelest owner in the state, who would whip him and chain him and force him to toil in the fields from morning until night?

The student responds, "I couldn't do that. You told me the murderer is white, and white people cannot be sold into slavery."

When the student gave this reply, was he simply imagining himself in 1850? Or could it also be that he was voicing his present-day sentiments? What emerges is that even in our century, white Americans do not want to think of a member of their own race, even the most vicious killer, being sold into slavery. (Would such a punishment stop with one, or might many whites have to worry about the possibility?) But no such mental difficulty arises when whites are asked to recall that kings and queens from Africa, as well as physicians and scholars, were wrenched from their homes and shipped across the Atlantic as chattels. While today one finds few defenders of slavery, whites can still "understand" how it happened that in America, only Africans were relegated to that status.

The recollections of the past that remain in people's minds continue to shape ideas about the character and capacities of black citizens. Is it possible to erase the stigma associated with slavery? After all, a very considerable number of black Americans have achieved impressive careers, winning many of the rewards bestowed by white America. Still, there is no way that even the most talented of these men and women will be considered eligible for the honorific of "white." They are, and will remain, accomplished blacks, regarded as role models for their race. But white Americans, who both grant and impose racial memberships, show little inclination toward giving full nationality to the descendants of African slaves.

TWO RACES: TIME OF DECLINE?

The subject of this book is race: in particular, America's two principal races, which, in Alexis de Tocqueville's words, "are fastened to each other without intermingling." As it happens, taken together, black and white Americans now comprise a dwindling share of the nation's population. Census counts over the last two centuries illuminate some of the changes.

At the time of the first census, in 1790, blacks were at their highest point as a proportion of the population. In each succeeding decade through 1940, their share grew smaller, because of growing waves of white immigration. Since 1940, the black quotient has been rising by about half a percentage point each decade, because of the fact that black Americans have a higher birthrate (although, as will be seen in a later chapter, the black rate is always a constant multiple of the white rate). Still, as the following table shows, each decade finds the two races accounting for declining proportions of the national population:

HOW AMERICA ADDED UP: 1970 AND 2000

Total Population

	1970	2000
White*	83.3%	69.1%
Black	10.9%	12.3%
Hispanic	4.5%	12.5%
Asian	1.1%	3.6%
Other**	0.2%	2.5%
	100.0%	100.0%

*Whites who are not of Hispanic origin.
**Native Hawaiians, American Indians, Pacific Islanders, and Arab-Americans.

As has been noted, Hispanics, Asians, Native Americans, and Hawaiians are now the nation's fastest growing groups. By 1990, they together outnumbered black Americans and were also helping to erode white predominance. For this reason, it might seem that a book that focuses on only two races will be woefully incomplete. Why not simply describe America's two nations as composed of whites and various people of color? Much can be said for such an argument. Certainly, all persons deemed to be other than white can detail how they have suffered discrimination at the hands of white America. Any allusions to racist attitudes and actions will find Cherokees and Chinese and Cubans agreeing with great vigor.

Yet, as has already been suggested in this chapter, members of all these "intermediate" groups have been allowed to put a visible distance between themselves and black Americans. Put most simply, none of the presumptions of inferiority associated with Africa and slavery are imposed on these other ethnicities. Moreover, as has also been noted, second and subsequent generations of Hispanics and Asians are merging into the "white" category, partly through intermarriage and also by personal achievement and adaptation. Indeed, the very fact that this is happening sheds light on the tensions and disparities separating the two major races.

CHAPTER TWO

RACE AND RACISM

INFERIORITY OR EQUALITY?

T HROUGHOUT THIS NATION'S HISTORY, race has always had a central role. Until recently, however, most notions concerning the races and relations between them either went unquestioned or remained relatively muted. As recently as two generations ago, white Americans in both the South and the North would say that their region had no overpowering racial problems. Most of them really wanted to believe that blacks and whites coexisted quite amiably; separately, to be sure, but that was a matter of mutual choice.

For almost a century after the abolition of slavery, America's black population subsisted under a system of controls. In the South, physical force was blatant and unabashed. The whims of a sheriff, an employer, even the driver of a bus, could hold black lives in thrall. In the North, intimidation and oppression were less explicit but nonetheless real. Fear of the police obviously helped to maintain this submission, for in those days precinct houses were less attentive to legal processes than they claim to be today. An equally effective control lay in the understanding that members of subordinate races did not touch or threaten their betters. This is not to suggest that black Americans were happy with their condition. Many were resentful, if not totally enraged. But given the panoply of power they faced, the most common posture was one of resignation: a minority held down and apart with barely an avenue of appeal.

Little attention was paid to the conditions under which black Americans lived. It was assumed, for example, that a docile pool would always be available for the arduous labors required by white society. No one thought to ask what domestic servants did after their working hours. Black Americans remained unobtrusive, and apparently uncomplaining, for all intents invisible to white eyes.

These were placid years for white Americans. No serious movements or organized protests arose to upset white sensibilities. No talk of black power was in the air, and only the barest whispers of egalitarian aspirations could be heard. Black Americans knew they were regarded as marginal members of the nation and realized that white America saw them as an alien appendage.

The real changes began during the Second World War, when for the first time black Americans were courted by white society. A shortage of civilian labor forced employers to offer jobs to workers who previously had been excluded. More than a million black women left domestic service never to return. At the outset of the war, blacks were drafted into the armed forces to serve in labor battalions. By its end, they were given the right to fight and die, as many did. Once a society has told men and women that it cannot function without their talents, they will not willingly revert to a subordinate status. Notions of civil rights and racial integration, of social equality and economic progress, received their impetus in those wartime years. During the decades that followed, they took coherent shape.

In particular, college students in the South decided it was time to end the ignominies inflicted on educated men and women, who could not even order a sandwich at a local lunch counter. Shortly thereafter, ordinary citizens began to demand that most elemental of rights, which was still denied to most members of their race; to be allowed to vote for the officials who legislate and tax and exercise power over you.

Most white Americans saw these sit-ins and similar activities as dignified and responsible and embodying legitimate aims. That black groups eschewed violence also set white minds at ease. Certainly, they felt safe with Martin Luther King, Jr., the most prominent leader in the civil rights movement. Not only was he a minister born into a patrician family, but he had studied and received a doctorate at a Northern university. Moreover, he welcomed whites to join in marches and demonstrations, making it a biracial cause.

So until the middle 1960s, there was little talk of a racial crisis or tensions that had grown out of control. Then came the so-called riots in cities like Los Angeles and Newark and Detroit, marked by looting and burning within black neighborhoods. In fact, these were not "race riots," if by that is meant actual confrontations of black and white citizens. The violence never reached downtown business districts or areas where whites lived. However, race became the central issue. The chief response, including gunfire, in which many blacks lost their lives, came from white police and National Guardsmen. To more than a few observers, the conduct of the police was much more callous and indiscriminate than that of the civilians they had been ordered to control.

After those disturbances, race relations never returned to their former plane. Whites ceased to identify black protests with a civil rights movement led by students and ministers. Rather, blacks were seen as trying to force themselves into places and positions where they were not wanted or for which they lacked the competence. As the 1970s started, so came a rise in crimes, all too many of them with black perpetrators. By that point, many white Americans felt they had been misused or betrayed. Worsening relations between the races were seen as largely due to the behavior of blacks, who had abused the invitations to equal citizenship white

America had been tendering. It is this setting that creates the context of racism.

RACISM IN ACTION

Something called racism obviously exists. As a complex of ideas and attitudes, which translate into action, it has taken a tragic toll on the lives of all Americans. Unfortunately, the term has been so used and overused that it loses serious meaning. It has served as a rallying cry, a bludgeon, and as a diversion from other issues. Indeed, virtually all white people will deny that they have racist tendencies, and they resent implications that they do. As a result, even raising the term "racism" turns them off, and makes them unwilling to listen further. But racism is real, an incubus that has haunted this country since Europeans first set foot on the conti-nent. It goes beyond prejudice and discrimination, and even transcends bigotry, largely because it arises from outlooks and assumptions of which we are largely unaware.

Racism expresses itself in three distinct but related ways. Of course, this or any trifurcation may seem oversimple and undoubtedly is. Still, a graphic presentation can expand our understanding of an elusive reality.

For the first kind, we can cite a familiar example. Taxicab driv-ers who refuse to stop for black riders base that decision on the only information they have: the race of the person raising his or her hand. Even if the driver has had some bad experiences, he understands that most black men are law-abiding citizens. At the same time, he knows that some have been known to pull a gun on taxicab drivers. And that "some" is enough to make him wary about every black man. Or when he drives by a middle-aged black woman without stopping, it is because he thinks she may ask to be taken to a part of the city he would rather not enter. Of course, he has no way of knowing her destination, but he does not want to take the risk. In these and similar cases, his decision not to stop is patently racist, especially since he then proceeds to pick up the first white passenger he sees farther down the block.

Racism has much in common with other "isms." We already have the term "sexism." Other generalizations may apply to height or weight or age or physical handicaps. "Homophobia" is also an "ism," although it carries connotations of hatred as well. Whether a taxi driver dislikes black people is not really the issue. He may actually feel sorry for the person he left standing in the rain.

In some cases, expressions of racism admit of no exceptions. This was the case with the Nazi ideology, which said that *all* human beings of Jewish origin carried the seeds of depravity. The fact that infants were included in mass exterminations made this conviction clear. (This is not to say that Jews are a race. Still, the Nazis' choice to see them that way is itself a fact.)

Racism need not be so rigid or absolute. In fact, few whites insist that the traits they dislike in some black people are to be found in every member of the race. Most are pleased to point to black men and women who are not like "the rest." They may watch black performers regularly on film or television, cheer them at athletic events, and even claim some black people as their friends.

Making—and acting upon—limited impressions is a part of ordinary life. Each day, like the taxicab driver, we base decisions on the one or two facts we gather about people, which may simply be their outward appearance, or their address on an application, or how they sound over the telephone. Such presumptions are obviously unfair to the individuals involved. Constraints of time do not always allow us to obtain the fuller information we would like or need.

Racism, we are sometimes told, rests largely on ignorance. If we get to know people better, we will discover that they are quite different from what we have been led to think they are. That is surely so. For example, very few white Americans have ever set foot inside a black family's home. They might be surprised to discover that simply in terms of furniture, appliances, meals, and television watching, blacks live very much like whites of their own class.

While some differences in style can be identified, members of the two races share many common characteristics. Quite obviously, the United States would be a much more harmonious nation if there were fewer racial barriers. Yet even blacks who attain economic and educational parity find that social obstacles remain. How often does one see two couples, one black and one white, on an outing together?

Still, racism is not always based on ignorance. There can be cases where stereotyped judgments contain some morsels of truth. While we can agree that taxicab drivers often make decisions on a racist basis, we might grant that in doing so they show a modicum of rationality. Some black men—a higher proportion than among whites—do have intentions that are in fact dangerous. It is one thing for a passenger to refuse to pay a taxi fare; it is another if he holds a loaded gun to the driver's head. And the latter has been a frequent enough occurrence to give many drivers pause. Sad to say, actions that are often unfair can also be reasonable, at least insofar as they are based on sufficient experience to give them a degree of validity.

To reply that taxicab drivers draw on rational odds hardly comforts those subjected to such calculations. Tendencies attributed to common felons get shunted onto black surgeons and scholars. Nor does it help to point out that this kind of unfairness is inevitable in a world where we can never come to know each individual in an intimate way. Judgments based on race cut more deeply and cause more harm than other presumptions Americans may make about one another. What every black American knows, and whites should try to imagine, is how it feels to have an unfavorable—and unfair—identity imposed on you every waking day.

INSTITUTIONAL RACISM

In addition to the outlooks and actions of individuals like taxicab drivers, there is a second set of conditions commonly called "institutional racism." The institutions can be colleges and churches, or business firms or governmental bureaus. The Federal Bureau of Investigation and the Los Angeles Police Department, for example, have long had reputations for antipathy toward blacks and other minorities. But not all organizations are so blatant in their biases. Most develop more subtle cultures of their own, which their members usually internalize, often without pause or reflection. Of course, organizational cultures take many forms. But in the United States, an overarching feature is that they tend to be inherently "white."

This is not to say that churches and colleges and corporations actually proclaim a racial preference. All will assert that they welcome parishioners and students and employees of every color, and they hope to increase that diversity. Executives at firms like General Motors and General Electric would be shocked if told that they headed racist firms, as would administrators at Cornell or Columbia. And three major companies—American Express, Merrill Lynch, and AOL Time Warner—can add that they have black chief executives. Indeed, the issue barely arises in the minds of their members. So if someone files a lawsuit, the complaint generally comes as a surprise. The organizations reply that they do not discriminate; more than that, most who speak this way truly believe what they say.

Simply stated, most white people prefer not to perceive their nation and its major institutions as "white" and consequently racist. They will say that the United States is a multiracial society and becomes more so every day. The same strictures, they will add, hold for its major organizations and associations. In their view, to claim that the white race holds so preponderant a sway is both untrue and gratuitous.

Black Americans seldom see the reality this way. Black students at Yale University, black members of the Omaha police force, even black passengers on an airline flight, never cease being aware of their white surroundings. When black Americans go to movies, turn on television, or simply scan the comic strips, it seems as if their nation hardly knows or cares that they exist. (They are quite aware of well-known black figures, ranging from Oprah Winfrey to Colin Powell. Still, institutional images are overwhelmingly white.)

American institutions begin with an initial bias against black applicants, since the presumption is that most blacks cannot or will not meet the standards the organization has set. Historically, virtually all of the people associated with Yale University, United Airlines, and the Omaha police force have been white, which has in turn created both the image of these institutions and the way they operate. In this sense, they are "white" organizations, from which it follows that their members are expected to think and act in "white" ways. This is not as difficult for white people, although some have to make an extra effort if they wish to master aspects of manner and style associated with a higher class. However, for blacks the situation is qualitatively different, since they see themselves as being judged by more coercive criteria, which call on them to deny large parts of themselves.

Black Americans spend much of their lives at a distance from white Americans, in part because they feel more comfortable that way and in part because their separation has been imposed by white America. As will be seen later, this helps to explain why even better-off blacks tend to do less well than whites on tests used by schools and employers. Since blacks of all classes are more likely to be raised in segregated surroundings, they grow up with less exposure to the kinds of reasoning that standardized examinations expect.

From slavery through the present, the nation has never opened its doors sufficiently to give black Americans a chance to become full citizens. White Americans often respond that it rests with blacks to put aside enough of their own culture so they can be absorbed into the dominant stream. Blacks can only shake their heads and reply that they have been doing just that for several centuries, with very little to show for it.

THE STIGMA OF SLAVERY: II

A third expression of racism has even deeper roots, evincing age-old attitudes about the continent of Africa. Many black men and women are concluding that they can best be described as African-Americans, considering how much their character and culture owe to their continent of origin. A pride in this heritage and history has helped them survive slavery and subsequent discrimination. Indeed, the nation as a whole has benefited from black Americans who bring to life the rhetoric and rhythms of their ancestral origins.

However, most white Americans interpret the African emphasis in another way. For them, it frequently leads to a more insidious application of racism. As has been reiterated, there persists the belief that members of the black race represent an inferior strain of the human species. In this view, Africans—and Americans who trace their origins to that continent—are seen as languishing at a lower evolutionary level than members of other races.

Of course, this belief is seldom stated in public. Still, the unhappy fact remains that most white people believe that compared with other races, persons of African ancestry are more likely to carry primitive traits in their genes. Given this premise—and prejudice—the presumption follows that most individuals of African heritage will lack the intellectual and organizational capacities the modern world requires.

Most whites who call themselves conservatives hold this view and voice it when they are sure of their company. Most liberals and those further to the left deny that present racial disparities are based on genetic inheritance. If they harbor doubts, they keep them to themselves. Their intellectual forebears were not so constrained. Thomas Jefferson provides a case in point.

As the principal author of the Declaration of Independence, he enunciated the new nation's commitment to human equality. Many Americans can recite his phrases from memory.

> We hold these truths to be self-evident: that all men are created
> equal; that they are endowed by their Creator with certain unalien-
> able rights; that among these are life, liberty, and the pursuit of hap-
> piness.

To refer to some truths as "self-evident" means that all reasonable people should be able to agree on their veracity, without need
for further proof or evidence. They are empirical first principles
and moral starting points. It is noteworthy that Jefferson set down
as the first of these verities the premise "all men are created equal."

There have been endless discussions over what "created equal"
could have meant to Jefferson and what it might convey to us
today. One thing can be said at the outset: it must refer to more
than the possession of equal rights, since those entitlements are
listed later and separately in the passage just quoted. Moreover,
those who take the egalitarian position are well aware of human
differences. No one will deny that some people are taller or gain
weight more readily or can run faster or have perfect pitch.

However, our current concern is not whether all human
beings everywhere are "created equal" in terms of personal potential but whether this tenet applies to the groups of individuals we
have come to call races. Here the terms of the argument can
allow for ranges of possible talents *within* racial groups. So what
racial equality *must* posit is that within each race there will be a
similar distribution of talents, if all members of all races are given
a chance to discover and develop those traits. Ideally, then, white
Americans and black Americans could be brought to a point
where both racial groups would have an essentially identical
range of IQ scores. Or, even more ideally, we might devise tests
that gauge more encompassing human qualities.

What is revealing is that while Thomas Jefferson was prepared
to affirm an equality among the people to whom the Declaration
of Independence applied, he was not so sure about that principle
when the slaves of his day were involved. In a letter written fifteen
years later, he said.

Nobody wishes more than I do to see proofs that nature has given to our black brethren talents equal to those of the other colors of men, and that the appearance of a lack of them is owing merely to the degraded condition of their existence in Africa and America.

This sentence deserves a close and careful reading since it shows several ideas converging in the author's mind. Can this be the same Jefferson who had earlier affirmed it was "self-evident" that all human beings everywhere are conceived with equal potential to pursue the fullest life? What, we may wonder, led him to single out blacks and say he now needed "proofs" that they had faculties equal to those of other races? We may also speculate about what manner of evidence would have been sufficiently persuasive to Jefferson to undo doubts that have proved so durable. One might think that even in his day at least some blacks had shown sufficient accomplishments to quell his misgivings. As has been noted, racial equality only asks us to assume a comparable range of potentialities within every racial group.

Jeffersonian doubts remain relevant for another reason. Note how much he *wanted* to believe that persons of African origin had capacities equal to those of other races. Why, then, could not Jefferson simply pronounce the inherent equality of blacks and whites also to be a "self-evident" truth? Any deficiencies he might find could be attributed to the oppressive environment of segregation and slavery. That has always been the egalitarian answer. Sadly, even for those who allude to blacks as their "brethren," a desire to believe does not always bring that result. Warring within the minds of Jeffersonians, both in his time and ours, is the hope that blacks are equal—accompanied by the suspicion that they are not.

The following vignette shows how feelings such as these could rise to the surface.

A professor calls on a student in his class—she happens to be white—and asks her to imagine that she has been in an awful traffic accident. She is brought to the nearest hospital, where she over-hears a nurse saying it will take the most expert skill in surgery to pull her through.

The professor continues setting the scene. He tells the student that before going into the operating room, she is told that this hos-pital believes strongly in patients' freedom of choice. Therefore, she is informed, two surgeons are available at this time, and she must select one.

The two surgeons come in. They are of the same gender, seem about the same age, and both belong to the hospital's staff. That is all she can know about them. Oh yes, there is one other thing. One of the surgeons is black, and the other is white.

Which of the surgeons will she choose?

The professor's purpose is apparent. Moreover, he knows that in virtually all cases, the student doesn't want to answer the ques-tion, at least not within the hearing of the class. Nor does he press her for a response. So he listens while she tries to evade the issue, perhaps by asking for further information, like which medical schools the surgeons attended. Someone else in the class may vol-unteer that the black surgeon could be better, since he had to work harder to get where he is. Another student, this one white, may wonder whether affirmative action had eased his entry to medical school. Still another may ask which of the surgeons their black classmates might choose.

What emerges, of course, is that the last thing these students want to talk—and think—about is what is really on their minds. Yes, most whites will grant, black people have many estimable tal-ents and impressive capacities. But is one of them the ability to meet the exacting standards of surgery in a highly scientific age? These students, like Thomas Jefferson, *want* to believe that per-sons of African ancestry have the same talents as members of other races. But, like Jefferson, they have not yet received the "proofs" they need to satisfy that belief.

THE "SCIENTIFIC" DEBATE

Not all expressions of racism have been as beset by misgivings as Jefferson's. Since Europeans first embarked on explorations, they have been bemused by the "savages" they encountered in new lands. In almost all cases, these "primitive" peoples were seen as inferior to those who "discovered" them. While they were often described as peaceful and pastoral, as innocent and caring, those were viewed as attributes of children, not of fully formed adults. On the whole, the presumption was that these natives could never attain to a stage where they might emulate European achievements.

Many people still hold views similar to these. Indeed, terms even cruder than "savages" can be heard in private interchanges. But in public discourse, ours is much more a scientific age. So those who believe in the inherent inferiority of certain races feel obliged to allude to research based on experimentation, evidence, and an objective point of view.

One of the most prominent has been William Shockley, a winner of the Nobel Prize, who argued that evidence showed people of African origin to be lower on an evolutionary scale. Another well-known name is Arthur Jensen, a professor of psychology at the University of California. His stated position has been that because black children are genetically inferior, even compensatory programs like Head Start will fail because the native talents are not there.

In the past, this field was called "eugenics," and it had practical as well as scholarly aims. For one thing, it hoped to warn people of supposedly superior strains that they should not mate with their genetic inferiors. The fear was of "mongrelization," a term then commonly used, wherein the best human breeds would marry down and produce lesser heirs. Today, such sentiments are seldom stated in so direct a way. Rather than counseling against intermarriage, it will be hinted that even social racial mixing can have deleterious effects. Hence the concern voiced in some quarters that allowing too many blacks into elite colleges will not only lower intellectual standards but will dilute the scholarly discourse that those august institutions have sought to achieve.

In rational terms, there is an easy rebuttal to research and reasoning based on racist suppositions. In simplest terms, it is the environmental answer. To begin, while conceding that heredity has a role in shaping human beings, its influences are best considered on an individual level. Thus, through parents or other forebears, certain attributes are passed on to successive offspring, although it is not always possible to trace who got what from whom. After all, many permutations and combinations are involved. For example, you may have traits much like those of one of your aunts or grandfathers.

Of course, races differ in some outward respects. Each race, taken as a group, carries a pool of genes that gives its members their identifiable color and anatomical structure. But even here there are shades and variations, since very few Americans belong to a "pure" race. (This is particularly true of the growing group of Hispanics.) However, despite more than a century of searching, we have no evidence that any one of those pools of race-based genes has a larger quotient of what we choose to call intelligence or organizational ability or creative capacities.

So if more members of some races end up doing better in some spheres, it is because more of them grew up in environments that prepared them for those endeavors. If members of other races had similar rearing they would display a similar distribution of success. Therefore, in terms of potential capacities, our best knowledge is that all races have a comparable range of geniuses and morons and people of average ability. We can test people as much as we please. But there is no way to factor out whether any part of the results reflect "racial" elements in some genetic sense, since we would have to adjust for every specific environmental influence as it has affected each individual. (Indeed, even when a white family adopts and raises a black infant, the child knows that she or he is "black" and that the self-image will affect the child's adaptation to a "white" environment.) An example may be found in Sweden, perhaps the palest-complected country. One of the most honored masters of that nation's own cuisine is a black chef of Ethiopian origin. He was brought to Sweden as an infant to be adopted by a white couple. While having been conceived by African parents may have given him "black genes," his rearing in Sweden gave him a "European environment," in which he excelled on his adopted country's own terms.

Of course, observations such as these will not deflect individuals like Arthur Jensen and William Shockley from sifting through research reports for evidence of race-based disparities. Other citizens who are not scientists will settle on conclusions of their own or cite accounts that seem to back their suppositions. Indeed, there is reason to believe that most white Americans still share Thomas Jefferson's belief that in terms of evolution and genetics theirs is the most developed race.

At a certain point, the suspicion arises that we are less in the realm of science than of ideology. Scientists, no less than lay people, have political dispositions. And, like the rest of us, the sentiments they hold give shape to what they see. More than that, even Nobel Prize winners can end up seeing not what is actually there but what they want to see. We are not talking about dishonesty or hypocrisy but the way human minds—indeed, brilliant minds—tend to work.

So it should not be surprising that scientists who stress the role of heredity tend to be politically conservative, while those who emphasize environment veer toward the liberal side of the spectrum. By the same token, lay people select scientific views that support their ideological positions. Even individuals who have never taken a science course feel free to cite some studies as authoritative, if they agree with their findings. Thus racism has always been able to come up with a scientific veneer. This is certainly true today of those who wish to claim that one race or another is by nature inferior. They are fully persuaded that they are citing biology, not displaying bigotry.

Thus the racism blacks face runs deeper than judgments about culture. From the premise of genetic inferiority, there follows the corollary that members of a lesser race should be content to perform tasks unsuited to other strains. This was the rationale for slavery, and it has by no means disappeared. (There are even hints of this in the plea to create more blue-collar jobs for black men.) Nor is the racism applied to blacks found only among persons of European ancestry. Today, inhabitants of every other continent like to think that they have evolved further than those who trace their origins to the region south of the Sahara.

Certainly, compared with other continents, Africa remains most like its primeval self. Even today, white Americans as individuals, and white America's institutions, are unwilling to fully absorb the people and patrimony of humanity's first continent. This expression of racism goes well beyond personal prejudice and discriminatory institutions. It rests on judgments about culture and civilization and who dictates the meaning of science and history.

WHO IS A RACIST?

All the observations offered thus far have focused on beliefs and behavior of white Americans. Quite obviously, racism arises in other places and guises. Most Japanese, for example, feel that they represent the highest evolution of humanity and have cited Chinese, Koreans, and Americans as their genetic inferiors.

And what about blacks in America; cannot they harbor racist sentiments as well? Some certainly seem to. Leonard Jeffries, a black scholar, has designated whites as "ice people," labeling them materialistic, greedy, and inherently driven to domination. By way of contrast, he calls blacks "sun people," whose chief traits are kindness and caring and communal responsibility. More than that, this scholar has argued, the melanin that makes for darker pigmentation imparts a mental and moral superiority to persons who trace their ancestries to Africa. So blacks can also employ stereotypes that impute inferiority to human beings of another race. Some whites worry about these views, seeing them as mirror images of white displays of racism, supremacy, and bigotry.

Some blacks reject that symmetry. Thus Coleman Young, a longtime mayor of Detroit, a predominantly black city, argued that blacks within the United States cannot be called racists for the simple reason that they are a subordinated people. Racism, he said, should be attributed only to those who have the power to cause suffering. What he suggested was that it is insufficient to define racism as a set of ideas that some people may hold. Racism takes its full form only when it has an impact on the real world. While most white people may have disputed the mayor's reasoning, he raised an important point. If we care about racism, it is because it scars people's lives. Individuals who do not have power may hold racist views, but they seldom cause much harm. (No one cares if homeless people believe the earth is flat.) The significance of racism lies in the way it consigns certain human beings to the margins of society, if not to painful lives and early deaths. In the United States, racism takes its highest toll on blacks. No white person can claim to have suffered in such ways because of ideas that may be held about them by some black citizens.

So ideas about equality and inferiority and superiority are not simply figments in people's minds. Such sentiments have an impact on how institutions operate, and opinions turn out to be self-fulfilling. If members of a minority race are believed to be deficient in character or capacities, the larger society will consign them to subordinate positions.

AN UNEQUAL CONTEST

America has always been the most competitive of societies. It poises its citizens against one another with the warning that they must make it on their own. Hence the stress on moving past others, driven by a fear of falling behind. No other nation so rates its residents as winners or losers.

If white America presides over this arena, it cannot guarantee full security to every member of its own race. Still, while some of its members may fail, there is a limit to how far they can fall. For white America has agreed to provide a consolation prize: no matter to what depths one descends, no white person can ever become black. As James Baldwin pointed out, white people need the presence of black people as a reminder of what providence has spared them from becoming.

If white people are compelled to compete against one another, they are also urged to believe that any advances blacks may make will be at white expense. Here government and politics reflect a harsh economy. Indeed, this country is less a society, certainly less a community, than any of the countries with which it compares itself. A reason commonly given is that the United States is a large and diverse country. What is less commonly acknowledged is that its culture makes a point of exaggerating differences and exacerbating frictions. This appears most vividly in the stress placed on race.

Competition and whites' fears of failure help to explain the resistance to ensuring opportunities for black Americans, let alone more equitable outcomes. Even allowing for interludes like the New Deal and the Great Society, government is expected to take on obligations only as a late and last resort. Hence the presence in the United States of more violent crime, more of its people in prison, more homeless families and individuals, more children created virtually by accident, more fatal addiction and disease, more dirt and disorder—why prolong the list?—than any other nation deemed industrially advanced and socially civilized.

A society that places so great a premium on "getting ahead" cannot afford to spare much compassion for those who fall behind. If the contest were racially fair, it would at least be true to its own principle of assessing all individuals solely on talent and effort. But keeping black Americans so far behind the starting line means most of the outcomes will be racially foreordained.

CHAPTER THREE

BEING BLACK
IN AMERICA

Most white Americans will say that, all things considered, things aren't so bad for black people in the United States. Of course, they will grant that many problems remain. Still, whites feel there has been steady improvement, bringing blacks closer to parity, especially when compared with conditions in the past. Some have even been heard to muse that it's better to be black, since affirmative action policies make it a disadvantage to be white.

What white people seldom stop to ask is how they may benefit from belonging to their race. Nor is this surprising. People who can see do not regard their vision as a gift for which they should offer thanks. It may also be replied that having a white skin does not immunize a person from misfortune or failure. Yet even for those who fall to the bottom, being white has worth. What could that value be?

Let us try to find out by means of a parable. Suspend disbelief for a moment, and assume that what is to be recounted could actually happen to someone who is white.

THE VISIT

You will be visited tonight by an official you have never met. He begins by telling you that he is quite embarrassed. The organization he represents has made a mistake, something that hardly ever happens.

According to their records, he tells you, you were supposed to have been born black: to another set of parents, far from where you were raised.

However, the official rules being what they are, this error must be rectified, and as soon as possible. So at midnight tonight, you will become black. And this will mean not simply darker skin, but the bodily and facial features associated with African ancestry. However, inside, you will be the person you always were. Your knowledge and ideas will remain intact. But outwardly you will not be recognizable to anyone you now know.

Your visitor emphasizes that being born to the wrong parents was in no way your fault. Accordingly, his organization is prepared to offer you some reasonable recompense. Would you, he asks, care to name a sum of money you might consider appropriate? He adds that his group is by no means poor. It can be quite generous when the circumstances warrant, as they seem to in your case. He finishes by saying that their records also show you are scheduled to live another sixty years—as a black man or woman in America.

How much financial recompense would you request?

When this parable has been put to white students, most seemed to feel that it would not be out of place to ask for $1 million for each future year they would be living as a black American. And this calculation conveys, as well as anything, the value that white people place on their own skin. Indeed, to be white is to possess a gift whose value can be appreciated only after it has been taken away. And why ask for so large a sum? Surely this needs no detailing. The money would be used, as best it could, to buy protection from the discriminations and dangers white people know they would face once they were perceived to be black.

Of course, no one who is white can understand what it is like to be black in America. Still, were they to spend time in a black body, here are some of the things they would learn.

In the eyes of white Americans, being black encapsulates your identity. No other racial or national origin is seen as having so pervasive a personality or character. Even if you write a book on Euclidean algorithms or Renaissance sculpture, you will still be described as a "black author." Although you are a native American with a longer lineage than most, you will never be accorded full membership in the nation or society. More than that, you early learn that this nation feels no need or desire for your physical presence. (Indeed, your people are no longer in demand as cheap labor.) You sense that most white citizens would heave a sigh of relief were you simply to disappear. While few openly propose that you return to Africa, they would be greatly pleased were you to make that decision for yourself. Indeed, from time to time, you find yourself recalling an essay Ralph Ellison wrote more than three decades ago, which he titled "What America Would Be Like Without Blacks." In it, he said that most whites harbor "the fantasy of a blackless America," in which black people voluntarily decide to live somewhere else. Of course, the vast majority of whites will deny that they hold any such view. At the least, they will say how much they revere the talents of black athletes and entertainers. Ellison did not offer evidence for his view, since it calls for plumbing the depths of individuals' minds. Yet once in a while, occasions arise in which the sentiments he described are in fact revealed.

A SEPARATE STATE

A prominent talk show featured a program on "What Future for Black Americans?" The three panelists were black. One spoke eloquently for integration, hoping that in a not-distant day, blacks and whites would live side by side. A second espoused the gospel of capitalism, saying that if blacks succeeded in making money, they could solve the rest of their problems.

At this point, it should be noted that the studio audience was almost entirely white. Most of them had written for tickets many months in advance, and learned of the subject only when they arrived. Still, they listened attentively and applauded politely.

The third speaker was a minister representing a lesser-known separatist sect. Looking straight at his white listeners, he announced: "My people don't want to integrate with you. In fact, we don't want to have anything to do with you. Our goal is to have a separate state of our own."

The audience took a collective gasp and then broke into wild applause, much longer and louder than that for the other participants. Indeed, it even seemed as if a few might be reaching for their checkbooks.

Your people originated in Africa, and you want to feel pride in your homeland. After all, it was where humanity began. Hence your desire to know more of its peoples and their history, their culture and achievements, and how they endure within yourself. W.E.B. Du Bois said it best: "two thoughts, two unrecognizable stirrings, two warring ideals in one black body."

Yet there is also your awareness that not only America but also much of the rest of the world regards Africa as the primal continent: the most backward, the least developed, by almost every modern measure. Equally unsettling, Africa is regarded as barely worth the world's attention, a region no longer expected to improve in condition or status. During its periodic misfortunes— usually famine or slaughter—Africa may evoke compassion and pity. Yet the message persists that it must receive outside help, since there is little likelihood that it will set things right by itself.

Then there are the personal choices you must make about your identity. Unless you want to stress a Caribbean connection, you are an American, and it is the only citizenship you have. At the same time, you realize that this is a white country that expects its inhabitants to think and act in white ways. How far do you wish to adapt, adjust, assimilate, to a civilization so at variance with your people's past? For example, there is the not-so-simple matter of deciding on your diction. You know how white people talk and what they like to hear. Should you conform to those expectations, even if it demands denying or concealing much of your self? After all, white America gives out most of the rewards and prizes associated with success. Your decisions are rendered all the more painful by the hypocrisy of it all, since you are aware that even if you make every effort to conform, whites will still not totally accept you as one of their own.

So to a far greater degree than for immigrants from other lands, it rests on you to create your own identity. But it is still not easy to follow the counsel of Zora Neale Hurston: "Be as black as you want to be." For one thing, that choice is not always left to you. By citizenship and birth, you may count as an American, yet you find yourself agreeing with the dramatist August Wilson when he says, "We're a different people." Why else can you refer to your people as "folks" and "family," to one another as "sisters" and "brothers," in ways whites never can?

There are moments when you understand Toni Morrison's riposte, "At no moment in my life have I ever felt as though I were an American." This in turn gives rise to feelings of sympathy with figures like Cassius Clay, H. Rap Brown, Lew Alcindor, and Stokely Carmichael, who decided to repatriate themselves as Muhammad Ali, Jamil Abdullah al-Amin, Kareem Abdul-Jabbar, and Kwame Touré.

Those choices are not just for yourself. There will be the perplexing—and equally painful—task of having to explain to your children why they will not be treated as other Americans: that they will never be altogether accepted, that they will always be regarded warily, if not with suspicion or hostility. When they ask whether this happens because of anything they have done, you must find ways of conveying that, no, it is not because of any fault of their own. Further, for reasons you can barely explain yourself, you must tell them that much of the world has decided that you are not and cannot be their equals; that this world wishes to keep you apart, a caste it will neither absorb nor assimilate.

You will tell your children this world is wrong. But, because that world is there, they will have to struggle to survive, with scales weighted against them. They will have to work harder and do better, yet the result may be less recognition and less reward. We all know life can be unfair. For black people, this knowledge is not an academic theory but a fact of daily life.

NEIGHBORHOOD APARTHEID

You find yourself granting that there are more black faces in places where they were never seen before. Within living memory, your people were barred from major league teams; now they command the highest salaries in most professional sports. In the movies, your people had to settle for roles as servants or buffoons. Now at least some of them are cast as physicians, business executives, and police officials. But are things truly different? When everything is added up, white America still prefers its black people to be performers who divert them as athletes and musicians and comedians.

Yet where you yourself are concerned, you sense that in mainstream occupations, your prospects are quite limited. In most areas of employment, even after playing by the rules, you find yourself hitting a not-so-invisible ceiling. You wonder if you are simply corporate wallpaper, a protective coloration they find it prudent to display. You begin to suspect that a "qualification" you will always lack is white pigmentation.

In theory, all Americans with financial means and a respectable demeanor can choose where they want to live. For over a generation, courts across the country have decreed that a person's race cannot be a reason for refusing to rent or sell a residence. However, the law seems to have had little impact on practice, since almost all residential areas are entirely black or white. Most whites prefer it that way. Some will say they would like a black family nearby, if only to be able to report that their area is "integrated." But not many do. Most white Americans do not move in circles where racial integration wins social or moral credit.

This does not mean it is absolutely impossible for a black family to find a home in a white area. Some have, and others undoubtedly will. Even so, black Americans have no illusions about the hurdles they will face. If you look outside your designated areas, you can expect chilly receptions, evasive responses, and outright lies; a humiliating experience, rendered all the more enraging because it is so repeated and prolonged. After a while, it becomes too draining to continue the search. Still, if you have the income, you will find an area to your liking. But it will probably be all black. In various suburbs and at the outer edges of cities, one can see well-kept homes, outwardly like other such settings. But a closer view shows all the householders to be black.

This is the place to consider residential apartheid—and that is what it is—in its full perspective. Black segregation differs markedly from that imposed on any other group. Even newly arrived immigrants are more readily accepted in white neighborhoods.

Nor should it be assumed that most black householders prefer the racial ratios where they currently reside. Successive surveys have shown that, on average, only about one in eight say they prefer a neighborhood that is all or mostly black, which is the condition most currently confront. The vast majority—usually about 85 percent—state they would like an equal mixture of black and white neighbors. Unfortunately, this measure of racial balance has virtually no chance of being realized. The reason, very simply, is that hardly any whites will live in a neighborhood or community where half the residents are black. So directly or indirectly, white Americans have the power to decide the racial composition of communities and neighborhoods. Most egregious have been instances where acts of arson or vandalism force black families to leave. But such methods are the exception. There are other, less blatant, ways to prevent residential integration from passing a certain "tipping" point.

Here we have no shortage of studies. By and large, this research agrees that white residents will stay—and a few new ones may move in—if black arrivals do not exceed eight percent. But once the black proportion passes that point, whites begin to leave the neighborhood, and no new ones will arrive. The vacated houses or apartments will be bought or rented by blacks, and the area will be on its way to becoming all black.

What makes integration difficult if not impossible is that so few whites will accept even a racial composition reflecting the overall national proportion of 12 or 13 percent. In this regard, one or two attempts have been made to impose ceilings on the number of black residents in housing projects and developments, so as not to frighten away whites. Spring Creek Towers, formerly Starrett City, in New York has used this strategy, as has Atrium Village in Chicago. According to some legal readings, these procedures are unconstitutional, since they treat racial groups differently. These developments create "benign quotas," which means that to preserve a racial balance, they specify how many residents of each race they will admit. And that requires them to maintain two sets of waiting lists. This has been necessary to ensure that the families chosen for vacant apartments will preserve the prevailing racial ratio. Given the preference of many blacks for integrated housing, quite a few tend to apply, and they outnumber the whites on the list because fewer whites want to live in integrated settings. The result is that black applicants have to wait longer and are less likely to get their first choice of accommodation.

Whites and blacks who want to achieve and maintain interracial housing—itself a rarity—find they are forced to defend "benign quotas" that are biased against some blacks, since there are fewer "black" places. Racial quotas also tend to put blacks on the spot. On the one hand, few are willing to publicly support a ceiling for people of their race. Even so, most of the black householders already in residence would prefer that the racial ratio remain stabilized. After all, they themselves underwent a wait because they wanted to live in a racially integrated setting. Yet preserving the equation pits them against other blacks who may be impatient to get in.

If many whites say they support racial integration in principle, even if this means having only a token black neighbor, at least as many do not want *any* blacks living near them at all. One question, certainly, is how far this resistance is based solely on race, or whether the reasons have more to do with culture or class. White people themselves vary in income and other symbols of status, and every part of the nation has hierarchies among its white neighborhoods. Even in an area where everyone earns essentially the same income, many residents would not want a homosexual couple on their block or a neighbor who parks a van marked "PARAGON PEST CONTROL" in his driveway every night. Simply being a fellow white is not enough to make a person a desired neighbor.

This granted, we can try to isolate the element of race by positing some "ideal" black neighbors: persons with professional credentials or those who hold administrative positions in respected organizations. Give them sophisticated tastes; make them congenial in demeanor; and have them willing to care about their property and the area as a whole. And allow, further, that a fair number of whites might not object to having one or two such households nearby. Why, then, would such open-minded neighbors start worrying if the number of black families—granting that all of them are impeccably middle-class—seems to be approaching a racial "tipping" point?

The first reason is that there is no assurance that the black proportion will stay below the "tipping" figure. Word gets around among black families when a "white" neighborhood appears willing to accept a measure of integration. Rental and real estate agents are also quick to note this fact and begin recommending the area to black customers. As a result, whenever homes and apartments become vacant, a visible number of those families coming to look at them appear to be black. Nor should this be surprising. Some black Americans want more interracial exposure for themselves and their children. Others may not share this wish, but they know that better schools and safer streets are more apt to be where whites are.

As has been noted, the white exodus gets under way even before the black proportion reaches ten percent. And the turnover can be all but total within a single year. Moreover, this happens even when the blacks who move in have the same economic and social standing as the white residents. What is it, then, that makes white Americans unwilling to risk having black neighbors? Some of the reasons are familiar and openly stated. Others involve fears less easily articulated or acknowledged.

To the minds of most Americans, the mere presence of black people is associated with a high incidence of crime, residential deterioration, and lower educational attainment. Of course, most whites are willing to acknowledge that these strictures do not apply to all blacks. At the same time, they do not want to have to worry about trying to distinguish blacks who would make good neighbors from those who would not. To which is added the suspicion that if more black families arrive, it would take only one or two undesirables to undermine any interracial amity.

Even if all one's black neighbors were vouchsafed to be middle-class or better, there may still be misgiving about their teenage offspring. To start, there is the well-known wariness of white parents that their children—especially their daughters—could begin to make black friends. Plus the fear that even less intimate contacts will influence the vocabulary and diction, or the academic commitments, of their own progeny. And if white parents are already uneasy over the kinds of music their children enjoy, imagine their anxieties at hearing an even greater black resonance. Along with the worry that some of the black youths on the block might display a hostile demeanor, clouding the congenial ambience most Americans seek.

Americans have extraordinarily sensitive antennae for the colorations of neighborhoods. In virtually every metropolitan area, white householders can rank each enclave by the racial makeup of the residents. Given this knowledge, where a family lives becomes an index of its social standing. While this is largely an economic matter, proximity to blacks compounds this assessment. For a white family to be seen as living in a mixed—or changing—neighborhood can be construed as a symptom of surrender, indeed as evidence that they are on a downward spiral.

If you are black, these white reactions brand you as a carrier of contaminations. No matter what your talents or attainments, you are seen as infecting a neighborhood simply because of your race. This is the ultimate insult of segregation. It opens wounds that never really heal and leaves scars to remind you how far you stand from full citizenship.

A WHITE STANDARD

Except when you are in your own neighborhood, you feel always on display. On many occasions, you find you are the only person of your race present. You may be the only black student in a college classroom, the only black on a jury, the sole black at a corporate meeting, the only one at a social gathering. With luck, there may be one or two others. You feel every eye is on you, and you are not clear what posture to present. You realize that your presence makes whites uncomfortable; some of them probably wish you were not there at all. But since you are, they want to see you smile, so they can believe that you are being treated well. Not only is an upbeat air expected, but you must never show exasperation or anger, let alone anything that could look like a chip on your shoulder. Not everyone can keep such tight control. You don't find it surprising that so many black athletes and entertainers seek relief from those tensions.

Even when not in white company, you know that you are forever in their conversations. Ralph Ellison once said that, to whites, you are an "invisible man." You know what he meant. Of course white people see you, and sometimes react with fright or aversion. What Ellison meant was that your African ancestry gives you a shadowy existence in the society white Americans have made. Yet for all that, you and your people have been studied and scrutinized and dissected, caricatured, and pitied or deplored, as no other group ever has. You see yourself reduced to data in research, statistics in reports. Each year, the nation asks how many of your teenagers have become pregnant, how many of your young men are in prison. Not only are you continually on view; you are always on trial.

What we have come to call the media looms large in the lives of almost all Americans. Television and films, newspapers and magazines, books and advertising and now the internet, all serve as windows on a wider world, providing real and fantasized images of the human experience. The media also help us to fill out our own identities, telling us about ourselves, or the selves we might like to be.

If you are black, most of what is available for you to read and watch and hear depicts the activities of white people, with only rare and incidental allusions to persons like yourself. Black topics and authors and performers appear even less than your share of the population, not least because the rest of America doesn't care to know about you. Whites will be quick to point out that there have been successful "black" programs on television, as well as popular black entertainers and best-selling authors. Yet in these and other instances, it is whites who decide which people and productions will be underwritten, which almost always means that "black" projects will have to appeal to whites as well. You sometimes sense that artists like Jessye Norman and Toni Morrison, Paul Robeson and Bill Cosby, Denzel Washington and Halle Berry, have had to tailor much of their talent to white audiences. You often find yourself wishing they could just be themselves, speaking to their own people.

At the same time, you feel frustration and disgust when white America appropriates your music, your styles, indeed your speech and sexuality. At times, white audiences will laud the originality of black artists and performers and athletes. But in the end, they feel more comfortable when white musicians and designers and writers—and athletic coaches—adapt black talents to white sensibilities.

Add to this your bemusement when movies and television series cast more blacks as physicians and attorneys and executives than one will ever find in actual hospitals or law firms or corporations. True, these depictions can serve as role models for your children, encouraging their aspirations. At the same time, you do not want white audiences to conclude that since so many of your people seem to be doing well, little more needs to be done.

Then there are those advertisements showing groups of people. Yes, one of them may be black, although not too black, and always looking happy to be in white company. Still, these blacks are seldom in the front row, or close to the center.

MORE HURDLES TO OVERCOME

To be sure, textbooks and lesson plans now include allusions to "contributions" made by Americans of many ancestries. Children are taught how the Chinese built the railroads and that Hispanics have a vibrant and varied culture. Even acknowledging these nods, the curricula of the nation's schools and colleges focus mainly on the achievements of white people. The emphasis is on English origins and how those settlers brought their institutions and ideas from the British Isles. Most Americans with European ancestors can identify with this "Anglo-Saxon" past. Descendants of slaves do not find it as easy. Whether black children are alienated by the content of the curriculum is a matter of controversy, which will be considered later on. At this point, it can be said that few teachers attempt to explain how the human beings consigned to slavery shaped the structure and sensibilities of the new nation. Apart from brief allusions to a Sojourner Truth or a Benjamin Banneker, your people appear as passive victims and faceless individuals.

In much the same vein, white children can be led to see how the travails of Shakespeare's heroes shed light on the human condition. Or that Jane Austen's heroines have messages for Americans of today. Nor is this impossible for black Americans. Ralph Ellison, raised in rural Alabama, recalled that reading Ezra Pound and Sigmund Freud gave him a broader sense of life. Jamaica Kincaid has cited Charlotte Brontë as her first literary influence. Yet no matter how diligently you think about these authors and their ideas, you find that much of your life is not reflected in European learning. You often feel that there is a part of yourself, your soul, that Europe cannot reach.

Well, what about assimilation? Here you receive the same message given immigrants: if you wish to succeed, or simply survive, adapt to the diction and demeanor of the Anglo-American model. But even if you opt for that path, you will never receive the acceptance accorded to other groups, including newcomers arriving from as far away as Asia and the Middle East. In the view of those who set the rules, if you are of African origin, you will never fully fit the image of a true American. Notice how even blacks who espouse conservative opinions are regarded more as curiosities than as serious citizens.

Whether you would like to know more white people is not an easy question to answer. So many of the contacts you have with them are stiff and uneasy, hardly worth the effort. If you are a woman, you may have developed some cordial acquaintances among white women at your place of work, since women tend to be more relaxed when among themselves. Still, very few black men and women can say that they have white "friends," if by that is meant people they confide in or entertain in their homes.

Of course, friendships often grow out of shared experiences. People with similar backgrounds can take certain things for granted when with one another. In this respect, you and white people may not have very much in common. At the same time, by no means all your outlooks and interests relate to your race. There probably are at least a few white people you would like to know better. It just might be that some of them would like to know you. But as matters now stand, the chances that these barriers will be broken do not appear to be very great.

Societies create vocabularies, devising new terms when they are needed and retaining old ones when they serve a purpose. Dictionaries list words as obsolete or archaic, denoting that they are no longer used or heard. But one epithet survives, because people want it to. Your vulnerability to humiliation can be summed up in a single word. That word, of course, is "nigger."

When a white person voices it, it becomes a knife with a whetted edge. No black person can hear it with equanimity or ignore it as "simply a word." This word has the force to pierce, to wound, to penetrate, as no other has. There have, of course, been terms like "kike" and "spick" and "chink." But these are less frequently heard today, and they lack the same emotional impact. Some nonethnic terms come closer, such as "slut" and "fag" and "cripple." Yet "nigger" stands alone with its power to tear at one's insides. It is revealing that whites have never created so wrenching an epithet for even the most benighted members of their own race.

Black people may use "nigger" among themselves, but with a tone and intention that is known and understood. Even so, if you are black, you know white society devised this word and keeps it available for use. (Not officially, of course, or even in print; but you know it continues to be uttered behind closed doors.) Its persistence reminds you that you are still perceived as a degraded species of humanity, at a level to which whites can never descend.

ARE YOU BEING INCONSISTENT?

You and your people have problems, far more than your share. And it is not as if you are ignorant of them or wish to sweep them under a rug. But how to frame your opinions is not an easy matter. For example, what should you say about black crime or drug addiction or out-of-wedlock pregnancies? Of course, you have much to say on these and other topics, and you certainly express your ideas when you are among your own people. And you can be critical—very critical—of a lot of behavior you agree has become common among blacks.

However, the white world also asks that black people conduct these discussions in public. In particular, they want to hear you condemn black figures they regard as outrageous or irresponsible. This cannot help but annoy you. For one thing, you have never asked for white advice. Yet whites seem to feel that you stand in need of their tutelage, as if you lack the insight to understand your own interests. Moreover, it makes sense for members of a minority to stand together, especially since so many whites delight in magnifying differences among blacks. Your people have had a long history of being divided and conquered. At the same time, you have no desire to be held responsible for what every person of your color thinks or does. You cannot count how many times you have been asked to atone for some utterances of Louis Farrakhan or simply to assert that he does not speak for you. You want to retort that you will choose your own causes and laments. Like other Americans, you have no obligation to follow agendas set by others.

As it happens, black Americans can and do disagree on racial matters, not to mention a host of other issues. Thus a survey found that 78 percent of those polled said they preferred to think of themselves as "black," and another 20 percent chose "African-American," while the remaining 2 percent stayed with "Negro." Another study by a team of black social scientists found that fewer than a quarter of the blacks they polled felt that black parents should give their children African names. Indeed, on a wide range of matters, there is no fixed, let alone official, black position. Yet it is amazing how often white people ask you to tell them how "black people" think about some individual or issue.

Then there are the accusations of inconsistency. As when you seem to favor taking race into consideration in some areas but not in others. Or that you support a double standard, which allows separate criteria to be used for blacks in employment or education. Well, as it happens, you do believe:

- That discrimination against blacks remains real and calls for radical remedies. Yet you cannot take seriously the argument that these compensatory actions will cause whites to suffer from "reverse" discrimination.
- That blacks have every right to attend dominantly white schools. Yet once they are there, they should not be taken to task for spending much of their time with classmates of their own race.
- That it is important to preserve historically black colleges. Yet you would feel entitled to object if some other schools were to designate themselves as "historically white."
- That racism is often the key reason why white voters rally behind white candidates. Yet when blacks support a candidate of their own race, you do not see this as expressing racism.
- That while you reject censorship, you would prefer that a book like *Huckleberry Finn* not be assigned in high school classes, since its ubiquitous use of "nigger" sustains a view of blacks that can only hurt your people. Nor are you convinced that white teachers can convey Mark Twain's sympathies to white teenagers.

It will often seem to you as if black people's opinions are constantly under scrutiny by the white world. Every time you express an idea, whites seem to slap it on their dissecting table, showing that blacks want the best of both ways. In fact, you have answers on these issues, but whites take so much delight in citing alleged "inconsistencies" that they hardly hear what you have to say.

UNREALISTIC EXPECTATIONS

You may, by a combination of brains and luck and perseverance, make it into the middle class. And like all middle-class Americans, you will want to enjoy the comforts and pleasures that come with that status. One downside is that you will find many white people asking why you aren't doing more to help members of your race whom you have supposedly left behind. There is even the suggestion that by moving to a safer or more spacious setting, you have callously deserted your own people.

Yet hardly ever do middle-class whites reflect on the fact that they, too, have moved to better neighborhoods, usually far from poorer and less equable persons of their own race or ethnic origins. There is little evidence that many middle-class whites are prepared to give much of themselves in aid of fellow whites who have fallen on misfortune. Indeed, the majority of white Americans have chosen to live in sequestered suburbs, where they are insulated from the nation's losers and failures.

Compounding these expectations, you find yourself continually subjected to comparisons with other minorities or even members of your own race. For example, you are informed that blacks who have emigrated from the Caribbean earn higher incomes than those born in the United States. Here the message seems to be that color by itself is not an insurmountable barrier. Most stinging of all are contrasts with recent immigrants. You hear people just off the boat (or, nowadays, a plane) extolled for building businesses and becoming productive citizens. Which is another way of asking why you haven't matched their achievements, considering how long your people have been here.

Moreover, immigrants are praised for being willing to start at the bottom. The fact that so many of them manage to find jobs is taken as evidence that the economy still has ample opportunities for employment. You want to reply that you are not an immigrant but as much a citizen as any white person born here. Perhaps you can't match the mathematical skills of a teenager from Korea, but then neither can most white suburban students. You feel much like a child being chided because she or he has not done as well as a precocious sibling. However, you are an adult and do not find such scolding helpful or welcome.

AN UNEASY ALLIANCE

No law of humanity or nature posits a precise format for the family. Throughout history and even in our day, households have had many shapes and structures. The same comments apply to marriage and parental relationships. All this requires some emphasis, given concerns expressed about "the black family" and its presumed disintegration. In fact, the last several decades have seen a weakening of domestic ties in all classes and races.

Black Americans are fully aware of what is happening in this sphere. They know that most black children are being born out of wedlock and that these youngsters will spend most of their growing years with a single parent. They understand that a majority of their marriages will dissolve in separation or divorce and that many black men and women will never marry at all. Black Americans also realize that tensions between men and women sometimes bear a violence and bitterness that can take an awful toll.

If you are black, you soon learn it is safest to make peace with reality: to acknowledge that the conditions of your time can undercut dreams of enduring romance and "happily ever after." This is perhaps especially true if you are a black woman, since you may find yourself spending many of your years without a man in your life. Of course, you will survive and adapt, as your people always have. Central in this effort will be joining and sustaining a community of women—another form of a family—on whom you can rely for love and strength and support.

If you are a black woman, you can expect to live six and a half fewer years than your white counterpart. Among men, the gap is seven years. Indeed, a man living in New York's Harlem is less likely to reach sixty-five than is a resident of Bangladesh. Black men have a nine times greater chance of dying of AIDS and out-number whites as murder victims by a factor of eight. According to studies, you get less sleep, and are more likely to be over-weight and to develop hypertension. This is not simply due to poverty. Your shorter and more painful life results, in consider-able measure, from the anxieties that come with being black in America.

If you are a black young man, life can be an interlude with an early demise. Black youths do what they must to survive in a hos-tile world, with the prospect of violence and death on its battle-fields. Attitudes can turn fatalistic, even suicidal: gladiators without even the cheers of an audience.

When white people hear the cry "The police are coming!" for them it almost always means "Help is on the way." Black citizens cannot make the same assumption. If you have been the victim of a crime, you cannot presume that the police will actually show up or, if they do, that they will take much note of your losses or suf-fering. You sense police officials feel that blacks should accept being robbed or raped as one of life's everyday risks. It seems to you obvious that more detectives are assigned to a case when a white person is murdered.

If you are black and young and a man, the arrival of the police does not usually signify help but something very different. If you are a teenager simply socializing with some friends, the police may order you to disperse and get off the streets. They may turn on a searchlight, order you against a wall. Then comes the command to spread your legs and empty out your pockets and stand splayed there while they call in your identity over their radio. You may be a college student and sing in a church choir, but that will not overcome the police presumption that you have probably done something they can arrest you for.

If you find yourself caught up in the system, it will seem like alien terrain. Usually your judge and prosecutor will be white, as will most members of the jury, as well as your attorney. In short, your fate will be decided by a white world.

This may help to explain why you have so many harsh words for the police, even though you want and need their protection more than white people do. After all, there tends to be more crime in areas where you live, not to mention drug dealing and all that comes in its wake. Black citizens are 2.7 times as likely as whites to become victims of robberies and in almost all of these cases, the person who attacks you will be black. Since this is so, whites want to know, Why don't black people speak out against the members of their race who are causing so much grief? The reason is partly that you do not want to attack other blacks while whites are listening. At least equally important is that while you obviously have no taste for violence, you are also wary of measures that might come with a campaign to stamp out "black crime." These reasons will receive fuller consideration in a later chapter. At this point, you might simply say that you are not sure you want a more vigorous police presence, if those enforcers are unable to distinguish between law-abiding citizens and local predators. Of course, you want to be protected. But not if it means that you and your friends and relatives end up included among those the police harass or arrest.

RESERVATIONS ABOUT PATRIOTISM

The national anthem sings of America as "the land of the free." The Pledge of Allegiance promises "liberty and justice for all." The Declaration of Independence proclaims that all human creatures are "created equal."

If you are black, you cannot easily join in during the anthem's refrain, recite the pledge, or affirm that your country is committed to equality. While you grant that the United States is "your" country, you may define your citizenship as partial and qualified. It is not that you are "disloyal," if that means having your first allegiance elsewhere. Rather, you feel no compelling commitment to a republic that has always rebuffed you and your people.

We know from surveys that during the Cold War era, black Americans felt less antipathy toward nations then designated as our enemies, since they saw themselves less threatened by the Soviet Union or Cuba or China than did most white Americans. Nor were they so sure why they or their children were asked to risk their lives fighting people of color in places like Vietnam and Panama and the Middle East. And as the United States finds itself increasingly at odds with Islamic countries or other movements in the Third World, even more black Americans may find themselves wondering where their own allegiances lie.

As you look back on the way this nation has treated your people, you wonder how so many have managed to persevere amid so much adversity. About slavery, of course, too much cannot be said. Yet even within living memory, there were beaches and parks—in the North as well as in the South—where black Americans simply could not set foot. Segregation meant separation without even a pretense of equal facilities. In Southern communities that had only a single public library or swimming pool, black residents and taxpayers could never borrow a book or go for a swim. Indeed, black youths were even forbidden to stroll past the pool, lest they catch a glimpse of white girls in their bathing costumes.

How did they endure the endless insults and humiliations? Grown people being called by their first names, having to avert their eyes when addressed by white people, even being expected to step off a sidewalk when whites walked by. Overarching it all was the terror, with white police and prosecutors and judges possessing all but total power over black lives. Not to mention the lynchings by white mobs, with victims even chosen at random, to remind all blacks of what could happen to them if they did not remain compliant and submissive.

You wonder how much that has changed. Suppose, for example, you find yourself having to drive across the country, stopping at gasoline stations and restaurants and motels. As you travel across the heart of white America, you can never be sure of how you will be received. While the odds are that you will reach your destination safely, you cannot be so sure that you will not be stopped by the police or spend a night in a cell. So you would be well advised to keep to the speed limit and not exceed it by a single mile per hour. Of course, white people are pulled over by state troopers; but how often are their cars searched? Or if a motel clerk cannot "find" your reservation, is it because she has now seen you in person? And are all the toilet facilities at this service station really out of order?

The day-to-day aggravations and humiliations add up bit by bitter bit. To take a depressingly familiar example, you stroll into a shop to look at the merchandise, and it soon becomes clear that the clerks are keeping a watchful eye on you. Too quickly, one of them comes over to inquire what it is you might want and then remains conspicuously close as you continue your search. It also seems that they take an unusually long time verifying your credit card. And then you and a black friend enter a restaurant and find yourselves greeted warily, with what is obviously a more anxious reception than that given to white guests. Yes, you will be served, and your table will not necessarily be next to the kitchen. Still, you sense that they would rather you had chosen some other eating place. Or has this sort of thing happened so often that you are growing paranoid?

So there is the sheer strain of living in a white world, the rage that you must suppress almost every day. No wonder so many black Americans, especially black men, suffer from hypertension. (If ever an illness had social causes, this is certainly one.) To be black in America means reining in your opinions and emotions as no whites ever have to do. Not to mention the forced and false smiles you are expected to contrive to assure white Americans that you harbor no grievances against them.

Along with the tension and the strain and the rage, there come those moments of despair. At times, the conclusion seems all but self-evident that white America has no desire for your presence or any need for your people. How else, you ask yourself, can one explain the incidence of death and debilitation from drugs and disease, the incarceration of a whole generation of your men, the consignment of millions of women and children to half-lives of poverty and dependency? Each of these conditions has its causes. Yet the fact that they so centrally impinge on a single race makes one wonder why the larger society has allowed them to happen.

This is not to say that white officials are plotting the genocide of black America. You understand as well as anyone that politics and history seldom operate that way. Still, you cannot rid yourself of some lingering mistrust. Just as your people were once made to serve silently as slaves, could it be that if white America begins to conclude you are becoming too much trouble, it will start contemplating more lasting solutions?

And there are grounds for this belief. After all, calls for more life sentences, the flow of funds for new prisons, and stepping up of executions, all largely affect your race. The same holds for demands that single mothers work. Perhaps most ominous is the renewed assertion that individuals of African ancestry are mentally inferior, and hence to be considered a subgrade of citizen.

CHAPTER FOUR

WHITE RESPONSES

RIGHT AND LEFT, GUILT AND SEX

LEFT AND RIGHT, we often hear, have lost their relevance in a complex and changing age. That view has validity for many issues, especially as fewer people see the world through an ideological lens. Yet race remains an area where it still makes sense to locate the attitudes of white Americans along a liberal-conservative continuum.

As used here, the term "liberal" will range from a moderate posture to the radical left. While liberalism is not a detailed doctrine with positions on every issue, it has a quite coherent outlook concerning what white America owes to its black citizens.

Conservatives also range across a spectrum; but, as with liberals, some generalizations can be ventured. Conservatives will be considered first, because their views are more straightforwardly stated and have a less ambiguous basis.

THE CONSERVATIVE STANCE

Most conservative Americans tend to disclaim responsibility for issues and tensions associated with race. They also reject the suggestion that they should bear any personal guilt. In their view, black Americans are the ones who should change their attitudes and conduct. Conservatives believe that for at least a generation, black people have been given plenty of opportunities, so they have no one but themselves to blame for whatever difficulties they face. Also, when among themselves, conservatives may be heard to wonder whether many blacks truly want to make an effort to adapt to the demands of this nation. Nor are they persuaded that many have the talents needed for positions of authority. For this and related reasons, in political contests involving a choice between candidates of different races, they usually end up voting for whoever happens to be the white candidate.

For their own part, conservatives prefer to believe that whatever success they have achieved has been due to their own efforts; and they feel this standard should apply to everyone. They may add that special assistance erodes the character of those so assisted, by allowing them to get by too easily. In objecting to calls for preferential treatment, they cite other ethnic groups that started at or near the bottom and have, by their own efforts, pulled ahead of black Americans. Conservatives tend not to be moved by arguments that immigrants face fewer obstacles than the descendants of slaves.

One of the more interesting hallmarks of white conservatives is the amount of energy they expend attacking policies intended to aid blacks. Among their targets are affirmative action in employment and education, along with contracts earmarked for minority businesses. At first glance, the sheer volume of these broadsides—books and articles and speeches, backed by lawsuits and administrative challenges—might seem a case of overkill given the impact of these programs. As will be noted in later chapters, the number of whites who have been adversely affected by affirmative action has been relatively small. Still, preferred treatment for blacks touches a conservative nerve. It is not simply that they want everyone to play by the same rules. In other areas, conservatives defend inherited privileges and advantages. With affirmative action, there is something about black recipients that bothers conservatives in ways they cannot always articulate in a coherent way.

On the whole, conservatives don't really care whether black Americans are happy or unhappy. At the same time, they remain vigilant for signs of discontent, especially if stirrings have ominous overtones. Hence their support for close police control of the black population. So when crime rates rise, conservatives do not call for confronting basic causes—unemployment, for example, or inferior education—but rather invoke a firmer use of force. Since they see themselves as bearing no onus for whatever problems blacks face, they do not really care if blacks feel aggrieved or unfairly treated. To support their position, they cite black conservatives—Thomas Sowell, Clarence Thomas, Shelby Steele—who assure them that blacks have played the victim too long and must be judged by the same standards as other Americans.

For the past several decades, a majority of white Americans have said that they support racial integration, equality of opportunity, and a better life for their black fellow citizens. Are these statements more than cosmetic?

What has changed in recent years is the way people speak in public. Indeed, even in private conversations, the coarser kinds of descriptions are less often heard. Hence recourse to roundabout phrases, like "underclass" and "inner city." There are several reasons for this shift. At the center has been the extension of schooling. The choice to go on with formal learning usually reflects a wish to raise oneself socially and professionally, which in turn calls for more caution in speech and demeanor.

Given these new sensitivities, it is not surprising that surveys find majorities of white Americans avowing that they would not object to having some black families on their block. Nor, they say, would they mind were their children's schools to have a greater mixture of races. Such responses should not be dismissed as dishonest or hypocritical, at least at a conscious level. For a further effect of education is to encourage people to think of themselves as tolerant and open-minded.

THE LIBERAL PERSPECTIVE

The term "liberal" tends to be associated with men and women who are at least minimally middle-class. (In contrast, conservative beliefs can be found on every rung of the social ladder.) What often distinguishes liberals from others at the same economic level is their greater willingness to pay for programs aimed at resolving social and racial ills. To that extent, then, they seem ready to share some of what they have with others less fortunate than themselves. In this respect, liberals like to feel they are altruistic and justified in criticizing conservatives for being tightfisted, if not downright selfish.

At the same time, the taxes liberals tend to propose are unlikely to be so severe as to reduce their own living standards in a serious way. However, few choose to live in multiracial neighborhoods and send their children to racially balanced schools. They may try to make up for this by expressing a willingness to pay taxes for social programs, as well as writing checks for progressive causes and organizations.

As was seen in Chapter Two, Thomas Jefferson used the phrase "our black brethren" to refer to fellow beings consigned to slavery, including those he owned himself. Liberals continue to profess this fellowship, affirming that in character and potential, blacks and whites are full and complete equals. Hence the inclination to empathize; to murmur, when seeing what so many blacks endure, that there but for an accident of birth, go I.

Moreover, liberals are also prone to accept personal responsibility for racial conditions that prevail in this country. Even if their forebears never owned slaves, they nevertheless believe that their own privileged status has contributed to keeping blacks in a degraded state. For example, liberals are ready to acknowledge how they have benefited from the availability of cheap black labor, whether as domestic servants or the people who pick the fruit and vegetables they buy. As an earnest of atonement, they may give larger tips to blacks who serve or wait on them.

Liberals also express more ambiguities than conservatives about the attainments of the white and Western world. They are more likely to focus on colonial conquests and exploitation, on technologies that destroy nature and corrupt the human spirit. Alongside the grandeur of Mozart and Michelangelo have been the horrors of Auschwitz and Hiroshima and chattel slavery. Thus on campuses, liberals urge a more multicultural content for the curriculum, which can mean compressing courses on Shakespeare to make room for offerings with less traditional origins.

Liberals also hold a theory about the sweep and tenor of human history. While this theory is seldom stated as a coherent philosophy, its premises occasionally become explicit. One such tenet is that the era of white dominance is coming to an end. If nothing else, birthrates dictate that the approaching century will belong to people of color, just as immigration is changing the texture of the United States. True, the Western world still has military might; but it lacks social goals and moral purpose. Hence the desire of liberals to find a place for themselves in the new era: so the future will note that they were among the few white persons who foresaw what was coming and were prepared to accept their diminished status.

Liberals seldom stop there. They frequently use psychology and the social sciences to excuse certain black behavior, on the ground that it is an understandable response to the way a subordinate race has been treated by an oppressive society.

This raises key questions about the meaning of crime and the rationale for punishment, which will be considered in a later chapter. What can be said here is that liberals are more apt to express compassion for the large numbers of black men and women currently languishing in prisons. They want to learn more about the conditions that may have turned these persons to crime, especially circumstances that might exonerate them from guilt. Seen in this way, individuals who have been condemned as culpable may be recast as victims, since they were driven to destructive conduct by forces beyond their control.

Liberals can thus conclude that the real guilt rests with white society, which forces blacks into demeaning segregation, consigns them to low-paid employment, and gives so many so little hope. That some black Americans may react in ways seen as antisocial should not be surprising, considering the constrictions on their lives. Of course, this raises the issue of how far individuals who have been treated unjustly should be held accountable for their acts. Conservatives have no problem with their answer. They believe that to exonerate irresponsible conduct is not only condescending but does little to improve the character of the culprits. Liberals tend to reply that the issue is not so simple. At the least, we ought to give more thought to the conditions that cause so many people who are black to end up being judged and condemned and punished by public opinion and official institutions.

WANTING APPROVAL

Liberals account for most of the white faces in the audiences for serious African and African-American music, art, and theater. A similar interest holds for books by black authors. Of course, white people of all ages and political persuasions are drawn to black entertainers, whether on television and movie screens or in athletic arenas. However, for those on the left, the attraction runs deeper than art and entertainment. For them, Africa—and much of black America—remains symbolic of a mode of life that the white and Western world has effaced or destroyed.

As has been intimated, white liberals want to be liked by black people, as if having their goodwill is a seal of approval. Hence the frequency with which they allude to black friends, black work-mates, and—when possible—black neighbors. (Having only a single black family in an apartment complex allows all the others to announce that they live in an "integrated" setting.) Hence also the mentions of black schoolmates their children may bring home, affirming their choice of integrated classes, even if in pri-vate schools. On the other side are the feelings of dismay when one receives rebuffs from blacks or simply the anonymous but scornful stares often encountered in public places. Liberals hope blacks will acknowledge that some whites—they themselves, as it happens—are not The Enemy but, rather, can be counted as friends and allies. For blacks to grant this, if only by bestowing a smile, serves to certify one's moral stature.

This search for approval also occurs in associational settings. Here we can observe an experience common among professional groups of professors, social workers, and librarians, which have large liberal memberships. These organizations usually elect their officers by ballots distributed through the mail. On an accompa-nying sheet, the candidates summarize their activities and affilia-tions, since in many cases they are not personally known to everyone taking part in the voting. If one of the persons running for office signals his or her race, perhaps by mentioning a position held in an African-American group, the odds are all but certain that he or she will end up among those elected. The individual's credentials may be excellent; however, that was not why that person got so many votes. Simply filling in the box by one or more "black" names allows a lot of white members to feel better about themselves.

Hence too the tendency to applaud longer and more vigorously following the remarks by a black participant in a panel discussion.

In many instances, of course, such praise is deserved: the panelist may have offered original and important observations. But it is also possible that the comments made by the black member are no more profound than those by the others at the table. If that is the case, then the prolonged applause is not so much to acclaim the presentation as to make someone who is black feel he is in the company of friendly whites. This will, they hope, serve as some recompense for the wrongs their race has done to his.

Often, in conversations where members of the two races are present, one or another of the white persons will say something that prompts a heated reply from a black member of the group. When it happens that the offending statement was made by someone who prides himself on being liberal, his reaction is usually to stammer plaintively, either retracting what he said or protesting that he had been misunderstood. Here, as elsewhere, liberals stand in dread of black disfavor, which must be mollified by admitting to oversight or error. This is especially evident when blacks charge whites with racism. Rather than deny the indictment, the liberal tendency is to admit to such bias and pledge renewed vigilance against future errors.

Upon hearing a report of a violent crime, many liberals find themselves half-consciously hoping that the perpetrator will turn out to be white. If that proves to be the case, their response will often be a sigh of relief. Given that liberals—much like everyone else—deplore violence of any kind, why should they have a preference about the race of the perpetrators?

The answer relates to the general tendency among Americans to associate blacks with crimes that threaten or inflict physical injury. As it happens, this belief has some basis in fact, since blacks do account for a disproportionate number of crimes like murder, rape, and robbery. As has been noted, an unfortunate consequence of this association is that law-abiding blacks find themselves perceived as possible criminals.

So, as liberals see it, any increase in the number of whites arrested for violent crimes would help to redress racial images in the public mind, which would in turn relieve blacks of the burden they bear because of current stereotypes about race and crime.

EXPERTS VS. AMATEURS?

Since the opening years of this century, America's variant of liberalism has maintained that governmental action can ameliorate serious social problems. Although less confident now than in the past, most liberals still put their faith in public policies. Hence the view that a variety of programs, many of them quite expensive, will be needed if black Americans are to be brought to parity with whites. By this time, the agenda is fairly familiar. Much more will have to be spent in areas such as education, health services, housing, and job training. Other programs would include better foster care for children, birth control education, and aid to men and women coming out of prison, along with drug treatment and counseling. The list could be easily extended in light of the disabilities besetting so much of the black population.

Liberals continue to have confidence in the competence of government to achieve social change. They do not view the Great Society of the 1960s as a failure. And indeed it had some signal successes. Head Start classes, for example, have enabled children to carry on through high school and beyond. Food stamps, really a kind of currency, have improved nutritional levels among millions of the poor. In both cases, black Americans were major beneficiaries. The sad part, liberals would add, is that funding for such programs was often reduced or rescinded just when results were beginning to show.

Therefore, governmental intervention is not just "throwing money" at social—and racial—problems. Liberals believe that both social science research and practical experience have amassed useful funds of knowledge. Thus, they would claim, we know how to make racial integration work and how to motivate youngsters to apply themselves in school. These aims have been attained in varied settings, and their lessons can be applied elsewhere. Faith in government rests on more than urging funding and authority for public agencies. It also arises from a belief in our ability to expand knowledge and understanding, a faith in the capacity of reason to triumph over prejudice, and the application of research to the betterment of society. So government should not be defined simply as a coercive force. It should also be seen as an instrument of service and a vehicle for organized action. Despite the presence of political pressures and parochial interests, we can still cite many cases where governmental agencies have pursued the public good and registered impressive successes.

As these arguments would suggest, liberals often rely on the presumed knowledge and objectivity of public-service professionals. Whether the area is child abuse, birth control counseling or managing low-income housing, liberals have sought a central role for experts with academic training. This has, however, stirred charges of "elitism," often with racial overtones, since the major decisions in health, education, and similar services tend to be made by white men and women with civil service tenure and graduate degrees. While these individuals have respectable credentials, questions have been raised concerning how much they truly know about the lives and aspirations of the people they are supposed to be assisting.

One consequence has been demands for "community control" of schools and other social programs, as a democratic counterweight to professional power. One proposal calls for giving committees of parents the authority to choose and supervise the principals of their youngsters' schools. In Chicago such a plan has been adopted, replacing a centralized system that had had little success in educating the city's children, especially in schools with enrollments that were largely or entirely black. Not surprisingly, most principals and many teachers have misgivings about giving over power to people they regard as amateurs. As a result, New York City has all but abandoned community control. This now means, among other things, that white administrators will pick the principals for predominantly black schools.

There is a real issue here, and it beleaguers contemporary liberals. Some have joined in the calls for community control, arguing that familiarity with local conditions should have higher priority than formal credentials and degrees. Others have resisted, saying that professional competence cannot be compromised. One resolution has been to co-opt more blacks as administrators and then use them as spokesmen for official policies.

All of these approaches are susceptible to perversion or corruption. Despite progressive intentions, social research can turn into arid methodologies of interest only to academics. Professionalism can become a wall of degrees and diplomas having little relation to the jobs that need to be done. Community control may end up with local groups diverting the resources of social agencies for purposes of their own.

If these and similar divisions sometimes daunt the liberal spirit, its faith in amelioration usually arises again. Despite the caricatures drawn by critics, few liberals go so far as to assert that the human condition is perfectible. But they do tend to affirm that progress is possible, that we can learn from experience, and that with goodwill and ingenuity, human beings can evolve new solutions that need not repeat the errors of the past.

THE GUILT FACTOR

Professions of sympathy and support have yet another source. Here the springs are more subtle, going beyond the way people want to be seen by the outside world. Rather, they reflect an unease within individuals stirred by distress over what this country has made of race.

Guilt is a tangled maze of emotions and reactions. Nor is there much consensus among psychologists about how it should be analyzed or explained. It is not a sentiment one can uncover by social surveys or opinion polls, since short answers to set questions seldom probe beneath the surface. Moreover, guilt can be rational or irrational. When it is rational, human beings admit that they have behaved badly, and they are right to blame themselves for such conduct. But guilt can also be irrational, in that people can flagellate themselves for conditions in which they did not participate. (Unless, of course, one believes that the mere fact of being white is enough to vest one with some responsibility for the plights of black Americans.) Some people enjoy feeling guilty, indeed savor the sensation. Guilt can also express a desire for punishment: as when a conscience-stricken oppressor asks to be told how he has erred so that he may mend his ways. We have seen how this operates with white people who seek the approval of blacks, which is taken as absolving them of racism.

Just what makes some people feel guilty, while others do not, cannot be answered in any conclusive way. We see that guilt is more apparent among academics and social service professionals than, say, corporation executives and self-made proprietors. It appears to run deeper among Jews and Congregationalists than, say, among Baptists or Mormons. But it is not enough to say that people have learned in their schools or from their families to judge themselves in certain ways. Imagine two sisters, raised in the same home during their formative years. Now, visiting them as adults, we find one sister plagued by racial guilt, while her sibling denies having any such feelings. Doubtless, close analysis of the two women could produce "explanations." We have no shortage of analysts willing to try their hand at psychobiography. In fact, though, we have little reliable knowledge about what may have moved one person in one direction and the other in another.

BEYOND GUILT

We now come to a more perplexing aspect of this subject of guilt: what to say about individuals who assert that they feel no guilt at all, who insist they have nothing to feel burdened about and dis-claim any responsibility for creating or maintaining the misfor-tunes of others. Are we to accept their own analysis and simply end the discussion there? For better or for worse, in our educated age, this is no longer possible. We have all experienced occasions when we feel we can see through a person's protestations. It is clear to us that they feel guilty about something but have set up barriers to avoid facing an unpleasant sensation. At one time or another, all of us have refused to admit certain truths about our-selves. By engaging in what Psychology 101 calls "denial," we seek to convince others—and ourselves—of our innocence of blame.

This said, it will be proposed here that all white Americans, regardless of their political persuasions, are well aware of how black people have suffered due to inequities imposed upon them by white America. As has been emphasized, whites differ in how they handle that knowledge. Yet white people who disavow responsibility deny an everyday reality: that to be black is to be consigned to the margins of American life. It is because of this that no white American, including those who insist that opportunities exist for persons of every race, would change places with even the most successful black American. All white Americans realize that their skin comprises an inestimable asset. It opens doors and facilitates freedom of movement. It serves as a shield from insult and harassment. Indeed, having been born white can be taken as a sign: your preferment is both ordained and deserved. Its value persists not because a white appearance automatically brings suc-cess and status, since there are no such guarantees. What it does ensure is that you will not be regarded as *black,* a security that is worth so much that no one who has it has ever given it away.

This helps to explain why white conservatives so vehemently oppose programs like affirmative action. They simply do not want to admit to themselves that the value imputed to being white has injured people who are black. Nor is this reaction sur-prising. Most people do not like feeling guilty. It can be an unpleasant, even painful, sensation. Hence the tendency to turn, often angrily, on those who stir us in this way. Rather than do something substantial to help people who have been treated unfairly, we find ourselves saying that they brought their afflictions on themselves. By this device, guilt can be made to disappear, or at least seem less burdensome. As we were also taught in Psychology 101, we erase our self-blame by projecting—or simply dumping—it onto someone else.

Every so often, something white people do shows evidence of misgivings. Here is an unexpected example. During elections, television stations conduct exit polls, in which individuals who have just voted are asked whom they supported. These findings are quickly collated and reported, and are used to forecast the results of elections before the ballots have been counted. On the whole, these surveys have been reliable, since people have no reason to lie to interviewers they do not know and will never see again.

But this is not always the case. In exit polls where the contest involves a white and a black candidate, more white voters will say they backed the black contender than in fact did. (It should be added that they do not give their responses on camera and that the interviewers are usually white.) This lying would suggest that a fair number of whites want to present a tolerant face, even to a total stranger. More than that, at least some may actually feel sorry for having voted as they did. They may have felt that the black candidate was better fitted for the job, yet they could not bring themselves to vote for him or her. To an extent, then, they are angry with themselves. So they take advantage of the exit poll, using it as an opportunity to atone.

Guilt is often associated with fear. In particular, fear of those aspects of ourselves we would prefer not to confront. This is why white people devised the word "nigger" and gave it so charged a meaning. It implies a creature so debased and degraded that such a person must represent a lower form of humanity. There was a need for such a term to justify slavery. And its current use rationalizes much of segregation and subordination today. James Baldwin, in *The Fire Next Time,* saw that the word served a further purpose. White people "need the nigger," he wrote, because it is "the nigger" within themselves that they cannot tolerate.

Construed in this way, "nigger" represents components of the human condition that may be found in all peoples and races. Whatever it is that whites feel that "nigger" signifies about blacks— lust or laziness, stupidity or squalor—in fact exists within themselves. Baldwin's message is that any person of any race can be a "nigger." The capacity is there, waiting to be released.

Needless to say, white people—paragons of civilization—cannot allow that "niggerness" is part of their being. Were that admitted, they would have to grant that they could plunge to a degradation from which their white skin could not shield them. So, Baldwin concluded, white people "need the nigger." By creating such a creature, whites are able to say that because only members of the black race can carry that taint, it follows that none of its attributes will be found in white people. This also explains why many whites react as they do to interracial marriage and mating and to rapes involving a black man and a white woman. There is the fear that the offspring of such couplings could dilute a superior strain with degraded traits.

RACE AND SEX

A half-century ago, Gunnar Myrdal observed that "sex and race fears are the main defense for segregation and, in fact, the whole caste order." In *An American Dilemma,* he cited the insistence of white men that they had to protect their women from advances of black men. Hence periodic lynchings, often accompanied by castration, to warn all black men that they would do well to avert their eyes when white women were in view. While lynchings are no longer used as means of control, anxieties over interracial sex have far from abated.

Myrdal was too polite a guest to draw out the full implications of the sexual emphasis he proposed. So he forbore from suggesting that white Americans also envy "the nigger" in ways they but dimly realize and are loath to acknowledge. Here we enter that very murky realm of sexual potency and performance, of sexual conquest and competition. Certainly, among the capacities that make for manhood, sexual potency continues to rank high even in our modern times. Compounding the ordinary insecurities most men have in this sphere, white men face the mythic fear that black men may outrival them in competence and virility. At issue, of course, is not whether this is actually true but the fact that the stereotype persists. Aggravating this unease is a further foreboding: that white women may wonder whether black men could provide greater sexual satisfaction than they get from their white mates. Notice, also, how white men glance a second time when they see a racially mixed couple: what, they seem to ask, does *she* see in—or do with—him? In a similar vein, white women may wonder whether they can provide the sexual abandon their own men may desire. What, they may ask themselves, draws so many white men to black prostitutes?

To be white is to be "civilized," which brings the acceptance and imposition of sexual constraints. True, the freedoms that arose with the sexual revolution permit more experimentation than in the past. Still, fantasies persist that black men and women are less burdened by inhibitions and can delight in primal pleasures beyond the capacities of whites. (The exhilaration displayed in black dancing has no white counterpart.) Nor is it surprising that much of the commentary concerning women on welfare adds the charge that they share their beds with successions of men. Underwriting their supposed indolence is bad enough. That taxes also subsidize sexual enjoyment stirs anger and, just possibly, envy. (Not the least reason for demanding that women on welfare be made to work is that they will have less time for recreational sex.)

REDEFINING THE STRUGGLE

There are signs that race now has a more problematical place on the liberal agenda. White support for racial justice reached its high point in the 1960s, when dogs and cattle prods were used on students and ministers engaging in peaceful protests. The viciousness and violence so common in the South shocked even white conservatives. When blacks organized for voter registration—the most elemental of rights—scores of their churches were burned to the ground. Local leaders such as Medgar Evers were gunned down, while civil rights workers were murdered with the connivance of public officials. Perhaps the most shocking act of all came in 1963, with the dynamiting of a black church in Birmingham, Alabama, taking the lives of four young girls attending a Sunday school class. Yet throughout these tragedies, there was something stoic, even saintly, about the demeanor of Southern blacks. Equally important for sustaining white opinion, blacks remained respectful of and deferential toward their liberal well-wishers.

If one person embodied these tendencies, it was Martin Luther King, Jr. He was—and remains—the leader that whites would have chosen for black Americans if they had had that power to choose. In white eyes, King was safe and respectable. It is hardly accidental that they invariably referred to him as "Dr. King," as if to draw assurance from the credentials he had earned in the white world. King stood for civil rights and peaceful change, as opposed to the fists of black power. (Shortly before his death, he was coming to conclude that sustained solutions would require a huge economic cost.) He also represented a mainstream religion, Baptist, which gave his movement moral impetus as well as political stature. Colleges and universities literally lined up to give him honorary degrees.

Of course, King was a genuine leader with an unequaled following. Still, his adoption by whites gave him an ambiguous status. One reason many white Americans worked to have his birthday made a holiday was to ensure that this honor would go to someone with whom they could feel comfortable. Blacks could not object, nor was that their wish. At the same time, they sensed that he was essentially a white choice. This feeling surfaced in New York at the time when the city council changed Harlem's 125th Street to Martin Luther King, Jr., Boulevard. Soon afterward, local residents aired their own sentiments by renaming Lenox Avenue after Malcolm X.

White attitudes began to shift when black activism started to show a more assertive posture. First came the urban disorders of the mid-1960s, where disaffection expressed itself in looting and burning. There soon followed the message that white advice and assistance were no longer wanted or needed. The deference blacks had shown earlier had come to an end; they now sought to define their own goals and pursue them on their own terms. This in turn led many whites to dissociate themselves from demands that moved beyond the basic entitlements covered by the rubric of civil rights. Affirmative action, autonomous control, and separate development made up a new agenda, in which whites were not asked to participate.

Most liberals who have reached middle age like to recall the fellowship they once felt in civil rights marches and integrated meetings. As liberals see it, the erosion of the interracial alliance did not come from a decline in white commitment. Rather, blacks turned from building bridges to shriller forms of politics that seem to indict all whites.

Racial relations have also been affected by the high incidence of crime, the fraying of family ties, and other behavior whites find frightening. Liberals can claim they worked for open housing, better schools, and vocational training. So some feel they have been let down, if not actually betrayed. In their eyes, rather than making the most of opportunities opened by progressive programs, all too many blacks appear to have embarked on self-destructive spirals, dooming themselves and taking a toll on the rest of society. Perhaps the most vivid evidence of altered attitudes comes from Democratic candidates and officeholders, who sense dwindling interest in wars on poverty and racial redress.

Recent decades have seen new issues command the concern and attention once given to race. One of the most prominent has been the environment. Here objects of compassion include whales, fur-bearing animals and those used in laboratories, along with rain forests and the ozone layer. While these are clearly worthy causes, working on behalf of flora and fauna brings an additional satisfaction. These beneficiaries never grumble or turn resentful or ungrateful.

PART II

CHAPTER FIVE

PARENTS AND CHILDREN

DO THE RACES REALLY DIFFER?

AT FIRST SIGHT, even the statistics are dismaying. Over two-thirds of black babies are now born outside of wedlock, and over half of black families are headed by women. The majority of black youngsters live with their mother; and in over half of these households, their mother has never been married. At last count, over half of all single black women have already had children, and among women in their mid-to-late thirties, less than half have intact marriages. These figures are from three to five times greater than those for white households and markedly higher than those recorded for black Americans a generation ago.

How people reside and reproduce can be sensitive subjects, so it would be well to guard against generalizations that oversimplify the facts. There is no generic "black family" any more than white families come in a single form. Black Americans account for almost thirteen million households, ranging from young adults in condominiums to suburban couples with two children and a swimming pool. So nothing in this chapter should be construed as claiming that specific domestic arrangements are "typical" for one race or the other. At the same time, it is possible to point to trends and tendencies, so long as it is understood that they refer to developments within a varied universe.

Similar cautions apply to interracial comparisons. Much of our knowledge of household life comes from government reports, which tally the race in separate tables. But even those figures must be placed in a larger context. Too great an emphasis on race can divert attention from forces that have been reshaping the entire society.

This becomes apparent from the figures in the table on the next page, which trace rates and ratios for families headed by women over the last five decades. As can be seen, the proportion of black families headed by women has always been higher than among white households and remains so today. But those numbers, by themselves, convey only part of the picture. An equally pervasive pattern emerges when the black percentages are transformed into multiples of the white figures. Once this is done, it turns out that the biracial ratio has remained remarkably stable throughout the fifty-year period. This raises the possibility that what we have been seeing are not so much racial differences as concurrent adaptations to common cultural trends.

MORE SINGLE-PARENT FAMILIES

During the past generation, single-parent households—which in most cases means homes headed by the mother—have become increasingly common in America and the rest of the world. That this arrangement now accounts for over half of black families has aroused great concern. For one thing, the loss of male breadwinners has done much to perpetuate poverty. More homes now lack a man's earnings, which means many are falling below the level of subsistence. In addition, some observers perceive an erosion of potential controls—especially over teenagers—which were once maintained by fathers in the home.

On the whole, these changes are relatively recent. In 1950, only 17.2 percent of black households were headed by women, actually fewer than today's white rate. So within living memory, homes with two parents present were very much the norm for blacks. This makes it difficult to describe the matrifocal families that preponderate today as being a "legacy" of slavery. Since legal servitude ended well over a century ago, the claim that it continues to exert a force should be made with some care. We know that in the slave system, pairings were denied legal standing, since owners did not want their chattels committed to lifetime covenants. Slaves were always subject to sale, which meant wives and husbands, parents and children, could be wrenched apart. Also, women had to

HOUSEHOLDS HEADED BY WOMEN: 1950–2000*

Year	Black	White	Ratio
1950	17.2%	5.3%	3.2
1960	24.4%	7.3%	3.3
1970	34.5%	9.6%	3.6
1980	45.9%	13.2%	3.5
1990	47.7%	13.6%	3.5
2000**	53.5%	19.1%	2.8

*Families with children under the age of 18 and no husband present. Figures after 1960 omit Hispanic families.
**Adds the families where children are living with their grandmother.

endure assaults by white men, including bearing their offspring. Such circumstances might not seem a forerunner for enduring marriages.

Yet it is now apparent that arrangements imposed by the owners were never accepted by the slaves themselves. Once freed, blacks sought the durable unions they had been denied. For almost a century following the Civil War, black families remained remarkably stable. Despite low incomes and uncertain employment, most black households had two parents in residence, even if bound by common-law marriages. Then as now, however, their rates for female-headed households always exceeded those of other races. But figures for even as recently as the 1950s show that such families were exceptions and not the rule. So it seems clear that more recent increases in homes headed by single parents cannot be attributed to a plantation past. Not only have other developments been at work, but they cut across racial lines. While many factors are at work, for present purposes two may be emphasized here.

One such force has been aptly described as "men's liberation." More married men than ever in the past apparently feel free to leave their wives and children, often to start again with a younger companion. Nowadays, they can do this with comparatively little social censure and often at small economic cost. Government studies show that most departing fathers end up either paying no child support at all or remit less than the agreed-upon amounts. Moreover, even the full payments seldom cover all the children's costs, leaving mothers to struggle with the bills. Ex-husbands are also more likely to remarry, in many cases starting a second round of children.

In the past, community opinion, religious canons, and an inner sense of duty kept most marriages intact. Legal divorces were also much harder to obtain. If passion and romance were less apt to be expected or experienced, spouses grew accustomed to one another and built settled routines. As has been seen, these conventions encompassed both races; black couples as well as whites spent their entire married lives together. A correlative duty was for young men to "do the right thing" when informed that a baby was on the way. Shotguns were seldom needed, since social pressure combined with conscience to achieve the desired result.

REPRODUCTIVE FREEDOM

A second development may be called "the right to reproduce." In theory, women have always been free to bear a child. (Despite much murmuring on the subject, forced sterilization has never been widely practiced.) In the past, girls who became pregnant usually got married before the baby came. When this did not happen, social censure set in. In some states, birth certificates were stamped "ILLEGITIMATE" in capital letters. Unwed women were often deemed unfit for parenthood. Prior to the Second World War, institutions assisting unmarried mothers made it clear that the women would not be allowed to keep their babies. (This is one reason why, in the past, more infants were available for adoption.)

Today, the decision of a woman to produce a child, under any conditions she chooses, is viewed as a personal right. Stated another way, no one can forbid her to follow through with her decision. Put still another way, the right of any woman—and fifteen-year-olds now receive this designation—to use her reproductive powers cannot be vetoed or overruled. Proponents of freedom of choice join with right-to-life activists in supporting the right of any teenager to use her body to make a baby.

Under the imprint of this freedom, more single women than ever before are deciding they want to be mothers. In the great majority of cases—currently well over 90 percent—those who decide to carry the pregnancy to completion also opt to take the infant home and raise it themselves. So if the liberation of men has helped to increase the number of households headed by women, the choice of single women to reproduce and start families of their own has pushed the figure even higher.

Perhaps the clearest racial parallel can be found in the basic natal measure: fertility rates, which represent the number of annual births per one thousand women from ages fifteen to forty-four, the most common childbearing years. Black women have always tended to have more children, due to a desire for larger families, coupled with less sustained use of birth control.

The facts and figures considered here suggest that much of the sexual behavior of black Americans may be defined less as "racial" than as within the national mainstream. Indeed, it would have been rather surprising had black men and women remained unaffected by such forceful currents. Given the ubiquity of these trends, little will be gained by lecturing only one race on its domestic duties. To ask black Americans to show greater discipline carries the implication that only they have deviated from national norms. In fact, if any strictures are in order, they apply equally to white Americans.

FERTILITY RATES: 1940–2001

Year	Black	White	Ratio
1940	102.4	77.1	1.33
1950	137.3	102.3	1.34
1960	153.5	113.2	1.36
1970	115.4	84.1	1.37
1980	90.7	62.4	1.45
1990	89.0	67.1	1.33
2001	71.6	57.6	1.24

Rates show the number of births each year for each 1,000 women between 15 and 44.

SOCIAL AND ECONOMIC CONSEQUENCES

Even given their ties to national trends, households headed by women and births outside of wedlock have become basic facts of life within much of black America. Most matrifocal families still adhere to the "nuclear" model of a mother on her own raising one or more children. Among black households, however, other configurations have begun to emerge. The fastest growing group consists of three generations residing in a single household. One common arrangement consists of a mother, one or more of whose adolescent daughters has come home from the hospital with her own child. Thus the original family headed by the mother, who has become a grandmother, now includes a "subfamily" headed by the daughter.

Since 1970, black multigenerational households have increased threefold. Three-quarters of the younger mothers have never been married, and many have dropped out of school to bear and care for their babies. While white daughters are also bringing babies home, these mothers tend to be older and have been married, and are now separated or divorced. Their sojourn home is more apt to be a relatively shorter stay, during which they prepare for becoming self-supporting.

Another growing group of black households consists of those where aunts and grandparents or other relatives are bringing up the children. According to the most recent census survey, one out of every seven black families is caring for youngsters not directly their own. Sometimes, the mother may have died or is being treated for an illness or drug dependency or simply lacks the resources to act as a parent. In other cases, she may be serving a prison term or has an occupation that keeps her from staying with her children. Not infrequently, she lives in a Northern state and has sent them to grandparents in the South.

This is not the place to debate whether optimal family life requires the full-time presence of two parents bound by a formal marriage. What can and should be stressed is that millions of American children have grown up in homes with a single parent, almost always their mother. Andrew Cherlin, a sociologist at the Johns Hopkins University who is an authority on marriage and divorce, notes it has yet to be shown that "absence of a father was directly responsible for any of the supposed deficiencies of broken homes." Still, single parents are more likely to experience emotional and physical exhaustion than couples, who can share parental responsibilities.

However, there is a social dimension as well. In depressed black neighborhoods, few of the households have a male parent in residence. As a functional alternative, boys spend much of their time with groups of youths of their own age, where they devise their own definitions of manhood. In many cases, their mothers all but cease having any influence over them. Indeed, even if more fathers were present, they would have their work cut out for them. Given the temptations of guns and drugs, as well as disdain for formal schooling, the most dedicated fathers might find it hard to impose a countervailing discipline.

The real issue, Professor Cherlin points out, "is not the lack of a male presence but the lack of a male income." If all too many families must live in dangerous terrain, it is because they cannot afford to move out. Many of those headed by single mothers get by at close to a subsistence level. In 2000, half of such households had incomes of less than $20,000 a year. Here is where the "feminization of poverty" takes its greatest toll. Thus 27.9 percent of white single mothers and 49.4 percent of their black counterparts are trying to feed and clothe their children on incomes below the poverty threshold. Many single mothers work hard at underpaid jobs and support their children in a creditable way. Yet only one in five manages to earn $35,000 a year. White women are more apt to be in this group, since they tend to have more education and to be older when they find they must manage on their own. At the same time, it should be noted that most black single mothers are self-supporting, and many on welfare do off-the-books work to supplement their stipends. Given the levels of public assistance, some outside income must be found to provide their kids with shoes and school supplies.

SINGLE MOTHERHOOD

As the table on the next page shows, close to two-thirds of black single mothers have never been married, which works out to over twice times the rate for whites and nearly five times what it was for their own race a generation ago. In the past, the chief reason black women ended up as heads of households was that their original marriages were dissolved by death or separation or divorce. Today, most such families come into being because an unmarried woman decides to become a mother. Nor does this always result from unfamiliarity with birth control or lack of access to abortion facilities. Often her pregnancy was intended from the start, all but assured by a refusal to use contraception.

Single status not only may be found on the welfare rolls, but is becoming common for middle-class professionals as well. Among black women aged thirty-five to forty-four who are college graduates, only 51.7 percent are currently married, compared with 74.2 percent of white women of similar age and education. One cause of the imbalance is that women tend to want a partner at their own educational level. Unfortunately, for every one hundred black women currently being awarded bachelor's degrees, only fifty-two black men are also receiving diplomas.

The pool of "marriageable" black men gets smaller every year. A traditional requisite for marriage has been having a steady job or the prospect of one, a status not readily achieved given current unemployment rates, which will be detailed in the next chapter. Currently, upwards of a million black men are in jails or prisons, and as many more could be sent there or returned if they violate their parole or probation. And perhaps as many as a million more have records as felons, not the best credentials for employment.

SINGLE WOMEN WHO HEAD HOUSEHOLDS

Race, Year, and Marital Status	Black 1960	Black 2000	White 2000
Divorced or Separated	64.5%	32.6%	66.1%
Widowed	24.0%	2.6%	4.1%
Never Been Married	11.5%	64.8%	29.8%
	100.0%	100.0%	100.0%

White figures for 2000 omit Hispanic household heads.

Another large group is debilitated by drugs or alcohol or mental illness. In addition, the death rates for younger men have reached terrifying levels. In the fifteen to twenty-five age group, the mortality rate for black men is now three times that for black women, with the principal cause being gunned down by a member of their own race. The fact that in some areas as many as 20 percent of the men are missed by the census would point to their lack of even a settled address. And of those who were contacted by the census, fewer than half had held full-time employment during the previous year.

When middle-class marriages break up, as millions do every year, economic reasons are seldom cited. This ought to remind us that low-income households can also fall prey to emotional tensions. (It is patronizing—and inaccurate—to presume that poorer people lack sensitivities found in the well-to-do.) For this reason, if no other, we should think twice before presuming that giving husbands steady jobs will keep poor families from falling apart.

What we do know is that some racial factors seem to have an influence of their own. For example, special studies conducted by the census allow us to look at the marital experience of black and white men of comparable ages and education. Among those aged thirty-five to fifty-four who have had five or more years of college, it turns out that black men are half again as likely to be separated or divorced. This need not mean that black men take wedding vows less seriously. Rather, it suggests that the strains that come with being black put extra burdens on a marriage. There is reason to believe that most black Americans, like Americans of every race, would like to settle in for a sustained period with someone they love. However, this eventuality is less and less likely, due to the factors and forces thwarting the aspirations of black Americans.

The increase in out-of-wedlock births is often taken as evidence that black Americans are evolving a separate sexual culture. Here, too, race-based explanations must be handled with care. As has been noted, many white women are making essentially the same decisions and usually for quite similar reasons. We have all heard of women with professional careers who decide to conceive a child without asking more from the father than a sperm donation. Still, there are racial differences. In far fewer white neighborhoods are out-of-wedlock pregnancies and motherhood seen as customary and ordinary. Moreover, we know that blacks are less apt to use contraception, which accounts for their higher pregnancy rates. And black girls are more apt than white girls to carry their pregnancies to completion. Moreover, it would be well to remind ourselves that the four basic steps—sex, pregnancy, birth, and keeping the baby—do not always follow from one to another. That is, not all sexual activity results in pregnancies; not all pregnancies end with births; and not all babies are kept by the mother.

Teenagers the world over are pubescent earlier and are increasingly independent; they are also exposed to similar erotic influences. In many other countries, young people are just as sexually active as they are in the United States; but youths elsewhere may take more care with contraception, which means that many fewer of the girls become pregnant. And if they do, they are more likely to arrange for abortions.

The next page gives figures for several countries, showing

how many of their teenagers become pregnant during a given year. The United States now leads other Western nations in out-of-wedlock births. In part, this is because other nations' schools and governments generally do more to encourage the use of birth control and make abortions available. But the chief difference is cultural. Young people in this country are less mature, less self-disciplined, and give less thought to their futures. (Not surprisingly, they also do less homework and register lower scores in academic skills.) True, there are cases where girls are forced into sex or never wanted a child. In many parts of the United States, abortion facilities are not readily accessible, often because of political opposition. (There is only one clinic in the entire state of South Dakota.) Still, a disheartening number of young Americans of both races cannot be bothered with birth control, either because they find it too much trouble or because a child is desired. A survey of teenagers who had already become mothers, by the National Center for Health Statistics, found that almost half—45.1 percent—said they had been pleased upon learning they were pregnant.

PREGNANCY RATES: SELECTED COUNTRIES (PER 1,000 TEENAGERS)

United States	
Black	186
White	93
England and Wales	45
Canada	44
France	43
Sweden	35
Netherlands	14

Such evidence as we have suggests that the forces propelling early parenthood cut across racial lines. One difference lies in the settings. Births among white teenagers tend to take place in depressed towns and rural areas, usually on the dreary side of the tracks where journalists seldom visit. Black out-of-wedlock births get much more attention, because more of them are clustered in central cities. Moreover, in low-income black areas, having babies outside of marriage is seldom seen as an act of rebellion, let alone defiance directed at parents or the larger society. Most black youthful parents are quite oblivious to whatever reactions they may be stirring elsewhere in the nation. For the young fathers, being able to point to a child they have sired is seen as tangible evidence of manhood, an important laurel for men unable to achieve recognition in other areas.

A CONSCIOUS CHOICE

At the same time, it should be noted that there is far less promiscuity among black teenagers than critics like to suggest. In almost all cases, a girl has no difficulty identifying whoever it was who fathered her child, although the young man's interest may soon pall after learning of the pregnancy. In fact, teenage mothers understand that the children will be their responsibility. They believe that having a baby to love will provide a focus for their lives. Given the surroundings so many of them have known, life offers few other options. So the act of reproduction becomes a way to validate yourself as a productive human being.* Also, it

---

*Of course, it takes two to create a baby, and a lot of young men are willing participants in the process. In many cases, they too feel their lives are not amounting to much, and siring a child is a way to show they can do something of substance. Hence the early urge to get the next generation started. While they may not cite this as their reasoning, it is something Charles Darwin would understand: even in the face of vicissitudes, every species seeks to ensure its own perpetuation.

offers a sphere of independence, including selecting the child's clothing and deciding how late it can stay up at night. Not least is the freedom to choose—or, even better, to make up—the baby's name. For many, discussing and comparing choices becomes a conversational staple in their early teens. Names like Equilla, Zanquisha, and Lakeisha are neither African nor Muslim, but schoolgirls' creations.

The real problem in our time is that more and more black infants are being born to mothers who are immature and poor. Compared with white women—most of whom are older and more comfortably off—black women are twice as likely to have anemic conditions during their pregnancy, twice as likely to have had no prenatal care, and twice as likely to give birth to low-weight babies. Twice as many of their children develop serious health problems, including asthma, deafness, retardation, and learning disabilities, as well as conditions stemming from their own use of drugs and alcohol during pregnancy. These conditions arise in part from a lack of clinics in rural towns and urban slums. But even when those facilities are available, younger mothers tend to be less conscientious about making and keeping scheduled appointments. Nor can they always find other sources of advice on matters like diet, their own during pregnancy and their baby's in its early years. And poverty is not the full explanation. Federal figures show that women of Mexican ancestry have healthier babies, despite low incomes and less access to medical attention. One reason may be that more of their families have preserved a traditional structure, with advice and authority coming from older members.

In the past, black families had their own support systems. These links had their origins partly in slavery, where relatives rallied round when parents were sold or sent away. After that, kinship was strengthened and sustained in the rural South. If a young woman found herself on her own with a baby, usually there was someone to take the two of them in. Nor was the assistance only economic; a new mother could count on guidance from relatives in the ways of parenthood. Also, most extended families had several working members; their earnings, however modest, ensured that there would be enough to go around.

Black families today still maintain deep and durable ties, often maintaining firmer roots than white households do. Yearly reunions are common, with relatives from all over the country returning to Southern counties they still regard as home. Black family members are also more willing to care for one another's children, sharing what they have. Still, the fact is that extended families can no longer take on these obligations in the ways they once did. For one thing, urban apartments are not as capacious as rural homesteads. In many cases, also, relatives have new burdens of their own. There is more unemployment, greater use of drugs, and a higher proportion of people in prison. But the key change has been in the balance of dependency. Instead of being the exception, single parents now outnumber two-parent households. This helps to explain why so many young mothers end up in shelters for the homeless or derelict hotels and motels. Studies by social service agencies show that they often began raising their babies at home but had to move out when another sister arrived with an infant, making the crowding intolerable.

WHO CHOOSES ABORTION?

Since at least half of black women have no wish for an early baby, it remains to ask what distinguishes them from those who do. Income and education play a role, as can religious convictions and parental influence. Still, these kinds of factors tell only part of the story. Imagine, for a moment, two friends from similar surroundings, who move in the same circles in their school and neighborhood. Call them Amy and Angela. And imagine, further, that each discovers she is pregnant. Amy will decide to bear and keep her baby. She may have some more later on, with the possibility that she will spend a prolonged period on the welfare rolls.

However, Angela will arrange to obtain an abortion, after which she will finish school and start a promising job.

There are obviously many such pairs. But why they take such divergent routes cannot be answered with any certainty. It could be argued that one lacked confidence in herself, whereas the other had greater inner strength and self-esteem. Perhaps one succumbed to the coaxing of friends who had already become mothers, while the other had an aunt who offered some timely advice. At the same time, it must be added that many who opt for early motherhood rearrange their lives later on and show they can support themselves. Still, explanations are elusive. As happens so frequently, we are watching the interplay of character and circumstance, the social and the personal, where the biography intersects with history. Neither psychology nor the social sciences can tell us much about why specific people pick the paths they do.

In 2001, a new high of 22.5 percent of all white births were recorded as occurring outside of marriage, compared with 68.6 percent of black births. It will be recalled that the racial ratios for households headed by women have remained relatively constant for the last half century. However, the figures for out-of-wedlock births, displayed on the next page, show the white ratio has risen to more than three times what it was in 1950. Put another way, even though the number of births to unwed black women has ascended to an all-time high, white births outside of marriage have been climbing at an even faster rate.

There is reason to suspect that in earlier years, reports on white out-of-wedlock births were kept artificially low by indulgent physicians and health officials. Still, the chief explanation for the decline in the multiple has been the availability of legal abortion. While it is not something one would guess from watching "freedom of choice" rallies, black women have been availing themselves of abortion to a far greater extent than white women. While they comprise only 13 percent of women of childbearing age, they account for almost a third of all women who have abortions performed.

Overall, 38 percent of pregnancies begun by black women end in abortions, which is more than double the 16.4 percent figure for white women. Unmarried women account for about 80 percent of all those who have abortions, and in this group, black women are 2.8 times more likely to obtain them than their white counterparts. It also turns out that among married women, the abortion rate for blacks is four times higher than for whites. The main reason is that black couples are less regular users of birth control. Many black men disdain condoms for themselves and often make it plain they do not want their partners using contraceptives either. So black women are more likely to return for subsequent abortions. According to one study, over half the black patients seeking abortions had had at least one previous termination.

Worth at least passing comment is that if the "right-to-life" movement achieves its goal of outlawing abortions, the impact will be felt most heavily by black women. As it happens, whites make up the great majority of those opposing abortion on prin-

BIRTHS TO UNMARRIED WOMEN

	White	Black	W:B*
1950	1.7%	16.8%	10.1%
1960	2.3%	21.6%	10.6%
1970	5.7%	37.6%	15.2%
1980	9.3%	56.4%	16.5%
1990	16.9%	66.7%	25.3%
2001	22.5%	68.6%	32.8%

*W:B gives the relation of the white figure to the black figure.

ciple. Their chief concern seems to be about better-off women who want full and frequent sex lives, with abortion available as a fallback. Left unaddressed is whether right-to-life activists wish a steep rise in the black birthrate, which could very well happen were abortions to be made illegal.

Another sensitive issue has to do with the motives that lead many whites to counsel greater use of abortion and birth control by black Americans. Some say quite openly that all too many blacks should not be bearing children. Sometimes this reflects a feeling that they lack the resources to raise youngsters properly, so they should have fewer than they do or, in some cases, none at all. The reasoning is that it is unfair to youngsters to bring them into a world of persisting poverty.

A good many black Americans discern other implications in these white concerns. As was noted earlier, black birthrates are not rising relative to those for whites, so it is not as if the black population is growing by leaps and bounds. In fact, indications are that Hispanics are already becoming the country's principal minority. Therefore, efforts to induce blacks to limit their birthrate are sometimes seen as a campaign to diminish the number of black Americans. To many blacks, the solution to social problems should not rest on curbing births but in creating conditions that will enable babies to have healthy and productive lives.

However, the space between white and black America is not an empty void. The table on the next page shows that the rates among ethnic groups span a spectrum ranging from 8.4 percent for Americans of Chinese ancestry to 58.9 percent for Puerto Ricans. The fact that the latter figure comes so close to that for blacks suggests that more than race is involved in such issues. After all, most Puerto Ricans identify themselves as white; they immigrated to the mainland voluntarily; and slavery played only a marginal role in their homeland's past.

In fact, Puerto Ricans, Hawaiians, and American Indians share a common history in one crucial respect, which may help to explain their behavior concerning births among unmarried women. All four began as indigenous groups, on either the mainland or outlying islands, which were later overrun by conquerors or colonizers from European powers, and then consigned to conditions of dependency. Of course, circumstances differed from group to group. American Indians were subdued by military means, with the survivors consigned to reservations. They and Hawaiians were turned into exiles within their own homeland, so newcomers could exploit those territories. They were kept underemployed, allowed to addict themselves to alcohol and subsist as tourist attractions or exotic relics. Puerto Rico was conquered first by Spain, after which it effectively became a colony of the United States, to which was added the option of easy migration to and from the mainland.

In the eyes of other Americans, all three of these groups continue to be viewed as less than full citizens. While never slaves,

NONMARITAL BIRTHS

Ten American Groups

Black	68.6%
American Indian	59.7%
Puerto Rican	58.9%
Native Hawaiian	50.6%
Mexican	40.8%
Cuban	27.2%
White	22.5%
Filipino	20.4%
Japanese	9.2%
Chinese	8.4%

they have been treated as subservient castes. Their conquerors chose to keep them apart and quiescent, allowing them to sustain remnants of their cultures rather than become full citizens. Consequently, many of their men drop out of school and lead listless lives, while high percentages of their women end up as unwed mothers due to lack of other options.

A RACIAL CONVERGENCE?

Until quite recently, white Americans felt free to comment on the state of black domestic life. In fact, the opening salvo came in 1965, during Lyndon Johnson's presidency, in a report called *The Negro Family: The Case for National Action.* It was a harsh analysis, filled with graphs and statistical tables, contending that black households were trapped in a "tangle of pathology." To underline this point, it noted that "nearly one-quarter of Negro births are now illegitimate," and "almost one-fourth of Negro families are headed by females." The author, a young official named Daniel Patrick Moynihan, cited his own race for purposes of contrast. "The white family," he said, "has achieved a high degree of stability and is maintaining that stability." Its out-of-wedlock rate, he noted, was one-eighth that for black births.

Following Moynihan's report, many white Americans stepped up their criticism of what they saw as a lack of domestic discipline on the part of their black fellow citizens. This campaign remained high on political agendas for several decades. Most recently, welfare rolls have been slashed and stipends stopped to halt what was viewed as licentious procreation by much of the black population. Americans whose forebears came from Europe felt they could make these judgments because they had set demanding standards for themselves. Indeed, it was their devotion to marriage and parenthood that allowed them to censure others for their failings.

But what once may have been white "stability" is now a thing of the past. The white out-of-wedlock rate now exceeds the black figure for 1960, around the time it was branded "patholog-ical." And the proportion of white households headed by women is now only one percentage point behind where the black rate was in 1950.

White suburbs now have almost as many divorces, defaulting fathers, and births out of wedlock as were once deplored in black urban neighborhoods. Whatever the causes of these white lapses, they cannot be blamed on a supposed legacy of slavery, since immigrants of European extraction came here willingly. Moreover, most white men and women are employed in white-collar occu-pations, so they cannot claim they have been shut out of a chang-ing economy. Nor can whites easily say that their tenuous family ties stem from racial discrimination. Indeed, broken homes and absent fathers are now common among whites in well-paid pro-fessional positions.

To this extent, the races may be converging. As has been noted, many black children have grown up in neighborhoods where women headed most of the families and not many full-time fathers were around. Youngsters who were in these households came to see those homes as fairly typical, and adapted to them. For example, it was more usual than not to have lost touch with your father. Each year finds this situation becoming more common for white children. In growing numbers of white suburbs, as well as urban private schools, teachers will tell you that as a third or more of their students are not living with both of their original parents. Most know where their father is; but it is sometimes a whole continent away, where he is now married to another woman.

On these and other subjects, it is noteworthy that while schol-ars have spent a lot of time and money and energy dissecting the "pathology" of black families, there has been little interest in putting white households under a similar microscope.

CHAPTER SIX

THE RACIAL INCOME GAP

HOW MUCH IS DUE TO BIAS?

Since their first arrival, and continuing after they started receiving wages, black Americans have figured disproportionately among the nation's poor. Of course, differences in incomes can have explanations apart from race. After all, a lot of white people are poor, and a number of blacks are very visibly rich. Even so, after other factors have been accounted for, race still seems to play a role in how people fare financially. A recurrent theme of this and the following chapter will be how being black or white affects economic opportunities and outcomes.

Any discussion of incomes and earnings will depend strongly on statistics. While we cannot measure equity with precision, numerical disparities represent real facts about the races. Each year, the census asks a national sample of Americans to estimate their total incomes during the previous year. The table on page 111 gives some of the results from the 2000 survey, reported first as median incomes and then by how much blacks received for every $1,000 that went to whites. (This means of comparison will be used extensively throughout this chapter.)

The listings for families and for all men and women include every sort of income, ranging from pensions and welfare payments to disability benefits and capital gains. The figures for employed men and women reflect only the earnings of individuals who held full-time jobs throughout the year. As will be seen, the relative incomes for black families as a group and for black men are embarrassingly low, in particular when compared with those for the earnings of black women.

In 2000, personal income received by everyone living within the country added up to a grand total of $6.7 trillion. While black Americans made up 12.1 percent of the adult population, they ended up with only 9.4 percent of the monetary pie. Earnings by some 150 million employed men and women accounted for $5.1 trillion of the income total. Black workers comprise 11.6 percent of that employment force, but received only 9.1 percent of all earnings. This chapter will focus on the conditions causing these gaps.

DOLLAR DISPARITIES

White households are more apt to have both a husband and wife present, which raises the likelihood of multiple incomes. As it happens, among married couples, a smaller percentage of white wives work: 61.9 percent are in the labor force, compared with 69.3 percent of black married women. Since the earnings of black men tend to be lower, fewer of their families can afford the luxury of full-time housewives. When white wives work, they are more likely to take part-time jobs, and their paychecks tend to be supplemental; whereas among black families, the husbands' and wives' earnings are often of equal value. And since more black families are headed by single women, a higher proportion of their households must make do with only one income. Moreover,

INCOMES AND EARNINGS

Medians (2000)	White	Black	Ratio
Families	$56,442	$34,192	$606
Men's Earnings	$42,224	$30,886	$731
Women's Earnings	$30,777	$25,736	$836

Earnings are for year-round full-time workers. Ratios show blacks' figures per $1,000 for whites.

when black single mothers work—and the majority do—it is generally at a job paying relatively low wages.

So the question arises whether income ratios would change if black families had the same mixture of single parents and married couples as white households now do. In theory, if this became the case, then more black homes would have someone bringing in the amounts of income that men ordinarily make. The problem is that black families that have husbands in residence still end up with only $817 for every $1,000 going to similar white households. So changing the black family structure won't help much so long as black men make less than their white counterparts. At best, it would only close the racial income gap by about one-half.

On the whole, increased education tends to bring in higher incomes. While we can always cite exceptions, for most people most of the time, staying in school does pay off. The figures in the next table show how the rule works along a racial continuum. To make the comparisons as firm as possible, the table covers only individuals who worked full-time throughout the entire year.

A steady economic progression is evident. Among black and white men and women, incomes tend to ascend with added years of school. The catch is that even when black men reach the same

EDUCATION AND EARNINGS:
RACIAL RATIOS

	Men	Women
Finished High School	$799	$944
Bachelor's Degree	$784	$1,117
Master's Degree	$778	$1,030

Earnings of black men and women for every $1,000 made by whites, for full-time year-round workers in 2000.

academic level as white men, their incomes still stay several steps behind. Let's see what happens with black men who complete college. True, they end up on average making 26.7 percent more than white high school graduates. But before the cheering starts, it would be wise to note that white men who finish college earn 61.6 percent more than high school graduates of their own race. So for black men, a college education gives them less than half the earnings advantage that accrues to white men who have college diplomas. Hence the advice so often given to blacks, that they should stay in school, seems valid only insofar as additional education will move them ahead of others of their own race. There is no evidence that spending more years in school will improve their position in relation to whites. On the other hand, as the table shows, black women actually earn somewhat more than white women with comparable education. Of course, there is less of an income range among women. Still, the question remains why black men do not receive a similar reward for investing in education.

If we want to find out how much income disparities result from racial bias, then we must do our best to compare similar groups, since additional elements like age and experience can distort comparisons. The most recent census figures for the earnings of male attorneys between the ages of thirty-five and thirty-nine show that the black lawyers averaged $744 for every $1,000 made by their white counterparts. Given that these men are in the same age range and have the same level of education, it could be argued that race accounts for at least part of the $256 earnings gap. Of course, we would have to know a lot more about the individuals in question. Factors like talent, intelligence, and temperament could affect the equation. Or the variance in earnings might reflect different law schools the men attended and how well they did there. After all, it hardly needs mentioning that not all educations are comparable. If more of the white lawyers in the cohort went to Harvard while the black lawyers were apt to have studied at Howard, then some people might use this fact to justify part of the $256 difference.

As it happens, black *women* lawyers in the same age group make $926 for every $1,000 going to their white colleagues. Moreover, this similarity holds even though black women attend the same spectrum of law schools as black men. So a question must arise: if black women in the legal profession are paid nearly as much as white women, then why don't black men make almost as much as white men? A suspicion cannot help but arise that some of the racial earnings spread among men stems from the fact that black men are given fewer opportunities to rise to better-paid positions.

Medians—like averages—can conceal important variations. The depictions on the next page show how incomes were distributed among black and white families in 2000. As can be seen, the range of black households takes the shape of a pyramid, if not quite in the classical form. The largest group of families makes less than $25,000, showing that poverty is disproportionately concentrated in their race. Above them, fairly equal numbers of families are found in each of the higher ranges. And that almost a third ends up with over $50,000 reflects the growth of a black middle class.

White incomes are essentially in an inverted pyramid, with a third of the households making $75,000 or more, and well over half above the $50,000 mark, which would be expected with a median income of $56,442. That as many as 16.5 percent of white homes are still living on under $25,000 reflects in part the growing number that are headed by single women, as was detailed in the last chapter.

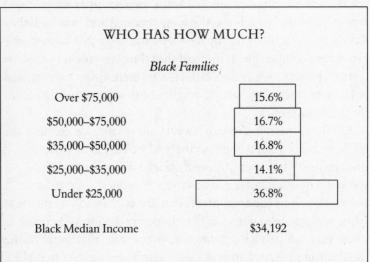

WHO HAS HOW MUCH?

Black Families

Over $75,000	15.6%
$50,000–$75,000	16.7%
$35,000–$50,000	16.8%
$25,000–$35,000	14.1%
Under $25,000	36.8%

Black Median Income $34,192

White Families

Over $75,000	33.8%
$50,000–$75,000	22.8%
$35,000–$50,000	15.6%
$25,000–$35,000	11.3%
Under $25,000	16.5%

White Median Income $56,442

While some black Americans have improved their economic status during the last generation, even more whites have been making comparable or greater advances. The best demonstration of this is in the pyramids: over half (56.6 percent) of white families have more than $50,000 a year at their disposal, while almost exactly half (50.9 percent) of black households are getting by on less than $35,000. Looking at individuals, 12.4 percent of white men are now making over $75,000, while only 3.6 percent of black men bring that much home. If there is now a much larger black middle class, more typically the husband is likely to be a bus driver earning $37,000 while his wife brings home $34,000 as a teacher or a nurse. A white middle-class family is three to four times more likely to contain a husband earning $100,000 in a managerial position, which allows him to support a nonworking wife. Nor is it easy to visualize these two couples living on the same block, let alone becoming acquainted with each other.

THE REALITY OF POVERTY

Some thirty years ago, federal officials devised a formula to designate which Americans could be considered poor. The poverty threshold is adjusted each year, to keep pace with the cost of living. In 2000, an older woman living by herself would fall into the poverty cohort if her income dropped below $8,259. A single mother with two children was counted as poor if her family's income was lower than $13,874. In most parts of the United States, $8,259 spells not simply poverty, but a good chance of malnutrition. Nor is it possible to bring up, say, two teenagers on $13,874 a year. Even adding in the dollar value of school lunches, food stamps, and Medicaid benefits, the formula only really counts the bottom stratum of the poor. Another problem is that the figures ignore variations in living costs. A widow might manage on $8,259 in rural Arkansas, but that amount would barely pay her rent in Boston or Brooklyn. Still, if we make appropriate adjustments, the official poverty percentages can tell us a lot about who is poor and why.

As the table on the next page shows, 25.1 percent of black children live below the poverty line, compared with 7.2 percent of white youngsters. So black children are 3.5 times as likely as white children to grow up in poor surroundings. The ratio runs higher for all black families and is somewhat similar for black people as a whole. However, the poverty figures have a much closer ratio (1.82) in households headed by women. For women who must raise children on their own, being white loses much of its advantage.

The poverty figures also show that almost three-quarters of poor white Americans live in small towns, suburbs, or rural areas. Anyone who has traveled along the back roads of outlying America has seen the homes of people who are white and poor. However, their homes are less likely to be clustered together in slum neighborhoods, unless one applies that description to decaying trailer parks.

Of course, there is a white underclass. Its members can be found among the addicted and the homeless, among men who have never held steady jobs and women who have spent many years on welfare. The nation's prisons still have plenty of white criminals, some of whom are quite vicious and others who have made careers in small-time larceny. Even so, neither sociologists nor journalists have shown much interest in depicting poor whites as a "class." In large measure, the reason is racial. For whites, poverty tends to be viewed as atypical or accidental. Among blacks, it comes close to being seen as a natural outgrowth of their history and culture. At times, it almost appears as if white poverty must be covered up, lest it blemish the reputation of the dominant race. This was not always the case. In the past, sociology textbooks dilated upon families like the Jukes and the Kallikaks, who remained mired in squalor from generation to generation. In earlier days, too, some white people were called "trash," whether along the tobacco roads or in pellagra-infested pine barrens.

POOR AMERICANS: RACE AND RESIDENCE

Percent in Poverty	Black	White	Ratio
All Persons	22.0%	7.5%	2.93
All Children	25.1%	7.2%	3.49
Female-Headed Families	44.7%	24.6%	1.82

Where the Poor Live	Black	White
Central Cities	60.6%	27.0%
Suburbs	24.0%	41.3%
Rural or Small Towns	15.4%	31.7%
	100.0%	100.0%

While class bias prompted these allusions, at least they granted that white people could occupy the lowest stratum of society.

MEN, WOMEN, AND WORK

Apart from people who are independently wealthy and those with generous pensions, enjoying the modest comforts of life requires having a decent job. Altogether, about 80 percent of Americans' personal income comes from wages and salaries or other gainful earnings.

Between 1940 and 1960, the earnings of black men relative to whites improved by over a third. Those who made the move to Northern cities relocated in search of employment. They were willing to take blue-collar positions once reserved for immigrants but which newer generations of whites were beginning to spurn. This period saw the emergence of a stable black working class, underpinned by two-parent families and orderly neighborhoods. If some saw themselves as "poor," that status did not have the connotations conveyed by "poverty" today. The earnings of black women also grew during this period, as they turned from domestic employment to better-paid occupations.

However, during the past thirty years, black men lost ground. Despite this being a period when affirmative action supposedly gave blacks preferences in hirings and promotions, the decline in blue-collar employment hit black men especially hard. Each year found the economy offering fewer factory jobs, while more were being created in the white-collar sector.

If black women have fared better, it is because more of them have been seen as suitable for office positions. Professional and clerical occupations generally call for attitudes and aptitudes associated with the white world. For reasons that will be considered later, black women apparently satisfy employers on these counts more readily than black men. By 1980, it was apparent that black women were making greater advances than black men. At the same time, white women were entering the labor force in large numbers, and their arrival on the scene brought pressures to move them into professional and supervisory positions, which has in turn compressed the pay gap between white and black women.

Black men, women, and children were brought to this country for a singular purpose: to work. Indeed, the demand for their labor was so great that slaves continued to be smuggled in even after that traffic had been banned. In the years following emancipation, former slaves found that their services would not necessarily be needed. Their labor, like that of other Americans, would be subject to the vagaries of a market economy. The capitalist system has been frank in admitting that it cannot always create jobs for everyone who wants to work. This economic reality has certainly been a pervasive fact of black life. For as long as records have been kept, in good times and bad, white America has ensured that the unemployment imposed on blacks will be approximately

EARNINGS OF BLACK WORKERS

1940–2000 (per $1,000 for Whites)

	Men	Women
1940	$450	$379
1960	$669	$696
1980	$751	$917
2000	$736	$943

double that experienced by whites. Stated very simply, if you are black in America, you will find it at least twice as hard to find or keep a job.

The ratios in the table on the next page make it clear that black Americans get jobs only after white applicants have been accommodated. In periods of prosperity, when the economy requires more workers, blacks who had been unemployed are offered vacant positions. But as last hired, they can expect to be the first fired. In bleak times, the jobless rate among blacks has exceeded 15 percent, as it did in 1985. From 1975 to 1995, unemployment rates for blacks remained at double-digit levels. And even when the rate fell to 8.1 percent, as it did in 2001, it was still over twice the white figure.

A BASIC RIGHT DENIED

It is frequently remarked that many black men and women lack the kinds of skills that modern employment requires. However, these charges are hardly new. They were also common in the past, when blacks were shunted to the end of the line even for laboring jobs. And today, whites who barely make it through high school continue to get the first openings in the building trades. Moreover, blacks who do stay in school soon learn there is no assured payoff. Those who finish college still have a jobless rate twice that for whites with diplomas.

Exacerbating the situation today is the fact that millions of jobs are being filled by legal and illegal aliens, largely from Latin America and Asia. Few of the positions they take call for special skills, so the question arises as to why these places haven't been offered to native-born black Americans. This issue is not new, since it has long been argued that immigrant labor takes bread from the mouths of citizens. In most cases, though, immigrants acquiesce to wages and working conditions that black and white Americans are unwilling to accept. Indeed, newcomers often put up with what are essentially Third World terms of employment to gain a foothold in the American economy. And if these workers are

UNEMPLOYMENT RATES: 1960–2001

	Black	White	Ratio
1960	10.2	4.9	2.08
1965	8.1	4.1	1.98
1970	8.2	4.4	1.86
1975	14.8	7.8	1.90
1980	14.3	6.3	2.27
1985	15.1	6.2	2.44
1990	11.4	4.8	2.38
1995	10.4	4.9	2.12
2001	8.1	3.4	2.38

exploited, it is often by employers or supervisors of their own origins who arrived here not much earlier. Nor is it likely that the pay for such jobs can be raised appreciably.

What black Americans want is no more or less than what white Americans want: a fair chance for steady employment at decent pay. But this opportunity has been one that the nation's economy continues to withhold. To be black in America is to know that you remain last in line for so basic a requisite as the means of supporting yourself and your family. More than that, you have much less choice among jobs than workers who are white. As will be seen in the next chapter, entire occupations still remain substantially closed to people who were born black.

A DISCOURAGED CLASS

That black Americans are willing or required to do arduous work cannot be questioned. When a new hotel announces that it will be hiring porters and chambermaids, a line largely composed of black men and women can be seen curling around the block. Black youths sign on for the armed services in disproportionate numbers because it is the only promising job they can get. And other young men and women can be found on sordid streets at all hours and in all weather, selling illicit services or merchandise. The baleful consequences aside, the fact remains that what they are doing is unquestionably *work*. For each one who sports a fancy car, dozens more serve as "stashers" or "spotters" in hopes of picking up a few dollars.

All in all, a greater proportion of black Americans lack regular employment than at any time since the 1930s Depression. Many of those who have jobs are needed for less than a day's work or for only part of the year. And in addition to men and women who are officially recorded as unemployed, at least an equal number have given up the search. Because they are now a substantial group, the Bureau of Labor Statistics has created a category it calls "discouraged workers." These are individuals who say they would like to work but have ceased looking because they have become convinced that they will never find a job. So they have been dropped from the "labor force" category and are no longer even counted among the unemployed.

On a typical day, the bureau is able to identify almost a million of these "discouraged workers." The true total has to be considerably higher, since many in this plight cannot be found for interviews or refuse to give out information about themselves. Of the recorded "discouraged workers," close to 30 percent are black, a much higher proportion than on the official list of the unemployed who say they are actively looking for work. As was just noted, some of these "non-workers" support themselves on the streets by providing products and services in the underground economy. Others resort to theft, which means that sooner or later they will join yet another cohort of the nonemployed: the growing number of Americans who languish in this nation's prisons.

It is sometimes proposed that the economy should create more semiskilled jobs at decent wages, which will be made available to black men. Just what kinds of positions they would be are seldom specified. As hardly needs mentioning, machines now perform many of the tasks once handled by human beings, while a lot of factory work once done within this country is being performed overseas. Moreover, recent trends have expanded the sectors of the workforce open to women. Even if special jobs were devised, it is not clear how they could pay what today's men regard as a living wage. For at least a decade, newly created positions have been offering wages and salaries lower than those of the jobs they replaced. As a result, they are usually taken by women or teenagers or immigrants, who are willing to work at those rates because they have no other option. Put another way, many native-born men cannot see how they can work for such wages and still maintain the self-respect integral to their identity.

But the larger point is that this country cannot revert to a

sweat-and-muscle economy of earlier eras. More than that, to contrive blue-collar jobs for black men would rouse not only charges
of preferential treatment but accusations of racism as well, since
it would imply that work requiring physical skills is all that black
men can be expected to do.

CHAPTER SEVEN

EQUITY
IN EMPLOYMENT

QUALIFICATIONS AND QUOTAS

MEN AND WOMEN of African origin number among the most highly paid people in the United States. Not surprisingly, their strongest presence is among athletes and entertainers. *Forbes* magazine's 2002 listing of their earnings was headed by Oprah Winfrey ($150 million), followed by Tiger Woods ($69 million) and Mariah Carey ($58 million). Farther down were Michael Jordan ($36 million) and Samuel L. Jackson ($34 million), Lennox Lewis ($28 million) and Mike Tyson ($23 million), Shaquille O'Neal ($24 million) and Kobe Bryant ($22 million), Barry Bonds ($18 million) and Ken Griffey, Jr. ($17 million), along with Venus Williams ($11 million) and Serena Williams ($9 million). Also visibly successful have been rapper-entrepreneurs like Sean Combs (formerly Puff Daddy), Andre Young (Dr. Dre), and Percy Miller (Master P).

Black men and women have headed important institutions, giving them significant responsibilities and imposing salaries. The

Ford Foundation had a black president, while baseball's National League and National Public Radio have been led by black executives. A black man also headed the College Board, the nation's principal testing agency. Another held the top position at TIAA-CREF, one of the world's largest pension funds. Black educators have served as presidents of Brown University, Colorado State University, and New York City's Cooper Union.

This, certainly, is the good news. At the same time, it is apparent that all the organizations just cited are governmental or in public service. The private sector has been less welcoming. During the last decade, only four black names have been on *Forbes* magazine's list of the richest Americans: John Harold Johnson, the owner of *Ebony* and *Jet;* Berry Gordy of Motown Records; the late Reginald Lewis, who acquired Beatrice Foods in a leveraged buyout; and Oprah Winfrey.

The so-called small business sector can also be a route to wealth and social status. The Census Bureau keeps count of the number of firms owned by black men and women. Its most recent survey found 823,000 such enterprises, numbering about 3.5 percent of the country's corporations, partnerships, and sole proprietorships. By and large, the black businesses are local concerns, with annual receipts averaging around $50,000, and they deal largely in products or services oriented to black clienteles. Indeed, only 93,000 of the 823,000 have any paid employees. In other words, 88.7 percent are one-person enterprises or family-run firms.

Many arguments have been given for the paucity of black-owned enterprises. There is the difficulty of getting start-up loans and capital from banks and investors stemming from biased attitudes about blacks' business abilities. Nor is it easy for blacks to get experience in corporate management as a prelude to branching out on your own. Some blacks have done well providing products and services to their own community. Still, the real challenge is to build a wider clientele. In fact, some firms have been successful in this sphere. Most whites who have bought

Parks's sausages and McCall's patterns do not know that those companies were owned and managed by blacks.

It has occasionally been suggested that black Americans do not have a "culture" that encourages entrepreneurship. But it is best to be wary of such sweeping explanations, since they imply that the roots run very deep. There may be some validity to the view that youngsters who grow up in areas with few locally owned enterprises lack models for business careers. But even this need not be an obstacle, since the decision to start up on your own usually comes later in life. As it happens, in the generation following emancipation, many blacks set up businesses in Southern cities, just as others prospered in farming. Haitian and West Indian immigrants have brought entrepreneurial ambitions with them; and it will be interesting to see what becomes of the West African sidewalk vendors who have become a New York fixture.

WHO GETS TO THE CORPORATE TOP?

In 1992, *Ebony* magazine printed a list of the "50 Top Black Executives in Corporate America." They were all with well-known companies, ranging from Xerox and Coca-Cola to American Airlines and the Campbell Soup Company. While their ages were not given, photographs of each were printed, and most looked as if they were in their forties or early fifties. While not all people who head divisions or reach vice presidential levels make it to the top, they are usually assumed to belong to pools from which chief executives are drawn. After all, they have thus far shown talents that earned them their promotions, and future advancement should be a likely prospect.

Fast-forward to ten years later, by which time most are at an age when people become corporation heads. Of the fifty on the 1992 list, two had got a top prize. One was Kenneth Chenault, who was named chairman of American Express in 2001. The other was Richard Nanula, who became CEO at Starwood Hotels and

Resorts in April of 1998. (But then, for reasons that were never fully explained, he resigned a year later.) Still, two out of fifty makes for a four-percent success rate.

Suppose, say, *Fortune* magazine drew up a list of the 50 top white executives below the CEO level. It would interesting to see how many of them would be heads of companies ten years later. The odds are good that their figure would be higher than four percent. And that, in turn, makes one wonder how many on the list of blacks were ever regarded as contenders for the top tier. Or had they simply gone as far as black managers could go?

In fact, in 2002, black men were serving as chief executives of three major corporations. Stanley O'Neal at Merrill Lynch, Richard Parsons at AOL Time Warner, and Kenneth Chenault at American Express. (In 1999, Lloyd Ward was named CEO of Maytag, but he resigned after eleven months on the job.) To say these appointments are impressive would be an understatement. Every firm wants the best person it can get for its top position. So far as O'Neal, Parsons, and Chenault were concerned, they were judged to be the finest out of large fields of candidates. And this has to mean that they were judged superior to quite a few white managers their companies were considering. So in no way can their elevation be regarded as part of some "affirmative action" program. That kind of preferment might happen at lower levels, but the selection of a CEO is viewed as too crucial to be used for meeting a racial goal or filling quota.

In the years ahead, it will be revealing to see how many other companies in the top 500 decide that someone who happens to be of African ancestry is their top choice. What can be said is that fewer of these posts are going to white men who were born in the United States. By the late 1990s, among the 800 largest American-owned companies, no fewer than 56 had CEOs who had been born outside this country. (This group doesn't include foreign-owned companies like Firestone and DaimlerChrysler.) The largest single number hailed from Canada (12), followed by Great Britain (8), France (6), Germany (5), and Australia (3). Also on the list of executives were names like Samir Bibara (born in Egypt), who headed Goodyear; Ray Irani (Lebanon) of Occidental Petroleum; Malik Hasan (India) of Health Systems International; Mory Ejabat (Iran) of Ascend Communications; and Roberto Goizueta (Cuba), who presided over Coca-Cola.

As has been noted, corporations conduct an extensive search, looking for the best possible individual they can find. So we are faced with the fact that fewer American-born white men, the group that has long dominated the executive pool, are satisfying their own firms'—and their country's—requirements for corporate leadership. A similar set of developments will be observed in the chapter on academic excellence.

HAS THERE BEEN PROGRESS?

Not so many years ago, entire spheres of employment were almost completely closed to blacks. As recently as 1980, the census could find only 254 black optometrists, 185 black actuaries, and 122 black auctioneers. In addition, blacks accounted for only 138 nuclear engineers, 89 theology professors, and 70 sheet metal apprentices. At present, it can be said that absolute barriers have been broken, and every occupation has some blacks among its practitioners. In many areas, however, the numbers remain exceedingly small. The table on the next page gives racial breakdowns for various areas of employment. Even now, blacks remain underrepresented in the professions of engineering, law, and medicine, as well as architecture and dentistry. Until lately, black students felt little incentive to train for these fields, since there were few if any prospects of obtaining a job. (Paul Robeson turned to acting because he had no serious offers after graduating from Columbia Law School.) While virtually all professions are saying they would like to have more blacks on their payrolls, it still remains to be seen whether they simply want a few faces for showcase purposes or if they mean jobs with real responsibilities.

BLACK REPRESENTATION IN OCCUPATIONS (I)

All Occupations in 2000	11.3%

Greatest Overrepresentation

Postal Clerks	35.3%
Nursing Aides and Orderlies	32.7%
Bus Drivers	28.6%
Parking Lot Attendants	27.9%
Security Guards	27.6%
Corrections Officers	26.8%
Telephone Operators	25.5%
Social Workers	24.5%
Taxicab Drivers	23.2%
Janitors and Cleaners	20.8%

Closest to Parity

Hairdressers	13.1%
Flight Attendants	12.6%
Police Officers	12.6%
Telephone Installers	11.8%
Upholsterers	10.9%
Elementary School Teachers	10.6%
Bank Tellers	10.6%
Registered Nurses	9.9%

Greatest Underrepresentation

Engineers	5.5%
Lawyers	5.1%
Dentists	4.1%
Tile Setters	4.0%
Designers	3.9%
Cabinetmakers	3.4%
Architects	3.1%
Bartenders	2.9%
Tool and Die Makers	2.6%
Dental Hygienists	2.5%
Geologists	1.9%
Airline Pilots	0.6%

But moving beyond the professions, how are we to account for the low percentages of blacks when it comes to waiting on tables and tending bar? These are hardly elite occupations requiring sophisticated training. The suspicion arises that proprietors of restaurants and lounges may feel that their white clienteles do not want their food and drinks handled by black employees. Or it could stem from the belief that if a place has "too many" blacks on its staff, it will drop to a lower status. (Obviously, there are exceptions: for example, New Orleans dining rooms that affect the "old-retainer" tradition.) Perhaps most revealing of all is the small number of black dental hygienists. While white patients seem willing to be cared for by black nurses, they apparently draw the line at having black fingers in their mouths.

Occupations where black workers have the strongest showing are not necessarily menial. Still, they do more than their share of janitorial chores and cleaning up after others, which have been traditional "black" positions. As the tabulations show, the positions where blacks have greatest representation tend to be jobs that whites are reluctant to take (janitors and nursing aides) as well as some at lower civil service levels (correction officers and postal clerks). Blacks now fill in at high-turnover occupations (as security guards and taxicab drivers). In some cases, the fields offering more openings (bus driving and social work) are ones serving clienteles that have become disproportionately black.

How much "progress" recent years have seen depends on how one interprets percentage losses and gains. The listings on the next page show a greater black presence in some office positions and skilled blue-collar fields. There are now more black electricians and firefighters, both decently paid occupations sought by high school graduates. However, not many people are lining up to become telephone operators and secretaries, jobs white women no longer find so attractive and that have consequently opened up to blacks. The picture is far from encouraging in some other fields. Four decades have passed since 1960, which presumably should have been enough time for increases among black college teach-

BLACK REPRESENTATION IN OCCUPATIONS (II)

	1960	2000
More Than Doubled		
Telephone Operators	2.6%	25.5%
Firefighters	2.5%	12.9%
Retail Sales	2.4%	12.6%
Librarians	5.1%	10.8%
Accountants and Auditors	1.6%	9.5%
Secretaries	2.0%	9.0%
Electricians	2.2%	7.7%
Lawyers	1.3%	5.1%
Small Increases		
Hairdressers	12.7%	13.1%
Automobile Mechanics	7.4%	7.5%
Skilled Metal Workers	5.0%	6.9%
College Faculty	4.4%	6.1%
Physicians	4.4%	5.6%
Decreased		
Domestic Servants	54.3%	12.1%
Chefs and Cooks	24.9%	17.4%
Commercial Painters	7.7%	7.6%
Aircraft Mechanics	4.6%	4.0%

ers and automobile mechanics. It would seem that even affirmative action programs have not done much to raise black representation in these areas.

That there are more black electricians is heartening. But what happened among commercial painters, where the black share has actually dropped? One answer is that much of home construction now takes place in suburbs or farther-flung locations, far from where most blacks live. So a real obstacle to workforce equity stems from the difficulties blacks have in finding housing in areas where jobs open up.

The past generation has seen the medical and academic worlds enter new areas. Both have become highly specialized, as well as dependent on research and technologies. Since 1960, membership in both professions has experienced a threefold expansion. However, most of the beneficiaries in this increase have been white women, along with a growing proportion of Asians. While recruitment efforts have raised the number of black professors and physicians, their growth rate nevertheless remains smaller than for other groups. For this reason, they have retained the ratio they held four decades ago or have actually fallen behind.

Domestic service deserves special attention because of the real and symbolic role it has held for black Americans. Virtually every black adult can tell of mothers and grandmothers who cooked and cleaned and cared for children in white people's homes. This was one of the few forms of employment open to black women; indeed, it was so poorly paid that even lower-middle-class families could afford black "help." In 1940, there were 2.4 million household servants in a workforce of 52 million. In 1960, the ratio was still relatively high, 1.8 million out of 68 million. By 2000, however, the number of people working in other people's homes had dropped to 715,000 in a workforce that had risen to 135 million. So relative to the employed population, there are now only a ninth as many servants as there were sixty years ago.

There are several messages here. In larger cities, women who are willing to work as servants—whether on an hourly basis or as full-time nannies for children—now demand higher wages, with the result that fewer households can afford domestic help. And in large stretches of the suburbs, it is difficult to find anyone available for this kind of work. One recourse has been to turn to aliens, many of whom will settle for off-the-books arrangements.

Equally noteworthy is that between 1960 and 2000, the black proportion among household servants fell from over half to 12.1 percent. One reason was cited earlier: job openings are now often in the suburbs, a long distance away. But there is a further consideration here, one having symbolic significance. In the memories of black women, domestic service represents not so much a job as something closer to servitude. Having to work within white homes recalls not only the condescension of employers but having to feign gratitude and a cheerful demeanor. While black women continue to do much of the nation's arduous work, most prefer the option of a hotel or hospital rather than mopping and dusting for the mistress of a house.

White employers can sense racial tensions and often seek to avoid them by hiring more acquiescent Filipinos or Hispanics. Some whites also worry lest having black servants will lower their status. Others of a more liberal bent fear that having blacks work in their homes may appear racist or exploitative. Families that once had black women look after their children now find it easier to work with—and converse about—their European au pairs.

Concerns over status may also explain the decline in black hairdressers and chefs. Sad to say, many white Americans feel uncomfortable in establishments that have a pronounced number of black employees. At best, they may go in once in a while, on a let's-try-it basis. By and large, however, they would rather not have black people taking charge of their hair or presiding over the kitchens where they dine. (This was not always the case in the past. In both Southern and Northern cities, for example, white men had their hair cut by barbers who were black.) One reason for the shift is that greater sophistication, including an international ambience, has come to be associated with coiffure and cuisine. As a result, more whites have entered these fields, bringing about a displacement of blacks.

A GENDER GAP

In recent years, black women have come to comprise a majority of the black workforce. The figures on the next page give the proportions of the positions within various fields that are held by black and white women relative to men within each of their racial groups. Thus black women account for 59.5 percent of all managers, whereas white women represent 44.9 percent of the whites holding those positions. In technical and professional positions, black women are even further ahead.

One reason is necessity. More black women must manage on their own, since they are less likely to have a housemate who brings in a second income. But even when they are married or live with someone else, they must still make a serious work commitment, since it often takes two black incomes to match what one white breadwinner can bring in. This is especially true for the middle class, where one white executive can make $100,000, but a pair of black schoolteachers hardly reach that level.

But this describes only one element in the equation. Of at least equal importance are attitudes and decisions among white employers. If and when organizations feel compelled to hire more black workers, they generally prefer to take on black women rather than black men. Black women, like all women, are perceived as being less assertive and more accommodating. Thus there is the hope that black women will show less resentment or hostility and will be less apt to present themselves as "black" in demeanor and appearance. A further concern of white employers, albeit not one openly stated, is that having black men and white women work together might lead to relationships that could either be misunderstood or have some grounding in fact.

In addition, black and white women tend to mingle more easily in workplace settings. This is partly because women tend to feel less tense about race. But there is also evidence that women can ignore racial lines in acknowledging common experiences, at least to a far greater extent than men are willing to do. At restaurants near their place of work, groups of black and white women can be seen enjoying lunch together. Far less frequently—if at all—does one encounter similar parties of men. Circumstances like these are not lost on employers, who may conclude that if they must have racially mixed workforces, things will go better if they consist largely of women.

EDUCATED AND EMPLOYED

Percentage of Degrees to Women

	M.D.	Law	Ph.D.
Black Women	61.0%	60.7%	61.2%
White Women	40.5%	44.0%	48.2%

Percentage of Women in Workforce

	All Workers	Managers
Black Women	53.4%	59.5%
White Women	46.8%	44.9%

Percentages reflect share of places held by women in their own racial group.

AN ADDED BURDEN

As has been noted, public and nonprofit organizations have become havens for much of the black workforce. Over a third of all black lawyers work for government departments, as do almost 30 percent of black scientists. Blacks account for over 20 percent of the nation's armed services, twice their proportion in the civilian economy. They hold about a third of all positions in the Postal Service and have similar ratios in many urban agencies. Unfortunately, this makes middle-class blacks vulnerable to public budget cuts.

On the whole, then, the business world has not done much to expand black employment. White executives worry about how large a black presence they want to absorb within their firms. Obviously, these thoughts are not committed to paper, nor are they specified in percentage terms. At the same time, racial considerations often figure indirectly, as when companies decide to move operations to suburban locations or open facilities in sparsely populated areas. When questioned, they usually allude to the lack of skilled people in central cities rather than confess to racial prejudice.

Companies realize that too few black faces could lead to charges of bias, causing unpleasant publicity. At the same time, they worry lest they are seen as having "too many" black employees or as promoting blacks too liberally. In this vein, they may fear that "too black" an appearance will jeopardize their image for competence and credibility. Firms also become uneasy if one of their products—a brand of outdoor wear, for example—becomes identified with a black clientele. Perhaps projecting some of their own anxieties, they sense that white customers will shy away from items they feel have become associated with black preferences and tastes.

All the while, businesses can be expected to protest that they are "color-blind" in both policy and practice, seeking only the best

talent they can find, regardless of race or creed or gender. If there
appear to be few black people on their payrolls, they will insist it
is because hardly any have applied or not enough live near their
facilities or have the necessary qualifications. What is not openly
addressed is how far possessing skin of a certain color might figure as one of those "qualifications."

Business has always been inherently conservative, waiting
until other sectors take steps toward social change. In part, this attitude stems from anxieties about how customers will react. Will
they buy, or buy as much, from salespeople who are black? And
can blacks join in the socializing so often needed to clinch a deal?
Will users of your product feel confident that a black technician
can work competently with complex equipment? Hence the tendency to play it safe, which usually means hiring as white a workforce as possible. (To combine competence and color, Asians
serve as acceptable surrogates.) There is also the worry that blacks
who are promoted to supervisory positions may not obtain the
best performance from white subordinates, who may be resentful
if not actually resistant. Chief executives may smile wanly and
agree that the problem is one of prejudice. Not their own, of
course, but those of customers and others who still cling to
stereotypes.

In more protected settings, white employees and supervisors
may be heard to say that they find blacks hard to work with ("We
had one, but he didn't work out.") They will cite cases of coldness
or hostility or chips on the shoulder compounded by a readiness
to imagine racial insults. Or they will allude to an unwillingness
of black men to relax in workplace relationships. Rather than
inquire why this reluctance persists or how it might be remedied,
the tendency is to evade the issue by hiring and promoting as few
blacks as possible. At that point, personal biases become trans-
muted into institutional racism.

Small wonder, then, that black Americans have always agreed
among themselves that if they want to get ahead, they have to work
harder and do better than white people. Given all the misgivings

of white executives and supervisors, it would seem self-evident that blacks must put in a lot more effort simply to satisfy the standards their employers set. It is not as if they could simply walk in and start doing a job. All eyes are on them, as if a Great Experiment were under way.

It is not easy buckling down to a job when you have to expend so much of your energy contriving a "white" personality—or at least the appearance of one—so as to put your white workmates at ease. Nor is it easy to establish one's authority, since simply having a black face raises doubts in many white minds. Added to which is having to read nuances and allusions that whites recognize as a matter of course. All this demands much more from black workers than is ever asked of whites. If white people have any doubts on this score, they might imagine spending their entire careers with a foreign company, where they find that no matter how much they study its ways, it is still supposed that they can never master the assignments at hand.

AFFIRMATIVE ACTION

With employment, as in education, interests and emotions can cloud discussions of "affirmative action." Indeed, the phrase has become an epithet for our time. Simply hearing it mentioned causes individuals to raise defensive bulwarks, as if the most vital of principles are at stake. The issues and reactions to them are often similar in both employment and education. However, preferential policies have some different implications in educational settings, and these will be considered separately in the next chapter.

Most simply, affirmative action in employment proposes—or requires—changes in hiring or promotion policies. It aims at bringing more of certain categories of people into an organization and then ensuring their representation at various levels. The intended beneficiaries may be women or persons with certain attributes or origins. However, the cases drawing the greatest attention have been those that focus on race.

Affirmative action is by no means new. It began in 1941, when President Franklin D. Roosevelt signed an executive order requiring defense plants to show that they were opening jobs to black workers. Roosevelt also established a Fair Employment Practices Committee to ensure that his ruling would be enforced. This body was continued under Presidents Truman and Eisenhower, and later Congress expanded its authority and renamed it the Equal Employment Opportunity Commission. The Kennedy administration coined the actual phrase "affirmative action," in a ruling that directed firms with federal contracts to take "positive steps" to have a racially representative workforce. Under the Civil Rights Act of 1964, passed by a bipartisan majority, Title VII banned employment discrimination that might be based on race, religion, sex, or national origin. President Lyndon Johnson, shortly after signing the law, illustrated the thinking that led to racial preferences. Speaking at Howard University in 1965, he said:

> You do not take a person who for years has been hobbled by chains, and liberate him, bring him up to the starting line, and then say, "You are free to compete with all the others."

Martin Luther King, Jr., stated the position in similar terms when he remarked that one cannot ask people who don't have boots to pull themselves up by their own bootstraps. It was President Richard Nixon, generally considered a conservative Republican, who took affirmative action a step further. In what his administration called "The Philadelphia Plan," companies were told that to keep federal contracts they would have to set numerical "goals" for hiring minorities. By 1972, Congress had amended Title VII so that courts could require affirmative action measures as a way of compensating for discriminatory practices.

GOALS OR QUOTAS?

Much has been made of whether affirmative action calls for setting "goals," which employers must make a good faith effort to reach, or if it imposes actual numerical "quotas." For many people, the latter term can have ominous overtones. In the 1990s, Senator Jesse Helms of North Carolina won reelection by stirring worries among whites that jobs they might have otherwise obtained would become unavailable to them. While it happened that his opponent was black, Helms's victory also sent a message to white candidates, alerting them to what could happen if they appear to favor quotas.

In fact, there have been cases where quotas were imposed. One of the first occurred in 1972, when a federal judge told Alabama officials that half of all new state troopers they hired would have to be black and that the order would remain in effect until blacks comprised one quarter of the force. Moreover, the Equal Employment Opportunity Commission has the power to file suit against private employers who do not appear to have enough black workers on their payrolls. In one case, the commission told a small Chicago firm that it had to hire eight more black employees, since statistical studies showed that it had an inadequate racial mix compared with other businesses in the area.

In increasing numbers of cases, however, employers do not wait for court orders or other official rulings. Rather, they take steps on their own to avoid litigation or bad publicity. In some instances, these moves arise from liberal motives, or at least from a wish to appear progressive. Thus a law firm may decide that no matter what, it will include at least one black graduate among its next intake of associates. Or the reasons can be semivoluntary. A construction firm may move black applicants higher on its hiring list to secure or retain a government contract, since many local and federal agencies want evidence of a multiracial workforce. More than a few corporations have integrated affirmative action policies into their human resources systems. Not only have they been successful in changing their racial ratios, but they have sought to educate their staffs on how to make the new procedures work.

THE RATIONALE

The purpose of affirmative action is not simply to avow good intentions but to register results. Showing you have tried to find qualified people will not suffice. Rather, its aim is to achieve a visible increase in the number of black men or women at various levels on the nation's payrolls. Justifications for these policies can take several forms.

(1) One is that blacks should figure disproportionately in hirings and promotions to compensate for past policies that excluded them from employment or allowed them entry only in token numbers. In these cases, those being hired will not necessarily be the same persons who suffered from discrimination in the past. So one presumption of affirmative action is that an entire race can deserve redress for unjust treatment. On this premise, at least some of the beneficiaries may come from later generations. An analogy might be that if a family's property was unfairly confiscated, restoration can go to descendants who were not even alive when the expropriation occurred. But not everyone accepts this view. Recent decisions by more conservative judges have declared that only specific individuals who can show that they were not hired or promoted due to racial bias can claim jobs or promotions or recover financial damages.

(2) Another rationale for affirmative action suggests a broader basis for increasing the number of black physicians and professors, as well as metalworkers and firefighters. Our society will be a better place if it has fairer racial representation in these and other occupations. If a country wants to vouchsafe that it has overcome discrimination and prejudice, visible evidence is necessary. Two hundred years ago, Alexander Hamilton said that the promise of

America was to allow every individual to "find his proper element and call into activity the whole vigor of his nature." To make good on this principle would not require that the membership of all professions precisely mirror the population as a whole. Not everyone will want to go into every field or speciality. Even so, no group chooses to have most of its members remain below the norm in pay and prestige. Nor does affirmative action aim at eliminating gaps between the well-off and the poor. Indeed, it accepts the economic inequalities characteristic of America's economic system. Thus it seeks to redistribute status and rewards with more concern for racial equity.

(3) A further justification for preferential policies relates to the "hobbles" Lyndon Johnson referred to in his Howard University speech. If black people are to have a fair chance in the nation's economic competitions, they must obtain enough training and experience to vie on an equal footing. To reach a higher status, you must first get to the step immediately below. America will not have additional black chief executives unless contenders can learn the ropes at vice presidential levels. In this view, affirmative action promotions are temporary expedients that may lapse once black representation becomes evident in all sectors of the system.

(4) A variant of this view may be found in "set aside" provisions, under which public contracts are awarded to firms owned by blacks and other minorities. In some instances, exact quotas for such contracts have been set by public agencies, but this has now been questioned by the courts. Until recently, under this system, minority-owned firms that put in bids have had a better chance of securing a contract. Here, too, the idea has been that once they begin to gain experience in construction or manufacturing or providing financial services, they will be able to compete without special subventions. Until recently, the Federal Communications Commission made it easier for minority owners to obtain radio and television frequencies. Nor should it be forgotten that government help for private firms is by no means new. Military contractors have been given quite costly subsidies, on the ground that

they need to build up the expertise to provide products or services the government requires.

Thus far, few minority firms can be said to have graduated from dependence on their "set aside" cushion. If the aim of the program is to get them to the point where they can compete with other businesses on an unassisted basis, it still has a long way to go. An additional concern is that some companies seeking "set aside" contracts have not in fact been owned by blacks or other minority entrepreneurs. As successive prosecutions have shown, firms have frequently been underwritten by white businessmen, with some black or other minority executives displayed as figureheads. In one egregious case, a white contractor won an award because he claimed he had a Native American great-grandmother.

QUESTIONABLE CRITERIA

The debate over affirmative action raises some basic questions about how people are selected for positions and promotions. Methods will obviously vary among industries and occupations. In some cases, personality plays a major role; in others, more formal criteria hold sway. Increasingly, however, credentials like degrees and diplomas are expected at the outset simply if you want to have your name considered. In public employment, standardized tests can be critical for civil service positions, and rules may specify that openings can go only to the persons with the highest scores. Many private firms now administer similar examinations to job applicants.

The problem is that most such tests have had "a disparate impact" when their results are broken down by race. Generally, blacks as a group do not do as well as whites on multiple-choice tests. Back in 1971, the Supreme Court confronted the impact of testing in *Griggs* v. *Duke Power Co.* The company had kept black employees in lower-level jobs, arguing that their test scores showed they were not "qualified" for better positions. The Court rejected this explanation, ruling that employers who hired and promoted on the basis of tests had to show that those examinations in fact provided good forecasts of how well people would do at their jobs.

Thereafter, companies could continue to use tests that disparate numbers of black applicants failed to pass only if they could demonstrate that those examinations served a "business necessity." That is, they had to show that only by using these tests could they find the best people, who were needed for the firm to perform profitably. Under this logic, even if test results display some racial bias, a business is still entitled to hire the people who will best benefit its balance sheet. Affirmative action proposals would then have to argue that considerations other than profits should also play a role.

Legal phrases like "disparate impact" and "business necessity" recur in the debate over affirmative action. Another term is "bona fide occupational qualification." In some professions, employers may ask that all candidates have an advanced degree, since that attainment stands as evidence that they have the "skills and aptitudes essential to the job." A good example is academic employment. As was seen earlier, black professors hold only 6.1 percent of all faculty positions, even after several decades of affirmative intentions by college administrations. The most common reason given is that the "pool" of qualified blacks is very small, and those who already meet its standards have a multitude of offers. As is well known, the basic qualification for college teaching is the Ph.D. Colleges argue that having it is their equivalent of a "business necessity."

In 2000, a total of 33,578 doctoral degrees were awarded to American citizens and aliens who intend to remain in this country. Of those doctorates, 2,220–or 6.6 percent—went to black men and women. Even if all of these individuals had joined college faculties, it would not have done much to improve the existing percentage. As it turns out, the largest single field for black doctorates is education, and most of the recipients were school administrators averaging over forty years of age. Altogether, only 94 black candidates received Ph.D.s in engineering, 71 in physics and chemistry, and 56 in business administration. Given the small size of these "pools," it seems that a lot of college departments will not have much success in their search for black colleagues.

But need a Ph.D. be mandated as a "bona fide occupational qualification" for everyone in college teaching? Most institutions do not place much emphasis on research. In fact, many professors cease being productive scholars or writers after they get tenure. Moreover, in fields like business and engineering, practical experience and an ability to communicate may actually make for better teaching than an advanced degree. Law is another practical calling, yet many law schools continue to limit their hiring to candidates who have published articles in professional reviews. This limitation led the Reverend Jesse Jackson to call on law schools to abandon these and other "archaic rules" and cease defining "who is qualified in the most narrow, vertical, academic terms." A law professor experienced in defending an inner-city clientele could have a lot to teach apprentice attorneys.

In actual fact, many job requirements are artificial or overly rigid and bar people of real talent from professions where they could do a lot of good. In medicine, we want physicians who have an intuitive flair for diagnosing maladies. Others may have personalities that put patients at ease, obviously an important element in treatment. Yet many of these potential healers may not score well on tests designed to assess abstract reasoning.

While everyone supports standards associated with "quality," the term can also conceal vested interests and biases. Why not say that an orchestra or a law school or a medical center should accept incorporating new people as a challenge? After all, there are literally dozens of fields where blacks have come to excel once opportunities started to open. (The military is an obvious case in point.) There is no reason why a more representative workforce could not be brought to match, if not surpass, standards set in more segregated days.

Public employment has been a prominent target in affirmative action cases, partly because it relies more heavily on tests and also because government is held to higher standards than enterprises committed to pursuing profits. Also, official agencies cannot use the defense of "business necessity" when their hiring practices are challenged. Of course, we all want public bureaus to do their jobs efficiently, and most of us believe they should provide better service than they currently do. Still, they are not businesses and do not usually have to vie with competitors for customers and revenues.

In 1979, in *United Steelworkers* v. *Weber,* the Supreme Court renewed its early support for affirmative action by approving plans that intended to "remove manifest racial imbalance" in hirings, placement, and promotions. This principle was applied two years later in New York City, where a lower court agreed that not enough black police officers were passing the test for promotion to the rank of sergeant. The question arose whether something about the test itself might have been racially biased. Certainly, the results showed a "disparate impact." It was not an easy test, and only 10.6 percent of the whites taking it received passing grades. However, among the black candidates, the passing proportion was a dismaying 1.6 percent. So the court ordered the police department to come up with a new examination, to be revised in ways that would enable more blacks to get passing grades.

The new test put less emphasis on reading and interpreting paragraphs of prose. Instead, the officers taking it watched situations acted out on videotapes. Even so, they had to fill in answer sheets that required them to know the meaning of words like "relevant," "disposition," "unsubstantiated," and "tactfully." When the results were computed, the number of passing black candidates was about as low as it had been before.

But this raises an issue similar to those considered with medical schools and college faculties: whether existing tests really have "a significant relationship to job performance." So far as police work is concerned, everyone agrees that we need more officers who can communicate with people in poorer and rougher neighborhoods. One could well argue that the knowledge and skills black candidates bring to law enforcement would more than make up for the lower scores they tend to receive on standardized tests.

At the same time, we now expect even officers on patrol to be well informed about complex constitutional issues. Investigations must be conducted to hold up later in court, where terms such as "disposition" and "unsubstantiated" inevitably figure. Officers are also expected to write reports with sufficient precision that they can withstand scrutiny if the case comes to trial. These arguments have been used to defend the need for literacy skills among police officers.

PREFERENTIAL TREATMENT?

Despite huge investments in research, even the experts have yet to devise tests that will be "race neutral" in their results. In theory, such tests would give all candidates the same chance to reveal their skills and intelligence, regardless of their racial origins or cultural backgrounds. But another expectation for "neutral" tests is that satisfactory numbers of black candidates will achieve passing scores. Since this has yet to happen, New York City resolved the problem by setting a lower passing grade for black police officers. This issue will be explored further in the next chapter, with regard to college admissions.

As has been noted, a frequent argument for affirmative action is that it will serve the nation's interests to have more black men and women serving as physicians and police officers and teachers, as well as in other professional fields. For one thing, they will be role models for youngsters: living evidence that hard work can be

rewarded. Moreover, in the occupations just cited, they can provide more effective service to patients, students, and citizens of
their own race. To the extent that black Americans have their own
culture, vocabulary, and styles, white practitioners may fail to
grasp important nuances and meanings. Even with goodwill and
careful training, it is unlikely that a white—or Asian or Hispanic—psychiatrist will be able to offer a complete diagnosis of a
black patient's mental state. And one reason so many white
policemen harass so many black youths is that they cannot catch
the clues that distinguish law-abiding young men from those
who are up to no good. One could hope that even black felons
would see more fairness in the justice system if they were tried and
sentenced by black judges.

But such a defense of preferential hiring comes close to suggesting that the skills of black professionals hinge on their ability
to serve clienteles of their own race. If that is why they should be
hired, then the question arises whether they can also serve the
more general population. If black police officers are hired prima-
rily for patrolling—and controlling—black neighborhoods, they
will soon begin to wonder whether they will be considered for
promotions and broader assignments. It will be revealing to see, as
more black physicians open practices, how many white patients
come to them for treatment.

Interestingly, an obverse argument is less often heard. That is,
that white students and patients and criminals would stand to gain
by being taught or treated or tried by black teachers and physicians
and judges. Given the everyday advantages that come with being
white, having to face black people with power may awaken whites
to realities about themselves and their society they have failed to
recognize.

A further concern with affirmative action is that colleagues and
patients and clients will wonder whether people promoted under
these programs made it on their merits or whether they got
where they are because of race-based preferences. Similar reactions have been expressed about those benefiting from the pro-

grams. How, it is asked, can people go through life knowing that they have been hired not on their inherent talents but to fill some quota or to satisfy appearances?

Not surprisingly, white people seem to do most of the worrying about this apparent harm to black self-esteem. In fact, there is little evidence that those who have been aided by affirmative action feel many doubts or misgivings. For one thing, most of them believe they are entitled to whatever opportunities they have received. The experience of being black in America cannot help but stir suspicions that in most cases you were never given a fair chance. So if preferential treatment comes your way, your response may be that it makes up for at least some of the inequities you have faced throughout your life.

Nor should it be forgotten that feelings of unworthiness seldom plague white Americans, who have profited from more traditional forms of preferment. For years, so-called selective colleges have set less demanding standards for admitting children of alumni. (This by itself should show that affirmative action has a venerable history.) These privileged offspring know full well that other applicants with better records received rejection letters. Yet few of them are seen slouching around the campus, their heads bowed in shame. Worries about the mental and moral health of persons labeled as undeserving can underestimate the readiness of individuals to justify good fortune. If nothing else, one can always rationalize: for years others have been favored; now it's our turn.

REVERSE DISCRIMINATION?

One reason the Supreme Court has given for permitting some affirmative action plans is that they do "not require the discharge of white workers and their replacement with new black hirees." The judges seem to be saying that whites should not suffer in order to bring about benefits for blacks. This principle has generally prevailed. According to the Court, white workers who hold jobs should not have to worry that they will be let go and replaced by blacks simply to change a racial ratio.

In fact, there have been such cases, although care is often taken to blur the connection. Thus a white college instructor whose contract is not renewed may have these suspicions when he discovers that his successor is to be a black professor. By and large, though, white fears focus less on losing jobs. A more pervasive concern has to do with not getting a position they may be applying for or being passed over for promotions. This worry is what gave rise to the case of Allan Bakke, a rejected medical school applicant, which came before the Supreme Court in 1978. He had sued the University of California, claiming that although his record entitled him to a place, it was given to a less qualified black candidate. He was rejected, he argued, simply because he was white. While Bakke did not use the phrase, his position was that he had suffered from "reverse discrimination." In other words, he argued that whites can also encounter bias; and in such cases, courts should find in their favor.★

No one can say with certainty how many white Americans may have been bypassed or displaced because preferences have been given to blacks. As was noted earlier, whites have not lost ground in medicine and college teaching, despite considerable efforts to open up those fields.

Still, it would be disingenuous to deny that some white men— and perhaps even some white women—did not get jobs that, in the absence of affirmative action, might otherwise have gone to them. Some of these individuals may be quite bitter about having been kept from positions they feel they worked for and deserved. So long as there are a limited number of desirable jobs and fewer avenues for promotions, there are going to be disappointed people. In some cases, they may be young men who had always

★The Court allowed California to continue preferential admissions for blacks, on the ground that colleges have always been allowed to select diverse student bodies. But it also told the medical school that it had to admit Bakke.

aspired to police careers or the building trades, perhaps following in their fathers' footsteps. In other instances, they may be administrators in public service organizations who believe that they did not get a promotion because those higher up felt it timely to have someone black in a visible position.

But given the disappointments that so often accompany having a black skin, it could be argued that whites could give way just a little. Even so, few white Americans feel that they should be held personally responsible for racial discrimination, either now or in the past. Thus they resent policies that would allow others to move ahead of them, and most of them sincerely feel that they have been subjected to "reverse discrimination."

In actual fact, talented advertising executives and successful surgeons have little to fear from minority preference. The whites who lose out are more generally blue-collar workers or persons at lower administrative levels, whose skills are not greatly in demand. One of the chief effects of affirmative action has been to pit whites with modest aspirations against blacks who want better lives for themselves.

WINNERS AND LOSERS

A few concluding comments are in order. The first is that such evidence as we have shows that white women have benefited more from recent workforce changes than have black men. And among blacks, women have gained more than have black men. Perhaps if the movement of women toward work and careers had come at another time, progress relating to race would have been given greater priority.

Much has been heard about the need to improve Americans' work skills, if only to maintain the nation's living standards and keep the country competitive in the world economy. Increasing numbers of companies have found they have to educate their own employees, often in collaboration with urban schools and community colleges. Firms like Motorola and Monsanto and Corning have made extra efforts to place black workers and other minorities in such programs. Nor is this always in response to official prodding or threats of litigation, let alone pressure to fill "quotas." In many cases, companies are finding that not enough whites entering the workforce are willing to consider blue-collar jobs. Benefits for employers include improved morale, retention of skilled people, and better company-community relations. Insofar as this is so, self-interest may force more businesses to devise their own variants of affirmative action.

But this may be wishful thinking. Companies that do not wish to pay the wages Americans expect have been turning elsewhere. In 2000, for example, Nike managed to sell $9 billion worth of footwear with a payroll of only 21,800 people. The reason is that it has no manufacturing operations within this country; all of its sneakers are made abroad. And rather than trying to teach white-collar skills to a local labor force, some insurance companies are flying their paperwork to places such as Ireland, where operators key it into computer systems. Indeed, architectural specifications can be sent by satellite, with the drafting done as far away as Bombay.

Here in the United States, many employers are quite open about preferring immigrants to native-born black workers. Apartment houses are more apt to choose Hispanics or West Indians for their service staffs, while retail shops look for Asians. A black owner of several fast-food restaurants in and around Harlem confessed that he confined his hiring to foreign-born applicants.

And, as has been noted, firms opening new facilities make a point of selecting sites with minimal black populations. This is especially true of foreign-owned corporations, an increasing source of American employment. Thus Toyota located an assembly plant in Kentucky's Harlan County, in which 95 percent of the residents are white, while Honda settled on a stretch of rural Ohio, where the white figure was 97 percent.

CHAPTER EIGHT

EDUCATION

ETHNICITY AND ACHIEVEMENT

Today, every college and university says it is committed to "equal opportunity" in faculty hiring and student admissions. On its face, the principle would seem unassailable: all applicants should be given full and fair consideration, regardless of age or race or sex or other characteristics and conditions, including physical disabilities. Under equal opportunity, standards would be set, and all would have the same chance in the competition. If this seems commonplace now, it was not always the case. In the past, colleges turned down qualified candidates because they were Catholic or Jewish and in many cases would not even consider black applicants. Now, as has been noted, some Asians are protesting that while they have satisfied admissions standards, they are not getting their fair share of college places. In a similar vein, some whites have complained that blacks with lower test results are given places sought by higher-scoring whites.

"Affirmative action" is rather different from "equal opportunity." No colleges today turn down black applicants who meet their academic criteria. Virtually all schools say they would like to attract even more black students, since small black enrollments have become a matter of embarrassment. In 2000, for example, Bates College in Maine could manage only 2.2 percent; and at the flagship University of Wisconsin campus at Madison, the black proportion was only 2.0 percent. Few schools simply wait for black candidates to apply; almost all mount recruiting drives.

The difficulty has been to find candidates the schools believe are qualified. Not only elite private schools but many state universities want to maintain minimal standards for the people they admit. Hence their quandary when too few black applicants meet those requisites.* To solve this problem, affirmative action programs have moved beyond recruiting drives and offers of financial aid. In other words, "action" must mean more than "opportunity"; it has to be able to point to results. To ensure that entering classes will display a certain racial composition, applications from black students are judged by a separate set of standards.

Separate standards can be rationalized in several ways. One argument is that preferential treatment is hardly new. For years, Ivy League colleges acted "affirmatively" by giving places to mediocre students from fashionable prep schools. It can also be argued that reserving places for athletes is a variant of affirmative action, as is greater indulgence toward candidates from distant states. The most common practice involves giving favored consideration to the offspring of alumni, even if their records are less impressive than those of other applicants. A study of Harvard, for example, found that about 35 percent of alumni children were admitted, compared with 16 percent among other candidates. At Princeton, 15 percent of the regular applicants got in, whereas acceptances went to 43 percent of those whose parents were Princeton grad-

---

*Of course, black students are not the only group "protected" (the official term) by affirmative action. Most programs also provide for Hispanics and Native Americans. Berkeley has added applicants from low-income families and persons with physical disabilities. The City University of New York, having decided it should have more Italian-Americans on its faculty, is allowed to judge candidates from that group by less stringent standards.

uates. (In response to inquiries from the U.S. Department of Education, Harvard officials said that alumni whose children were admitted gave more generously to the university. However, they later confessed that they had no figures to support this supposition.)

DIVERSITY OR DISCRIMINATION?

Almost everyone approves of diversity. And most people would probably agree with Justice Lewis Powell's statement in the 1978 *Bakke* case that recruiting a varied student body "is a constitutionally permissible goal for an institution of higher education."*
At the same time, individuals can differ on what constitutes diversity and where it may be found. Students at North Carolina's Appalachian State University, which is 94.2 percent white, may tell you their classmates come from different religious and economic backgrounds and hold a range of attitudes and views. Much the same might be heard at Louisiana's Grambling State University, where 95.5 percent of the students are black.

But affirmative action, as a policy, has construed "diversity" in terms of race and national origin. So its focus has been on attributes individuals were born with, rather than traits they developed themselves. Thus schools have not invoked affirmative action to bring more conservatives to a campus that was heavily liberal. Instead, with the emphasis on race, the diversity of a college could be gauged by strolling around its campus and looking at students' faces. The reasoning for the policy at Berkeley was summed up in a report by its Faculty Senate. The report said that students

*As it happened, Powell was one of six justices who published opinions in the *Bakke* case; but none of the six opinions got over four votes. So that case produced no single "majority" holding on affirmative action. This means that the current Supreme Court can hear new cases and perhaps hand down new rulings.

of varied races and origins would create "a more dynamic intellectual environment and a richer undergraduate experience." In order to bring about such a mixture, some applicants might have ancestries that would become a "qualification" for admission.

In 1981, only 3.8 percent of Berkeley undergraduates were black. Soon thereafter, an affirmative action program was instituted, under which black applicants would be evaluated and selected by separate standards. By 1988, after these new rules were in place, blacks accounted for 11.4 percent of those who were offered admission.

But during this time, Berkeley and other schools were not raising their total enrollments. So if students from some groups were being admitted in greater numbers, that meant rejection letters for others. In 1988, for example, white applicants were allocated only 38.9 percent of the acceptances, less than half of their share only a few years earlier. (Also figuring in the equation was a rise in Asian applications, which will be discussed shortly.)

Many white students and their parents resented seeing what they viewed as "their" places going to applicants who, to their minds, had weaker credentials. Their response came in 1996, when Proposition 209, which would ban affirmative action, was placed on the California ballot. It passed by a comfortable margin, mainly because white voters, who made up almost three-quarters of the electorate, gave it their strong support. Due to its passage, state universities could no longer take note of ancestries in making admission decisions. By 1998, of the 8,034 students who were accepted by Berkeley, only 191—or 2.3 percent—were black. In other words, their share had dropped below the 1981 figure, before affirmative action had been introduced.

In other states, persons opposed to affirmative action filed suits in federal courts. In Texas, for example, the state university's law school had set lower admission thresholds for black and Mexican-American applicants to ensure that more of them would be accepted. Under the Texas system, white candidates were expected to have scores of 199 or higher to be considered. And in fact, among those in a lower 189 to 192 range, only six percent of white applicants were admitted. However, because of affirmative action, all of the black students in that bracket were offered admission, as were most of the Mexican-Americans.

In 1994, Cheryl Hopwood and three other white applicants who had been rejected by the law school filed a suit, contending that the application process had discriminated against them because of their race. A judge at the district level ruled against them, saying that affirmative action was justified for several reasons. One was that if the 199 cutoff were applied to all candidates, there would be only nine black students in a class of about five hundred, or just 1.8 percent of the total. He also remarked that the law had school had a "reputation in the minority community" as a "white" institution, because students of that race dominated its enrollment. In his view, setting separate standards was the only feasible way to attract a "diverse student body."

Two years later, the Federal Court of Appeals for the Fifth Circuit unanimously overturned the district decision. It held, very simply, that a public institution "may not use race as a factor in deciding which applicants to admit." The court explained that if persons of one race were favored, then those of other races would suffer. A practice that harms whites, it said, is just as bad as one that injures blacks. On this ground, it ruled that "achieving a diverse student body is not a compelling interest under the Fourteenth Amendment." More than that, the court rejected the idea that having varied races on a campus produces diversity:

> The use of race, in and of itself, to choose students simply achieves
> a student body that looks different. Such a criterion is not more
> rational on its own terms than would be choices based upon the
> physical size or blood type of applicants.

Because of this ruling affirmative action programs were banned in public institutions within that circuit, which includes Texas, Mississippi, and Louisiana. Somewhat later, a circuit covering

Alabama, Florida, and Georgia invalidated affirmative action in those states.

Some 1,400 miles from the University of Texas, the University of Michigan was also using affirmative action at both its law school and undergraduate college. At the college, for example, applicants were rated on a 150-point scale, and students who were black or Hispanic or American Indian received an extra twenty points for their origins. This bonus was equivalent to raising their academic average by a full letter grade. Here, too, white students who had been rejected by the two schools claimed it was due to their race.

But there, in the Sixth Circuit, the appeals court upheld the university's claim that "a racially diverse student body produces significant educational benefits because of the current state of segregation and separation along racial lines in America." These judges were in effect replying to their Texas colleagues, pointing out that being black or white is not like having different heights or blood types. In America, the races tend to be raised separately, and often view the world in divergent ways. So in a campus setting, the court ruled "minority and majority alike" can learn a lot from one another.

This decision meant that public schools in Michigan, Tennessee, Kentucky, and Ohio could keep on using race in making admission decisions. (Private institutions are not affected by these cases, since they are given more freedom in making admission decisions.) At about that time, affirmative action was also approved by the circuit that extends across nine states, ranging from California and Hawaii to Idaho and New Mexico. So, by the close of 2002, six states had been ordered by federal courts to end their affirmative action program, whereas schools in another thirteen states could continue using them.

Needless to say, the parties that lost in each of the circuits have submitted appeals to the U.S. Supreme Court. The justices will be asked to decide which position will prevail for all fifty states. One approach argues that the presumed value of racial diversity should allow a college to set up admissions policies to achieve that goal. The other is that using race always has discriminatory effects, because while some people may benefit from having a certain origin, others are shut out due to their different background. The justices may well be holding hearings, or even have rendered a decision, while you are reading this book. And that ruling will decide whether the Texas or the Michigan reasoning—or even some compromise—will become the law of the land.

ASIANS OR CAUCASIANS?

All this noted, the scholastic statistics for several ethnic groups invite attention and explanation. White students generally get decent scores on the SAT, but it would be surprising if they didn't considering where they start. As the table on page 165 shows, 59.7 percent of them have parents who graduated from college, so that from infancy they were raised in homes attuned to higher education. Not only that, almost a quarter of the white students—23.6 percent—are from families with incomes exceeding $100,000. This means they probably live in areas with high-performing schools and take preparatory courses for the SAT. True, not all white students have these advantages; but enough do to explain why their race's average is as high as it is. If black and Hispanic students came from comparable backgrounds, their scores would probably be equally high.

Perhaps the most revealing figures on the table are those that show the relationship between improvement in scores and income gain. Those numbers represent the gap between students from families making under $20,000 and those with $100,000 or more. Latin American and Asian students show considerable progress as their economic situation improves; and the same holds for black students, although to a lesser degree. One striking point is that the rise for white students is relatively small. And one reason is that the scores for top-income whites are not especially impressive. Perhaps because they have had advantages, they don't feel they have to study hard or give full attention to the test. An earlier chapter showed how white adults are displaying less of the dedication once associated with family stability. Might it be that at least some of their children are showing similar signs?

What is certainly clear is that Asian teenagers are passing whites on several scales. As the graph on page 167 shows, they register better scores at every income level. Not only that, the gap between the groups grows greater with each subsequent bracket, from four points to thirty-two to fifty to sixty-three. In theory, white students whose families earn from $80,000 to $100,000 should do as well as their Asian counterparts. It is true that Asian students have well-educated parents, but often those degrees are from foreign universities. Indeed, over a third of Asian students are from homes with incomes under $30,000 and where English is not the first language, which suggests that their families are new to the United States. Yet despite those constraints, they outscore whites, almost all of whose parents and grandparents are native to this country.

At least some white Americans continue to be impressed with what they feel is the historic superiority of their race. The fact that they have been falling behind in the educational arena is making it more difficult to substantiate that claim.

Let's take another look at California's public universities. By 2000, Asian students were outnumbering whites at its three most selective campuses. These shifts led a local humorist to remark that UCLA now stands for "Unhappy Caucasians Lost among Asians."

	UCLA	Berkeley	Irvine
Asians	37.1%	40.2%	53.8%
Whites	33.9%	30.5%	22.1%

In these and other selective schools, Asians have been winning their places on merit in a fair competition. And this was happening even in the years when affirmative action was in place. Even then, when credentials were added up, not enough whites were getting grades and scores equal to those of Asian candidates. As a result, many of the white students were rejected, and ended up in campuses like Riverside or Davis, or Fullerton or Fresno. Some of them—or their parents—looked for someone to blame. But they couldn't easily claim that Asians, who had superior records, were unfairly taking places. So they made black and Hispanic students their targets, even though they had displaced far fewer whites than their Asian classmates had.

Studies of attrition suggest that affirmative action programs may do some students a disservice, by placing them in colleges for which they are not properly prepared. To stem dropout and failure rates, Pennsylvania State University has created "Black Incentive Grants" and "Black Achievement Awards," under which students must achieve a certain average to keep their scholarships. These grants have stirred some controversy, since they are confined to students of one race. Harvard has sought to avoid the attrition problem by ensuring that most of its black students come from middle-class homes and have attended predominantly white schools. As an admissions officer explained, "It is right for Harvard and better for the students, because there is better adjustment and less desperate alienation."

Most colleges remain committed to their affirmative action programs. The reason is that many professors and quite a few students regard the paucity of black faces on their campuses as a cause for shame. To raise the minority presence eases a lot of academic guilt. The fact that the newly admitted students themselves may bear a burden is hardly ever mentioned in campus discussions. Even with intensive remedial programs, teenagers from inner-city high schools are unlikely to be lofted to Ivy League levels.

The question frequently arises why affirmative action must specify race. After all, it can be argued, the whole intent of the civil rights drive was to remove race as a factor, since it was long used to bar blacks from enrolling in many colleges. Yet today, preferential policies for blacks mean that some whites are being shunted aside simply because they are white.

Hence the argument has been made that if a college wants a diverse student body, it could gear preferential admissions and aid to *all* low-income students, regardless of their ethnic origins. And because a higher proportion of black applicants come from families of modest means, they should get more than their share of low-income places and scholarships.

There is only one problem with this proposal. Among the black, white, Asian, and Hispanic high school seniors who took the Scholastic Aptitude Test in 2000 (its name has recently been changed to Scholastic Assessment Test), a total of 116,955 had family incomes under $20,000. The table on this page shows the average SAT scores of low-income students from four ethnic groups. Since all could claim economic need, admissions and aid would presumably be decided by academic merit. But gauged by SAT scores, low-income whites and Asians would end up with almost all of the "race-blind" awards, since most of them have better records from a strictly scholastic standpoint. This is why affirmative action that aims at helping blacks must take race into account.

AVERAGE SAT SCORES OF STUDENTS
FROM LOW-INCOME FAMILIES

White	26,763	973
Asian	15,723	946
Hispanic	23,221	825
Black	27,280	789

The kinds of abilities the SAT actually evaluates has been the subject of much debate, and some of those issues will be considered momentarily. At this point, it can simply be said that doing well on the SAT shows how well students have prepared themselves—and have been prepared—for the admissions competition as it currently exists.

The next table gives SAT scores for the same ethnic groups, along with some background information about those taking the test. The gap between the average scores of black and white students—more than two hundred points—has received a great deal of attention and need not be belabored here. Further insights can be obtained if the black and white groups are compared not with each other but with two other cohorts. This approach makes sense, since in terms of parental income and education, the Hispanic and black students taking the SAT have fairly comparable backgrounds. The Asians and whites are also quite similar so far as parental education is concerned.

Yet Hispanics average seventy-nine points higher than blacks, which might be considered surprising since two-thirds of the Hispanic students come from homes in which English is not the pri-

STUDENTS TAKING THE SAT: 2001–2002

Black	Hispanic		White	Asian
857	936	Average Score	1060	1070
212	265	Point Gain: Low to High Income	144	259
37.0%	31.4%	Parents College Graduates	59.7%	58.3%
2.9%	32.4%	English Not First Language	2.1%	36.8%
45.7%	46.1%	Family Income Under $30,000	11.8%	35.5%
5.1%	7.1%	Family Income Over $100,000	23.6%	15.0%

mary language and may not be spoken at all. So it is impressive that they score as well as they do, since their families are often new to this country or live in Spanish-speaking neighborhoods. That Asians do ten points better than whites is at least equally striking, since English is not the principal language in most of their homes, and their economic status is relatively modest. And, as is apparent from the depiction on the next page, they move further ahead of whites as their economic standing improves.

This is not the first time that immigrants and their offspring have surpassed native residents. Hard work and ambition still pay off, as they have in the past. However, there is another factor at work. While today's newly arrived immigrants tend to start out with lower incomes, many of them belonged to the middle class in their countries of origin, and they bring those values with them. Over half of the Asian students taking the SAT have parents who attended college, as do almost a third of the Hispanics. Also, immigrants who arrive today are less beset by culture shock. In the global village of an electronic age, most are prepared for American ways.

THE PROBLEM WITH THE SAT

The SAT has become the closest thing we have to a national IQ test. So it is best that we be clear about what this three-hour examination measures. Clearly, it does not gauge "intelligence" or "aptitude" in a broad sense. At best, it rates a narrow range of academic-oriented skills. Some have argued that, as much as anything, scores simply reflect how adept people are at taking that kind of test. As it happens, the sponsors of the SAT have known for many years that their test fails to identify how people will do in later life. A follow-up of Yale University graduates revealed that "no significant relation could be found between original scores and . . . honors and standing within their occupations." A similar study concluded that "no consistent relationships exist between

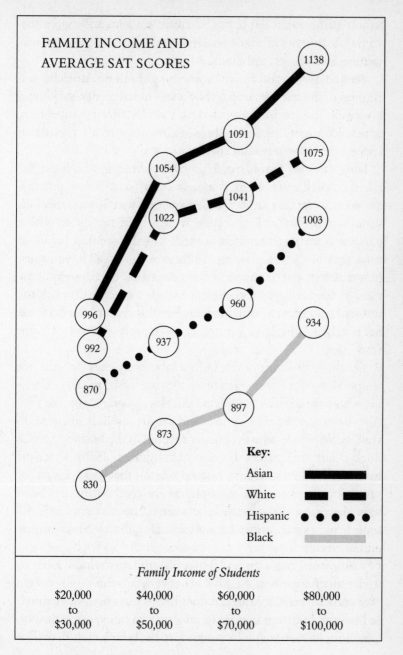

FAMILY INCOME AND
AVERAGE SAT SCORES

Key:
Asian
White
Hispanic
Black

Family Income of Students

| $20,000 to $30,000 | $40,000 to $50,000 | $60,000 to $70,000 | $80,000 to $100,000 |

Scholastic Aptitude Test scores in college students and their actual accomplishments in social leadership, the arts, sciences, music, writing, and speech and drama."

Yet SAT scores still convey something about the attitudes and abilities of the nation's teenagers. As was noted earlier, they show how well students have prepared for the admissions competition, which in turn reflects a willingness to adapt to a structure of success set up by the adult society.

Most of us are familiar with the SAT format, in which you are asked to pick the correct response from four or five possible answers. Some are mathematical problems, with several specious solutions. In the reading section, you may be presented with a paragraph on an unfamiliar subject, say, the feeding habits of migratory birds. After taking a minute or so to read it, you must pick which of several sentences "best describes" the contents of the passage. For each question, there is a single correct answer that the test makers expect you to identify. For this reason, the SAT has been called "objective," since there is only one set of right responses.

Do the tests discriminate? Quite obviously they do, and not simply along racial lines. First of all, they are biased in favor of people who have a knack for solving puzzles at a one-a-minute rate. Also teenagers drawn to music and the arts are less likely to do well, as are people who eventually succeed in the business world. Such disadvantages can be eased for students from better-off homes, who are more apt to attend schools that make a point of preparing them for the multiple-choice method. As has been seen, there is a close association between economic status and SAT scores, and this accounts for a great deal of the variation among ethnic groups.

The record of Asian and Hispanic students would seem to undercut charges that the SAT is basically a "white"—or even a "Western"—test. Of course, it does have a class bias, since much in the verbal portion alludes to information or experiences with which middle-class children are more likely to be familiar. The two questions shown on this page, which are much like those used by the SAT and similar tests, show the kind of agility that is being assessed.

These puzzles are not impossible to solve; rather, high scores go to students who are able to crack each item's code in approximately a minute. For this to happen, a teenager must not only have absorbed a large vocabulary, but also have developed a mental matrix consistent with the structure of the test. This type of logic originally emerged in Europe, and still underlies much of its intellectual culture. That so many young Asians and Hispanics have shown themselves able to master the SAT would suggest that they have adapted to this "white" world. Nor is it simply that they cram for the tests. Asian high school students have been found more likely than whites to take the full academic program recommended by the National Council on Excellence in Education, which includes intensive work in American history and literature.

So it may be more accurate to say that tests like the SAT now reflect not a racial or national corpus of knowledge but a wider "modern" consciousness. In the past, the word "modern" tended to have white and Western connotations. Today, however, the

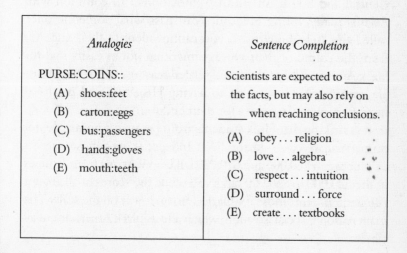

Analogies	*Sentence Completion*
PURSE:COINS::	Scientists are expected to _____ the facts, but may also rely on _____ when reaching conclusions.
(A) shoes:feet	(A) obey . . . religion
(B) carton:eggs	(B) love . . . algebra
(C) bus:passengers	(C) respect . . . intuition
(D) hands:gloves	(D) surround . . . force
(E) mouth:teeth	(E) create . . . textbooks

term has a far broader range. Much of Asia and Latin America has become modernized, to degrees few would have predicted a generation ago. Taiwanese and Costa Rican teenagers arrive in the United States already schooled in advanced mathematics and the multiple-choice method. So "modern" now stands for the mental and structural modes that characterize the developed world. It calls for a commitment to science and technology, as well as skills needed for managing administrative systems. The modern world rests on a framework of communication and finance, increasingly linked by common discourse and rules of rationality. Indeed, evidence from the educational scene suggests that even within this country, young people from immigrant backgrounds are showing themselves to be more "modern" in these commitments and skills than many of their native-born classmates. In recent years, over half of the Westinghouse science-competition winners have been immigrants or the children of immigrants.

Aspiring middle-class Hispanics have outlooks similar to those found among Asians. In fact, the term "Hispanic" underscores the European element in their origins, rather than aboriginal American links or ties to Africa. (An alternative, "Latino," carries Central and South American connotations.) In common with Asians, many young Hispanics can pass what someone once called the "telephone test": you cannot identify their ancestry from the sound of their voice, something not as easily said for black Americans. For these and related reasons, white Americans are considerably less averse to having Hispanics and Asians as neighbors or as classmates for their children.

It is striking that black students from better-off homes do not do particularly well on the SAT. Indeed, those whose parents earn between $60,000 and $70,000 fall below Asians from families in the $20,000 to $30,000 range. So while the scores of all groups rise with income, those for blacks remain lower on the scale. The main reason is social isolation, which affects black Americans of all classes.

Surveys of neighborhoods and schools show that black Americans spend more of their lives apart from other groups than even some immigrants. One outcome of this isolation is that they grow up with less sustained exposure to the rules of "linear reasoning" that are expected on the SAT and IQ tests. To be sure, blacks with middle-class jobs generally adapt to this regimen. Even so, their children tend to move among members of their own race, where they develop alternative intellectual styles. The result is that black modes of perception and expression become impediments to performing well on the official menu of standardized tests.

CHOOSING PHYSICIANS

Critics of affirmative action say that separate standards lead to the admission of unqualified students. As has already been noted, these charges are seldom leveled against children of alumni or applicants from distant states, who are often admitted with lower grades and scores. We actually have information on comparative outcomes. The University of California's medical school at Davis has long had a "special admission program" to increase its minority enrollment. A study published in the *Journal of the American Medical Association* tracked the careers of regular and special students over a twenty-year period. It concluded:

> The experience of the special admission students was very similar to that of regular admission students. There was no difference in completion of residency training or evaluation of performance by residency directors. The practice characteristics of the two populations were remarkably similar.

Moreover, the formal indicators usually used as "qualifications" fail to predict students' subsequent performance as physicians:

The student with higher MCAT scores and GPAs were not significantly more likely to become licensed, attain board certification, or enter the full range of career opportunities than were students admitted under special admission.

If this is true with a demanding career like medicine, it casts doubts on the use of scores and grades for admission to graduate schools of law and business management, as well as undergraduate liberal arts programs.

CHAPTER NINE

SEGREGATED SCHOOLING

VOLUNTARY AND IMPOSED

A HALF CENTURY AGO, virtually all black students who attended college enrolled in all-black institutions. In part, this was because most of them then lived in Southern or border states, where higher education was strictly segregated, and even private colleges banned black undergraduates. And since schools elsewhere in the country accepted only token numbers of black applicants, many Northern blacks traveled to segregated colleges in the South. Limited admissions persisted in the postwar period. Amherst College, reputedly a "liberal" institution, could display only two black faces among the 258 seniors at its 1951 graduation.

Today, close to half of all black Americans live in the North, and what had once been all-white Southern institutions now take in applicants of all races. As a result, seven out of eight black undergraduates now attend schools that can be described as "integrated," if by that is meant having student bodies that are predominantly white. Nor is this surprising, since whites still make up the majority at most colleges. (It is mainly at urban campuses that black students surpass ten percent of the enrollments.)

At most colleges, black students are relatively few in number and continually aware of their minority status. All too often, when they enter a classroom, they discover that they will be the only one of their race in the class. Even after official welcomes and overtures expressing goodwill, they soon sense that they are seen as an alien presence at what still remain essentially "white" institutions.

Given the struggle to enter schools that once barred them, all indications are that black students are far from happy once they get there. A study entitled *Blacks in College* surveyed several thousand black undergraduates in both Northern and Southern states. According to its author, Jacqueline Fleming, most of those attending integrated colleges said they felt "abandoned by the institution, rebuffed by fellow students, and inhibited from taking part in any but all-black organizational activities." It was also found that the majority of those who stayed to the senior year showed signs of "intellectual stagnation" and "frustrated academic drives." Many diverted their disappointment "into less constructive outlets," including attacking the school's administration or its curriculum.

THE BOUNDS OF FREE SPEECH

It must be borne in mind that most undergraduates are teenagers or in their early twenties, not a group notable for tact or immune from displays of bravado. They are at an age where they try to impress one another, often with heavy-handed humor and ill-considered pranks. There are still plenty of beer brawls, especially along fraternity row. While undergraduates often express liberal sentiments on social issues, many come to college never having known black people their age. Nor should this be surprising, since most attended schools that were almost or wholly white or where the races tended to go their own ways.

There is something about a college setting that makes race a visible issue. Campuses tend to be closed-off communities, where professors and students have a lot of free time, much of which they spend inflating the meanings of local events. It often turns out that colleges with liberal reputations receive the most recriminations, not least because protesters know how to play on the feelings of white faculty and students, many of whom need little prompting to plead guilty to racism.

Colleges also care more about the principles of free speech, which is certainly to their credit. But because they are compacted settings, it takes only one statement or expression to ignite an entire campus. Moreover, the freedoms in question seldom involve a "speech" in the sense of an extended presentation. True, there can be debates over whether a Louis Farrakhan or a David Duke should be invited to give a lecture or about what they may say if they actually come. Even so, speakers like Farrakhan and Duke are more ideological symbols than expositors of intellectual positions. Still, no one has ever said that to be counted as "speech," talk must be reasoned or profound or, for that matter, even truthful. What can be said, though, is that if a Farrakhan or a Duke appears on a campus, the event is unlikely to improve comity between the races.

Even today's Supreme Court has agreed that "speech" can also include expressive action, such as burning a flag or printing a slogan on a shirt. In 1991, some Harvard undergraduates hung Confederate flags inside their dormitory windows, which were visible to passersby. This also was defended as "speech," since it was a message aimed at arousing reactions. Not surprisingly, some observers saw the flag as defending slavery, perhaps even proposing its return. They felt that this display hardly helped interracial relations at Harvard, which they saw as a more important goal than the freedom to hang a piece of cloth in a window.

Brown University, another Ivy League citadel, actually expelled an undergraduate for shouting "nigger" and several other slurs in a well-trafficked part of the campus. The administration reasoned that his words were not a "speech" but, rather, an "action" that impaired the college atmosphere. To black people, certainly, to be called a "nigger" barely differs from an actual slap across the face. And all the more so on a predominantly white campus, where blacks are never sure of their welcome. Nor can it be argued that shouting "nigger" constitutes an argument or an idea, although one can sense the general sentiment, which is essentially one of hatred. Of course, the student had his defenders, who argued that even insulting shouts must be tolerated, lest we open the door to censoring more coherent expressions.

Bigoted behavior among white students often comes as a reaction to the more assertive attitudes that can be found among many of their black classmates. If we want to know why students put up Confederate flags or set crosses on fire, one explanation is that these are ways of telling black undergraduates that they have been making themselves too pronounced a presence. While no one says so in public, many white students still believe that blacks should be grateful simply for having been admitted, and they have no business criticizing their benefactors.

Perhaps the greatest problem is that legal determinations focus on balancing personal freedoms with preserving public order. What the law cannot readily do is deal with the subtler sensibilities that make for social relationship. If colleges that are mainly white wish to become amicable interracial communities, they will have a hard time achieving that end if some of their students insist on hanging flags in their windows or venting their animosities. To point this out is not to argue against free speech but simply to note some of its effects. As matters now stand, the First Amendment covers a very wide area. It could be used, for example, to protect some students on a predominantly white campus who decide to set up a table and then spend the day shouting "nigger!" at whatever black students happen to pass. Whether this will ever occur is not the point. But there is hardly a black student who cannot visualize such a scene.

AN ISOLATING EXPERIENCE

As a matter of fact, college enrollments are more multiracial than at any time in the past. Overall, 86.2 percent of college-bound blacks go to integrated schools, where they make up 9.7 percent of the overall student body. (When those at predominantly black schools are added in, blacks account for 11.1 percent of all college enrollments.)

Until relatively recently, black undergraduates who chose white campuses knew they would find few classmates of their own race. Most spent a lonely four years, whether in the classroom or residence halls. Any misgivings they might have had about the curriculum were usually kept to themselves. Things are now very different, due to the increase in black undergraduates on integrated campuses. At many schools, there is now a large enough pool of black students to create their own organizations and social centers. At some colleges, black freshmen come early for their own orientation sessions. This more pronounced presence has had practical consequences, leading to calls for more black professors and programs that focus on their racial experience.

Black students are frequently berated for sticking closely together, especially at campus dining tables. Whites who talk this way seldom think about how they too have a circle of white companions. Indeed, they almost invariably sit at "white tables." But, it may be replied, there are many kinds of white people, and white students select their friends on the basis of shared temperaments or interests, not simply because they belong to one's own race. If white students cared to look, they would see that blacks do not simply sit down alongside any other blacks. They also have friendships based on outlooks and affinities. At the same time, they do have a shared experience of belonging to a black minority on a largely white campus. Compounding this sense of isolation is the fact that the communities surrounding most campuses tend to be virtually all white. Black students who seek to do a little shopping in Ithaca or Palo Alto find themselves objects of wary attention. As the figures on this page show, very few "integrated" colleges have black enrollments that are at or even near the 10 percent figure.

THE ATHLETES' QUANDARY

There is another route by which black students come to white campuses. Here the schools involved are less likely to be liberal arts colleges or Ivy League universities but, rather, institutions

BLACK STUDENT ENROLLMENT

Private Institutions		Public Institutions	
Amherst	7.8%	California	
Bates	2.2%	Berkeley	4.3%
Caltech	1.4%	UCLA	4.3%
Carleton	2.9%	Irvine	2.0%
Chicago	4.3%	Santa Barbara	2.6%
Dartmouth	5.5%	Indiana	3.9%
Duke	9.4%	Kansas	2.6%
Emory	9.1%	Michigan	7.8%
Harvard	7.1%	Naval Academy	6.0%
MIT	6.3%	New York City	
Notre Dame	3.3%	Brooklyn	28.7%
Oberlin	7.1%	Queens	10.4%
Reed	0.6%	Oregon	1.6%
Smith	5.1%	Wisconsin	2.0%
Stanford	7.3%	Wyoming	0.9%

intent on having winning athletic teams. These colleges, which make sports a moneymaking business, have been shameless in recruiting black players, many of whom have barely made it through high school.

In 2002, the National Collegiate Athletic Association released a study of the 115 schools in its Division IA, which have the biggest athletic budgets. Altogether, 51.4 percent of their football players were black, as were 61.9 percent of those on men's basketball teams. But few of these colleges seem committed to recruiting black students for academic programs. For example, black men accounted for proportionately six times as many athletes as nonvarsity men in the student body. At more isolated schools, like the University of Wyoming and Western New Mexico, black athletes may be virtually the only members of their race on the campus.

These athletes seldom excel at their studies. The NCAA report found that of black football players who entered as freshmen, 44 percent graduated, while 32 percent of those who transferred did. On their basketball teams, only 26 percent who came as freshmen earned degrees, as did 28 percent of the transfers. The report also cited twenty-five schools where not a single black man recruited for basketball made it to graduation. The list contains well-known institutions like the University of Minnesota, Florida State University, Georgia Tech, Louisiana State University, and the University of Nevada at Las Vegas. This failure to graduate is hardly surprising, since most tend to lack the level of preparation that ordinary college work requires. There are also the long hours of practice, trips to distant games, and the sheer exhaustion from an all-but-professional regimen. Nor are the demands only physical. Today's athletes are expected to memorize, analyze, and apply the voluminous playbooks compiled by their coaches, assignments that are easily as arduous as those in many college courses. The system uses student-athletes for as many seasons as possible, abetted by cynical interpretations of eligibility and academic standing.

With few exceptions, these semiprofessionals have never really been "students," nor do the colleges view them as such. They were not admitted on an academic basis, nor were they given financial support to encourage their studies. It has been contended that regardless of the reasons for their admission, once they have been officially enrolled, the institution has a duty to such students to foster their education. However, the magnitude of such an effort should not be understated; it would call for scholastic tutelage at least as demanding as the athletic coaching they currently receive. At this point only a few schools, like Georgetown and Notre Dame, take such commitments seriously.

Many coaches reply that these teenagers take up athletic offers of their own free will. They have few illusions about their options and believe this is the best chance they have to make something of themselves. They may have been raised in segregated surroundings, but they know enough about the real world to realize the odds they face, whether at home or on a campus. So there is probably not much point in telling them that they are unlikely to get a degree, let alone be chosen by a professional team. Hope springs eternal, and that as much as anything sustains this unsavory offshoot of higher education.

SEGREGATED VS. INTEGRATED

Altogether, 103 colleges and universities describe themselves as "historically black" institutions. Of these, eighty-eight are four-year schools, some of which offer graduate programs; two are independent medical schools; and one is a theological seminary. Forty-seven are under private control, and forty-one are affiliated with public systems. All but four are located in Southern or border states. (The exceptions are Ohio's Central State and Wilberforce, plus Pennsylvania's Lincoln and Cheyney.) All of them began as segregated schools, either by law or by choice. Their purpose was to offer higher education at a time when public and private colleges took hardly any black students or barred them altogether. That is their history. Of more than passing interest are the roles that they still serve, as well as arguments over whether states should be allowed to sponsor schools intended for members of only one race.

For *Blacks in College,* Jacqueline Fleming also interviewed students who had chosen to attend predominantly black colleges. Their responses were much more heartening. By and large, she found, "black students in black schools show more academic progress than their counterparts in white colleges." Not least, their rates of retention tended to be higher. Her report makes only modest intellectual claims for these institutions. At Morehouse in Atlanta, widely known as a selective black school, the SAT scores of its incoming freshmen averaged 1070, while the figure for Texas's Prairie View A & M University is 824. At none of the historically black schools do the average scores approach those at comparable white institutions.

But Fleming's study adds that the strength of black colleges rests on their "unique experience in providing higher education to students from inadequate secondary schools." In other words, they take their applicants as they find them and then help them move along from there. In an all-black setting, students have a more relaxed social life and a wider range of extracurricular activities. Fleming makes a strong case that black colleges "impart the orientation and skills that allow black students to function well in the larger society." Having achieved academic success, they graduate with fewer feelings of resentment or emotional strain. At the forty-seven predominantly black private colleges, attrition rates are lower than for black students at integrated schools. Moreover, studies of alumni suggest that black colleges do as well as racially mixed schools in preparing their students for graduate study and careers in a dominantly white society.

There should not be any objections to a private college calling itself a "historically black" school, just as Brigham Young University can refer to itself as a "historically Mormon" institution. If these schools are in any way segregated, they are so by choice and not by imposition. But what of the forty-one "historically black" campuses that remain parts of state systems? Their persistence would seem to betoken governmental sponsorship of racial segregation. It is true that in some cities, many public schools have all-black enrollments. But this is because they are located in neighborhoods where virtually all the children are black. However, this situation does not usually hold for state colleges, which draw their undergraduates from many parts of the state.

While predominantly black state colleges were originally set up in the years when segregation was required, they now continue with predominantly black enrollments on a voluntary basis. The table on the next page gives the racial breakdowns for eighteen public colleges in nine states. While all of these states have sizable black populations, their flagship campuses still have quite modest black enrollments. On the other hand, all have one or more campuses that are predominantly black, and these schools would seem to have loyal clienteles. Indeed, there is reason to believe that a fair number of the students at, say, Maryland's Morgan State would have been accepted at the College Park flagship campus had they chosen to apply.

Schools like Morgan State and Fort Valley State, in Georgia, have become embroiled in controversy over whether their high black enrollments make them "segregated" and hence in violation of the 1964 Civil Rights Act. True, they and others like them are not legally required to be blacks-only institutions, as they had been in the past. In varying proportions, some whites can and do attend.

SEGREGATED BY CHOICE

North Carolina's public system offers a good example of how self-segregation works. It is a state with a considerable black population; according to the 2000 Census, blacks made up 21.6 percent of the total. This is one reason it maintains five "historically black" colleges, plus eleven others that once barred blacks but are now deemed to be integrated. Altogether, black students represent 19.2 percent of the 160,982 students in this dual system.

As the table on the next page shows, none of the schools is solely of one race. Even at the historically black colleges, nonblack enrollments range from 11.8 percent at North Carolina Agricultural and Technical to 28.5 percent at Fayetteville. Black attendance at the once all-white schools goes from 2.9 percent at Appalachian to 19.2 percent at Pembroke.

All told, a clear majority 59.9 percent of the black students attending the state system chose its five historically black schools. And because so many black students avoid the eleven "integrated" branches, the black ratios at the latter are seen as embarrassingly low. After all, in a heavily black state like North Carolina, even a 10 percent black enrollment would fall below the goal of true integration, prompting the conclusion that public higher education in the state remains basically segregated. Indeed, it

BLACK STUDENT ENROLLMENT

Flagship Campuses		Predominant Black Campuses	
Alabama	14.5%	Alabama State	90.1%
Maryland	13.8%	Morgan State	94.1%
Mississippi	12.1%	Mississippi Valley	95.1%
North Carolina	11.2%	North Carolina A&T	88.2%
Tennessee	6.0%	Tennessee State	75.3%
Florida	6.0%	Florida A&M	91.6%
Georgia	5.9%	Fort Valley State	92.7%
Pennsylvania	3.9%	Cheyney	90.3%
Texas	3.4%	Prairie View	87.8%

could be argued that for all practical purposes there are two systems, one for each race.

For many people who believe in integration, separate racial systems signify more than segregation by choice. The largely black schools receive less funding, have fewer academic programs, and rank lower in prestige (although apart from the Chapel Hill campus, faculty salaries are now roughly comparable.) So it can be contended that the states are still sustaining an arrangement

NORTH CAROLINA'S PUBLIC UNIVERSITIES

Predominantly Black Campuses	Black Students
North Carolina A&T	88.2%
Central	81.8%
Winston-Salem	81.7%
Elizabeth City	75.4%
Fayetteville	71.5%

Predominantly White Campuses	Black Students
Pembroke	19.2%
Greensboro	18.7%
Charlotte	17.3%
East Carolina	13.6%
Chapel Hill	11.2%
North Carolina State	10.3%
School of the Arts	7.9%
West Carolina	5.4%
Wilmington	5.0%
Asheville	3.6%
Appalachian	2.9%

where the colleges for whites are superior to those attended largely by blacks. In Louisiana and Mississippi, court decisions have prompted moves to merge some black public colleges with nearby white institutions. As it happens, these proposals are being protested by many black students and faculty members. In the case of professors and administrators, careers are at stake. Most know they would not get equivalent positions if transferred to predominantly white schools. In the students' view, if these colleges are segregated, it is not because apartheid has been imposed from the outside. As has been noted, these undergraduates have opted for black colleges over integrated schools. Moreover, these and other historically black colleges do not aim to keep whites out. Legally, anyone is free to apply and attend, even if whites may sense that they are not particularly wanted. Still, at the predominantly black Alabama A&M, white students now account for 18.4 percent of the enrollment, while at Tennessee State University, white attendance reaches 24.7 percent.

If many black students choose predominantly black schools, it may be a very rational choice. As has been noted, some make this choice because they wish to avoid the racism and alienation they may encounter at largely white campuses. And given the level of high school preparation many black students have received, they will probably do better by enrolling, say, at a school like North Carolina Central than by applying to the flagship campus at Chapel Hill.

ASSUAGING WHITE CONSCIENCES

There are several analogies here. Some women argue that even today they cannot receive full intellectual encouragement at coeducational schools. The very presence of men, they say, inhibits women's participation in classroom discussions and extracurricular activities. Women's colleges that are under private control can still legally refuse to admit men even if the schools receive some public funding. The same freedom applies to private all-male schools. The law also allows colleges to affirm their religious affiliations or to let it be known that they stress Chicano culture or have "historically black" antecedents.

However, there is one American group that is not allowed to announce that a college it sponsors is intended mainly for its own members. Nor can it make such an announcement even if it adds that it is willing to admit persons who do not belong to its group. Nor may this group point to the institution's history as a way of describing its identity and orientation. All of which is a roundabout way of saying that not even private institutions can publicly call themselves "historically white," even if that happens to be an accurate description.

Are double standards being tolerated here? When blacks or women or Mormons say they prefer being educated among people of their own background, sex, or faith, they are generally seen as having that right. (So far, this position has been sustained only for private schools. Thus Texas Woman's University, a state institution that once admitted only one sex, must now accept applications from men.) But if a private college described itself as a place where white people would feel comfortable, it would face charges of using a discriminatory identification.

The differences have to do less with logical consistency than with the consequences of exclusion. When people who have dominant power set up organizations that keep others out, they do so to exclude those they have barred from sharing their advantages. That is why businesswomen wish to break down barriers that deny them admission to men's clubs. It is why, in earlier generations, Jews and blacks sought more equitable admissions to Ivy League colleges. No one will deny that persons with less power also on occasion wish to associate among themselves. That is a major reason black colleges persist. Even so, it cannot easily be shown that the existence of all-black colleges causes harm to whites in the way that whites-only policies have injured blacks.

That many blacks wish to attend "their own" colleges lifts a burden from many white consciences. Most white Americans feel uneasy in the presence of blacks, unsure of what to say, and uncertain about what overtures to make. So if blacks want to go off on their own, not many white persons will complain. One reason is that most whites would like black Americans to "be happy." So if blacks say they are happier among themselves, that would be a double benefit.

By and large, whites prefer not to inquire about what goes on in black colleges, so long as the students seem satisfied there. For this reason, racial self-segregation is supported by many whites. For one thing, it reduces pressure for affirmative action. The University of Texas's flagship campus at Austin can say that it has tried to attract more black applicants, but they seem to prefer Prairie View. For another, it means less attention need be given to improving conditions for blacks on white campuses, whether with remedial programs or simply by striving to create a more hospitable atmosphere. What is barely acknowledged is that it is the racial mood at so many white schools that prompts large numbers of black students to choose predominantly black schools.

CHAPTER TEN

WHAT'S BEST FOR BLACK CHILDREN?

IN 1954—almost five decades ago—the Supreme Court handed down its *Brown* v. *Board of Education* decision, telling states and localities they could no longer maintain school systems that separated pupils by race. The Court's reasoning, simply stated, was that the schools set aside for blacks would always be inferior. This did not result from their deficient facilities, although that was usually the case. Even if separate schools for blacks were well-financed showcases, that would not solve the problem. The crucial fact, as the Court saw it, was that segregation based on race sent the message to black children that whites did not want them in their schools. And that isolation, the justices concluded, "generates a feeling of inferiority as to their status in the community that may affect their hearts and minds in a way unlikely ever to be undone."

Brown was the most sweeping of a series of decisions affirming that if black Americans are to feel that the United States is truly their country, they cannot be excluded simply because of their color. Since that time, courts have ordered that everything legally possible must be done to ensure that white and black children will share the same schools and classrooms.

While state and local laws requiring segregation have been nullified, the goal of racial integration has not been achieved. According to research by Gary Orfield of Harvard University, in the eighteen states where 70.3 percent of the country's black children live, more than two-thirds of these youngsters still attend racially segregated schools. In part, the failure has stemmed from a lack of political leadership. But the crucial determinants have been the attitudes and actions of white parents, who have made it clear that they will accept integration only on the most minimal of terms. In consequence, the United States has few genuinely integrated schools.

Usually the reason is residential. There are few if any neighborhoods with populations that reflect the nation's ethnic makeup. Black households are not spread around the country evenly; indeed, such dispersion is less likely in their case than for any other group. To the extent that schools draw their students from local communities or officially defined districts, enrollments mirror racial demography. Many large cities and a growing number of suburbs no longer have enough white families to give their systems a white majority. Nor, in most cases, will parents or authorities send suburban children in to integrate city schools.

As the table on the next page shows, California is in second place on the most-segregated list, even though only 8.6 percent of its students are black. And almost three-quarters of Wisconsin's black youngsters are having a segregated education, despite the fact that they make up only 9.8 percent of the state's students.

Segregation statistics tell us about racial enrollments for individual schools but not about what happens within those buildings. For example, while black pupils represent 16 percent of all public school students, they make up almost 40 percent of those who are classed as mentally retarded, disabled, or otherwise deficient. As a result, many more black youngsters are consigned to "special education" classes, which all but guarantee that they will fall behind their grade levels. Even if their diagnoses are couched in clinical terms, too often the message is that their behavior fails to

PROPORTIONS OF BLACK STUDENTS IN MINORITY SCHOOLS★

New York	86.2%
California	84.7%
Michigan	82.3%
Illinois	81.3%
Mississippi	77.5%
Maryland	77.0%
Louisiana	75.8%
New Jersey	74.1%
Texas	73.4%
Wisconsin	73.0%
Georgia	71.3%
Connecticut	70.3%
Ohio	70.2%
Pennsylvania	69.8%
Tennessee	68.8%
Alabama	68.6%
Missouri	67.2%
Arkansas	67.1%

★ Schools where black or Hispanic students make up the majority of the enrollment.

mirror middle-class demeanor. Slower tracks also become repositories for pupils whose conduct teachers find bothersome or inappropriate.

If a community cannot have all-white schools—although many towns and suburbs clearly do—white parents and officials strive for segregation within the buildings. The most common method is "tracking," which is always defended on scholastic grounds, with race never mentioned. At the elementary level, schools that have two or more classes for each grade often assign children according to their presumed potential. In some cases, teachers' reports play a part in tracking decisions; but as often as not, the key factor will be how pupils have scored on standardized tests. High schools have even more elaborate divisions, ranging from courses at the college level to sections for students deemed to be barely literate. Once put in lower tracks, even pupils who show promise tend to stay there throughout their school careers. Not surprisingly, black students are more likely to end up on lower—and slower—academic tracks.

The arguments for academic tracks are familiar. How, it will be asked, can students prepare properly for Princeton if they must share lessons with classmates who hold them back? The idea of integrating students having varied levels of preparation ("mixed-ability grouping") no longer has an avid following. In reply, one could note that many Americans were once educated in small untracked schools and went on to impressive careers. Some educators contend that brighter students will do even better if they are asked to explain materials and methods to less sophisticated classmates. However, parents anxious about college are unlikely to volunteer their offspring for such assignments. So even in an arithmetically integrated school, whites prefer to minimize their children's contacts with black classmates. (In fairness, it should be added that many black middle-class parents feel much the same way, although they see the issue as one of class rather than race.) Perhaps the last word should go to an Alabama legislator. "Before the 1960s," he remarked, "we had separate and segregated schools. Then came tracking, so while black and white students now walk through the same school door, they get segregated once they are inside."

DOES INTEGRATION WORK?

In some communities, integration is possible because blacks form a small portion of the population, and their presence does not stir white anxieties. In other settings, however, integration can be achieved only if some children are sent to schools outside their neighborhoods. This was the aim of what came to be called "forced busing." By and large, it has operated in only one direction. That is, officials have been reluctant to transport white children to schools in black neighborhoods or to schools that have appreciable black enrollments. Indeed, even suggesting such assignments can spur a white exodus out of the school district.

In some cases, the use of buses has been effective. Sometimes, a few black pupils travel to schools in dominantly white districts. In Hartford, for example, some inner-city youngsters arise early for trips to the suburbs. Of course, there is an implicit selection process at work since these students are usually enrolled in the program by involved parents. In another use of busing, white parents will let their children travel some distance to attend "magnet schools," where programs and facilities promise high-quality education. At the same time, such special schools succeed only if parents are assured that they will limit their black enrollments. On the whole, these variants of voluntary busing have not done much to reduce the number of schools that are basically all black or all white.

One unresolved debate concerns the effect of integrated learning on black pupils who do enroll in predominantly white schools. What some psychologists call a "transmission-of-values" hypothesis underlay the original *Brown* decision. It was argued that if black students were placed in classrooms where they would be outnumbered by whites, they would absorb and emulate the values of academically inclined classmates. And since teachers would gear their lessons to the white majority, black pupils would be motivated to use their best abilities. Also, once released from segregated settings, black children would begin to view themselves in a more positive light, since they were now integrated into the "white" system. According to some scholars, this has in fact been the experience of black students. One study concluded:

*Children who have attended desegregated schools tend to have more friends who are of another race, to work in higher-status jobs, to attend and graduate from multiracial colleges and universities, and to live in integrated neighborhoods.

But other scholars, who also observed black children in integrated schools, found "no systematic evidence supporting the idea that the majority can change deep-seated values held by the minority." In fact, there is "little meaningful contact, let alone contact that would permit learning about each other as individuals." Even worse:

*Thrusting the black child into a predominantly white status-oriented classroom does nothing to enhance the black child's self-esteem. Instead, we find that self-esteem diminishes after desegregation.

There are real contradictions here. One problem is that the studies seldom tell us how the black students in question had come to attend white schools, if their parents had expressly asked for such transfers, or whether their families had moved to or near white neighborhoods to take advantage of schools there. What we do know is that proportions play a role. If the school is heavily white, then the few blacks may feel isolated. Only those willing to adapt to white expectations will succeed, and not all want to move in that direction. According to some research, optimal achievement can be expected when black pupils make up about 20 percent of the school's enrollment. That level provides a sufficient pool for friends and support groups, as well as whatever advantages accrue from attending a school with a racially balanced student body.

This is a good place to inquire how far feelings of alienation have a racial basis. A study of high school dropout rates in New York City, released in 1990, found that while 25 percent of black students were failing to graduate, this was also the case with 32 percent of Hispanic students and 21 percent of those having Italian-American backgrounds. The high attrition for Italian-Americans suggests that white students can also be turned off by the ambience and expectations of secondary education. Sitting for much of the day in classrooms is not something they particularly enjoy, or at least not as that regimen is imposed in New York City's schools. Since the proportion of black students who drop out exceeded the Italian-American figure by only four percentage points, it would appear that factors related to culture and class have at least as great an impact as those associated with race.

EXPANDING THE CURRICULUM

In recent years, the United States has become less white, less "European," and less bound by a single language. As the 2000 census has made clear, the country now has a greater variety of cultures than at any time in its history. This has resulted largely from the rise in immigration, mainly from Latin America and Asia, but also from Eastern Europe and the Middle East. In addition, some native-born Americans are saying they can no longer identify with prevailing cultural perspectives.

One reaction has been to call for official recognition of heritages beyond those of the Western world. Much of the controversy has centered on classrooms and campuses and, particularly, on the content of curricula and the makeup of college faculties. As in all such debates, advocates often claim they represent ignored and inarticulate constituencies.

Black Americans, in particular, have objected to what some call the "Eurocentric" orientation to life and knowledge that has been imposed on their children. In a report submitted to the commissioner of education in New York State, several black educators advanced the view that minority pupils have "been the victims of an intellectual and educational oppression," due to the "Euro-American monocultural perspective" that dominates most school curriculums. This insensitivity, they asserted, has had a "terribly damaging effect on the psyches of young people," whose "cultures are alienated and devalued."

Many white Americans have been put off by epithets like "monocultural" and "educational oppression." Some have replied that Europe itself is a varied continent, stretching from Inverness to Istanbul, and the "Euro-American" immigrants came from Spitsbergen and Salonika and many points in between. Even so, it can be replied that whether they are Christians or Jews or from Poland or Portugal, persons of European origin have shared a common culture and civilization. Moreover, this country's schools have always reflected the literary and scientific side of that tradition, which came with the first English settlers and has essentially endured.

Until now, that hegemony has been accepted or at least has not occasioned wide protests. In past generations, immigrants who arrived from the rural reaches of Ireland or Sicily found that the school systems felt no obligation to acknowledge their customs. Nor did educators devise special curricula when they set up separate schools for liberated slaves or Indians on reservations. Black youngsters in Alabama and Cherokee children learned essentially the same lessons as were taught in white schools. The schools were to stoke the proverbial melting pot, which meant accepting the society as it had been shaped by those who came before. Few thought to ask if this might have, as the New York educators now claim, a "terribly damaging effect on the psyches of young people," because their ancestral cultures were "distorted, marginalized, or omitted" in lessons and textbooks.

Ours is much more an age of psychology and social science, as well as expressly ethnic politics. We also have a growing industry of ethnic writers eager to tell of injuries they suffered from having to conform to the dominant culture. Along with loss of language and tradition have been strains between immigrant parents and assimilating children. There is a real issue here, and it should not be minimized. To some observers, the erosion of older values explains much of the aimlessness and self-indulgence so common in this country. We may now be paying a heavy price for marginalizing so many cultures.

At the same time, the promise of America has been the chance to make it on one's own, which often calls for loosening older ties. Moreover, the United States cannot be accused of false labeling, at least so far as voluntary immigrants have been concerned. All came here freely, aware of the pressures they would face. However, not everyone's ancestors came here by their own choice. Many were brought in chains, while others were overrun and conquered in the name of a "Euro-American" manifest destiny.

The New York report warrants mention because similar efforts have begun in many parts of the country, including calls for new courses to be required at the college level. As might be expected, they propose expanding the curriculum to give major attention to cultures outside the European sphere. In particular, pupils would learn much more about the customs and contributions of blacks and Hispanics, as well as Asians and Native Americans. Nor will short summaries suffice. Under the Asian umbrella are Chinese, Koreans, Filipinos, and at least half a dozen other nationalities that differ in significant ways. The same holds for the Hispanic grouping, within which Mexicans, Cubans, Puerto Ricans, and many others have distinctive histories and cultures. Nor can justice be done to Native Americans with some well-meant generalities. Rather, the New York report insists, "curricular materials must be developed so there is equity in the coverage of . . . Mohawks, Oneidas, Cayugas, Onondagas, Senecas, and Tuscaroras."

DIFFERING LEARNING STYLES

That black children have not been well served by the schools hardly needs recounting. In the view of growing numbers of black educators, the reasons are inherently racial. In all parts of the country, as they see it, school systems are organized and administered by white officials who have little understanding of the needs of black children. Even in schools that have black principals and are staffed largely by black teachers, statewide rules shape most of the curriculum, often limiting the choice of books and imposing uniform testing. To a casual visitor, such a school may seem "all black." Yet further observation reveals the influence of white power and authority. Saddest of all, abilities and aspirations of black children often remain unrecognized, if not discouraged or destroyed.

Some proposals are quite modest and should not give rise to debate. One group of black educators has pointed out that "it takes nothing away from Shakespeare or Emily Dickinson to include the dramas of August Wilson and the poetry of Langston Hughes as an integral part of the school curriculum." These educators also stress that many black children learn a distinctive language in their homes, one with rules and expressions of its own. White teachers, they point out, must come to realize that "black English possesses a grammar, a system of deep cultural meaning, and a linguistic integrity on a par with that of standard English." Among those supporting this position have been such well-known figures as Roger Wilkins, Eleanor Holmes Norton, and John Hope Franklin. While they do not urge classroom lessons in black English, they want teachers to be conversant in it and draw on its usages when necessary, as happens in bilingual programs for children new to this country. Still, black pupils must come to show proficiency in standard English. In later life, they can decide for themselves which speech they will use in varied circumstances and settings.

A related question concerns whether black and white children have different "learning styles." This, too, has become a sensitive subject, with education and ideology very much entwined. Many black educators have proposed that white teachers should be taught to recognize the strengths—and enthusiasms—black youngsters bring to school. In the early years, for example, black pupils should be given more opportunities for expressive talking, since black culture gives as much attention to the style as to the substance of speech. Here, too, it has been found that black youngsters apply themselves more readily to lessons involving actual people than to more abstract situations. Similarly, teachers should be tolerant of more casual approaches to syntax, time, and measurement. Professor Asa Hilliard of Georgia State University has found that white children tend to tell stories in a "linear" fashion, while black children are more apt to employ a "spiral" style. When given an assignment, they frequently "skip around to several apparently irrelevant topics before they come back to the theme, and then they begin to work on it."

Black children are also more attuned to their bodies and physical needs. So, some educators argue, they should be allowed more leeway for moving around the classroom. "Michael Jackson, Michael Jordan, Bill Cosby, and Eddie Murphy would be a kindergarten teacher's worst nightmare," one black professor noted. "She would wind up telling Michael Jackson to sit still, Michael Jordan to sit down, and Bill Cosby and Eddie Murphy to shut up." Similarly, it has been found that black pupils are more apt to work to full potential if their teachers identify with them in a caring and solicitous way. For this reason, they may perform best with teachers of their own race.

From nursery school through graduate school, most black students have most of their classes with white teachers. Due to seniority and union rules, even schools in all-black neighborhoods can still have a majority of white faculty members. Everyone agrees on the need for more black teachers, partly to serve as role models and also because they understand the needs of black pupils. In recent years, sad to say, their proportion in faculty positions has actually been declining. To make matters worse, black undergraduates currently account for only 7.1 percent of the college students who are majoring in education. In common with many of their white classmates, a lot are choosing better-paid fields or those with more prestige. Another reason has been that most states have introduced so-called "competency examinations" not only for beginning teachers but also to recertify those with classroom experience. The pass rates for black candidates have not been impressive, and an awareness of these results may have signaled at least some students to stay away from careers in education.

A CASE FOR A "BLACK" CURRICULUM

As was seen in the previous chapter, colleges that choose to call themselves "historically black" say they would be pleased to consider applicants of any race. At the same time, they let it be known that they don't really solicit such applications, since they wish to maintain their distinctive atmosphere. The same message could be sent by high schools having similar aims.*

Elsewhere in the country, new curricula have been developed for classes composed of black students. Here the emphasis is on African history and cultures, as well as the accomplishments of black Americans and peoples of African descent throughout the world. Here are some sample lessons:

- The fact that some Pre-Columbian sculptures have what could be seen as Negroid features strengthens the supposition that it was Africans who first sailed across the Atlantic to America.
- The draftsman Lewis Howard Latimer, who worked closely

*New York City has a Harvey Milk High School in Greenwich Village for homosexual teenagers. While in theory it is open to everyone, thus far no heterosexual youngsters have applied.

with Alexander Graham Bell, should be recognized as the coequal inventor of the telephone.

- In 1879, an African surgeon performed successful cesarean sections, a procedure European physicians had yet to perfect.
- Vaccination against smallpox was introduced to North America in 1721, by a slave who brought the method over from Africa.
- Carbon steel was manufactured in blast furnaces in Tanzania before the birth of Christ. Early Africans also built ships that could carry as much as eighty tons, one of which transported a cargo of elephants from Kenya to China in the thirteenth century.

Attention to the African heritage pervades all these lesson plans. Instead of having black children dress up as Pilgrims for Thanksgiving pageants, they would celebrate Kwanzaa, the simulation of an African harvest festival. Given the richness and variety of tribal customs, there should be no shortage of source materials, ranging from coming-of-age rituals and herbal healing to the role of Islam in modern Africa. In some schools, students might be invited to adopt African names, following the lead of Molefi Kete Asante of Temple University, a prominent curriculum consultant, who started life as Arthur L. Smith in Valdosta, Georgia.

There may be a conflict between the multicultural approach described earlier and the curricula proposed for racially separate schools. Some black educators see attention to other cultures as a tactic to deflect black students' attention from their unique heritage. Leonard Jeffries, a professor of black studies at New York's City College, has gone so far as to attack the whole multicultural idea as "mental genocide."

In 1954, the Supreme Court outlawed officially segregated schools on the ground that they generated in black students "a feeling of inferiority as to their status in the community." Now, more than a generation later, it is being argued that blacks who go to schools with predominantly white enrollments can end up with the same inferior feelings. There is no inconsistency here. Today, the people proposing separate schools want those who enroll to sign up voluntarily. And, at least as important, these schools should be under black control.

The question black Americans will deal with for themselves is how much attention they wish to give to African and African-American history and culture and how much to mastering the skills needed to succeed in a highly technical world. In theory, this need not be a difficult choice. In a history class, students can learn about how slaves resisted their masters and then, in the next period, work in a computer lab where they study mathematical models. This already happens in Orthodox Jewish yeshivas, some of which have sophisticated scientific programs; pupils study the Talmud in the morning and spend the afternoon mastering bio-chemistry.

Insofar as black Americans want their fair share of what a modern world has to offer, it will be for them to decide how far they can retain the fruits of their heritage and also prepare themselves for the tests the impending era will set. Some may, of course, conclude that they do not wish to adapt to a world dominated by technology, administration, and corporate priorities. (Many whites make similar decisions; but most of them still possess—and rely on—modern skills more than they may admit.) Still, the possibility of pursuing "black" careers will depend largely on the number of such positions that white society is willing to underwrite. While black men and women can and do succeed on their own, they also realize that white America largely decides how many black people will be promoted and rewarded. And here white motives run across a spectrum, ranging from a desire for entertainment to a wish to pay off moral debts or the hope of buying social peace.

IDENTITIES: AFRICAN AND EUROPEAN

The accent on African identities comes at a time that finds growing numbers of white Americans less engaged with their European origins. The causes are not difficult to discern. As the passage of years dims memories of forebears, so the increasing incidence of intermarriage has diluted single-country ancestries. More white Americans now live and work and play in ethnically heterogeneous settings, where Old World origins are seldom mentioned. Indeed, with each passing year, more and more white Americans are becoming "nonethnic" in character and culture. A recent study of Americans of Irish, Italian, and Polish origins found that insofar as they displayed an "ethnic" demeanor, this tended to take place "in private rather than public realms." Fewer than one in three had occasion to use "words or phrases from their ancestral language" or expressed an intention to "teach their children about their ethnic background." The most common "ethnic experience" was an affinity for "special foods or dishes," and this was volunteered by fewer than half of the respondents. Moreover, this affirmation came mainly from Italians, whose cuisine is well established in America. And even with cheap airfares and chartered tours, only one in ten had visited his or her ancestral region on a European trip.

Of course, the United States is becoming host to new clusters of immigrants, who bring their languages, customs, and cultures with them. Undoubtedly, many older adults in these groups will retain much of their personal past. But it should not be assumed that younger immigrants and their children intend to retain their parents' ways. Indeed, there is not much evidence that immigrant parents are entranced with proposals for "multicultural" lessons: most want their children to learn about their new homeland and the modern world it represents. Evidence of this emerges in the number who object to having their offspring assigned to separate "bilingual" classes. So the United States need not necessarily become more "multicultural." Rather, the process of assimilation adhered to by earlier arrivals is once again getting under way. Of course, the culture and society to which new arrivals adapt change with each era. But, as has been noted, the format remains essentially Anglo-European, even after generations of mutations and transfusions.

AN INVERTED GENDER GAP

A study by the American Council on Education has pronounced that "black men are disproportionately at risk in American society." All too many black men, it added, "begin life in circumstances that diminish their chances of educational attainment." By now the litany of causes is familiar, ranging from misplaced bravado to drugs and death at an early age. The report also points out that "educational institutions tend to have low expectations of black males," while "the dominance of elementary and secondary education by women diminishes the number of role models in the schools."

Among those who do complete high school, many enlist in the armed services instead of applying to college. In fact, this can be a very sensible choice, since in the military they can upgrade their educational and vocational skills, as well as get their lives together, and then decide whether to remain in uniform or pursue careers in the civilian sector. Rather less heartening is the fact that the country now has more of its black men locked in prisons and jails than are attending classes on college campuses.

In the early 1960s, black women began to outnumber black men at institutions of higher education. This trend has continued, with each autumn finding fewer black men continuing beyond high school. As it happens, however, it is not only black men who are dropping away. As the table on the next page shows, since 1976, white and Hispanic men have also lost their majority status among enrolled undergraduates and degree recipients, and Asians also now have a majority of women. So it would seem that young men generally are an endangered gender, since whatever forces are at work cut across racial and ethnic lines.

Studies by the National Center for Education Statistics have found that high school girls have better academic records than boys, even allowing for their slower starts in mathematics and science. Teachers at all levels report that many more girls now volunteer in class. At the same time, girls submit more readily to classroom discipline, where they take better notes and turn in assignments to their teachers' liking. They also put in more time doing homework at both the school and college levels. Unfortunately, fewer boys have a makeup suited for twelve or more years of sustained sitting. Perhaps that was always the case, but in the past more of them endured the regimen.

The general success of women in education helps to explain why more are moving into occupations once the preserves of men. The other side of the equation is that each year finds more young men—white as well as black—lacking the diplomas and degrees expected in a modern economy.

WOMEN'S SHARE OF BACHELOR'S DEGREES

	1976	2000
White	48.5%	56.7%
Black	57.1%	65.8%
Hispanic	45.0%	59.7%
Asian	44.6%	54.0%

CHAPTER ELEVEN

CRIME

THE ROLE RACE PLAYS

WHAT MANY AMERICANS regard as "black crime" has become a preoccupation of public and private life. Black men and the offenses they commit are viewed differently from other felons and felonies. Of course, this kind of characterization is not altogether unique. While no one speaks of "white crime," since it would have too broad a compass, the phrase "Italian crime" has meaning for most people, implying the involvement of "the Mafia." After all, men of Italian ancestry seem to figure disproportionately in certain illegal activities, especially those involving extortion. The same might be said of "Colombian crime," insofar as it centers on cocaine trafficking. Even so, the damage done by Colombian and Italian criminals causes less public concern than the prospect of being accosted by a young black man after nightfall. If movies have rendered murders by Italian mobsters as comedy, it is hard to imagine scenes of "black crime" evoking many chuckles.

Interestingly, we never hear allusions to "white crime" as if there were no offenses characteristic of the nation's major race. Of course, a great deal is said about "white-collar crime," but with the understanding that "white" refers to items of apparel rather than pigmentation. Yet the fact remains that "white-collar" law-breaking is usually perpetrated by white people, ranging from the middle class to the very rich. While most people agree that these can be serious felonies, reactions to them are more subdued. It is almost as if they are not regarded as "real" crimes, perhaps because committing them calls for brains rather than brawn.

We certainly know that virtually all the individuals who looted billions of dollars from companies like Enron, WorldCom, and Tyco were white. So are almost all the corporate executives who fix prices illegally or pad costs on government contracts. The same is true of financiers who lure citizens into bogus invest-ments. The Internal Revenue Service estimates that persons who conceal income and otherwise evade taxes cost the rest of us at least $150 billion each year, and it seems clear that most of those in a position to do so are white.

There is even a weekly newsletter, called the *Corporate Crime Reporter,* that keeps large companies and their counsel up-to-date in this area. Indeed, one expert it interviewed acknowledged that "white collar and corporate crime injures society far more than all street crimes combined." During 2002, here were some of the offenses the newsletter summarized for its readers' benefit:

- Beverly Enterprises, a nursing home chain, pleaded no contest to charges of "felony elder abuse," and paid $2 million in civil penalties, due to the deaths of patients from "infected bed-sores."
- The Lockheed Martin aircraft company paid $2,122,603 to set-tle a federal suit for "mischarging on Trident missile con-tracts."
- PricewaterhouseCoopers, a leading accounting firm, paid a $5 million fine for "violating auditor independence rules," due to "improper accounting" for Avon, the home-sales cos-metics company.
- Twenty-nine states filed suit against Bristol-Myers Squibb, for

having "monopolized the market. To maximize its profits" on TAXOL, a cancer-fighting drug.

- Carnival Cruise Lines pleaded guilty to six "felony counts for falsifying records of oil discharges at sea," and paid $18 million in fines.
- The DamlerChrysler Corporation pleaded guilty to pouring industrial wastes into the public sewers of Kokomo, Indiana, and its plant manager was sentenced to "six months of home detention."
- The Sony movie theater chain paid a $325,000 fine for having its own employees give "street interviews" praising the films it was showing.
- Citibank paid a $1.6 million fine for "unfair and deceptive practices," in which it charged customers "for products and services they did not knowingly agree to purchase."
- Eight McDonald's managers were arrested for "fraudulently manipulating promotional contests" and keeping $13 million in prizes for themselves.

It should not be necessary to say that the lawbreakers here were not impersonal institutions but, rather, real people, with names and faces, who planned and perpetrated these offenses. Moreover, most had impressive salaries, resided in exclusive suburbs, and undoubtedly took pride in their European antecedents.

But even when a swindler has made away with millions or if corporate felonies inflict tremendous costs on customers and taxpayers, seldom does one hear demands for twenty-year prison terms. Since it is usually their "first offense" and the crime was not "violent," a six- or seven-year sentence is usually thought to suffice for white-collar convictions. This is a far cry from the demand for "three strikes and you're out" (which really means you're in for life) involving crimes for which most of those to be locked away will be black.

It could be argued that violent crimes evoke a special dread, making them far worse than those involving fraud. So it is not without misgivings that the bulk of this chapter will be devoted to the kinds of physically threatening offenses that most Americans have in mind when they worry about "crime." In a book about race, at least equal attention should be given to the felonies more likely to be committed by the nation's most numerous race. Unfortunately, neither the government nor private bodies seem interested in collating such information. Even the FBI, which records every single arrest for gambling and prostitution, has no statistics on how many lawyers and accountants and executives are indicted and convicted each year on criminal charges.

Such information as we have about crime can be calculated in several ways. The starting point is that black Americans make up 13.1 percent of persons in the age groups most likely to be incarcerated. In virtually all spheres—offenders, victims, prisoners, and arrests by the police—the rates for blacks are greatly out of proportion to their share of the population. Thus black men and women account for 41.3 percent of the individuals awaiting trial in local jails or serving terms there. They also constitute 46.3 percent of the inmates in state and federal prisons and 42.7 percent of all persons under a sentence of death.

In 2000, according to a study by the Justice Policy Institute, there were 791,600 black men behind bars, exceeding the 603,000 who were studying on college campuses. Twenty years earlier, the figures were 143,000 black inmates and 463,700 pursuing degrees. Put another way, for every 100 students in 1980, there were only thirty-one prisoners. Now, for every 100 studying, there are 131 in cells. In some states, the proportions are much greater. For every 100 enrolled in college in Tennessee, 388 are locked up. In Indiana, the ratio is 100 students to 582 serving sentences. All told, relative to their shares of the potential college-age population, black inmates outnumber whites by a factor of nine to one.

Another set of figures enumerates annual arrests, which the Federal Bureau of Investigation collects from local law enforcement agencies. In 2000, nine million Americans were arrested, on charges ranging from embezzlement and counterfeiting to van-

BLACK PROPORTIONS
OF PERSONS ARRESTED

Gambling	64.4%
Robbery	53.9%
Murder and Manslaughter	48.8%
Motor Vehicle Theft	41.6%
Prostitution	39.5%
Receiving Stolen Property	39.1%
Weapons Possession	36.8%
Drug Violations	34.5%
Embezzlement	34.1%
Rape	34.1%
Assault	34.0%
Disorderly Conduct	32.6%
Fraud	31.5%
Forgery and Counterfeiting	30.0%
Domestic Violence	29.6%
Burglary	28.4%
All Arrests	27.9%
Curfew and Loitering	24.7%
Arson	21.7%
Vandalism	21.6%
Drunkenness	13.7%
Driving Under Influence	9.6%

Black men make up 13.1% of men in the age groups most likely to be arrested.

dalism and vagrancy. Within these and other categories, the suspects are identified by race. The table on the previous page shows what percentage of the persons arrested on various charges were black. (Unfortunately, the FBI does not classify suspects by their economic status or other ethnic origins. So we have no measures for, say, Jews and Italians or business executives and investment advisers.)

Quite clearly, the phrase "black crime" does not make people think of tax evasion or embezzling from brokerage firms. Rather, the offenses generally associated with blacks are those that carry the threat or actuality of bodily injury. In a word, crimes involving violence: most particularly, murder, robbery, and rape. As the table shows, while blacks comprise only 13.1 percent of the relevant population, they account for over half—53.9 percent—of all robbery arrests, and about a third of suspects detained in cases of rape. Overall, black arrest rates are disproportionate for every offense except drunken driving.

Still, figures based on arrests may have a built-in bias, since police may be more apt to stop and detain black suspects. This certainly seems the case with violations like gambling and prostitution, since blacks in those trades tend to do so in the open, where they can be more easily apprehended. Whites, on the other hand, apparently perpetrate more of their felonies in offices or behind other doors.

LIMITED OPTIONS

A good check on FBI reports is the annual "victimization" survey conducted by the Census Bureau. This study polls a cross section of the nation's households, asking if any of their members had been a victim of a crime during the preceding year. If they were, they are asked to indicate their own race and that of the criminal. One purpose of the survey is to measure the extent of crime, since all offenses are by no means reported to the police, and not all of those that are reported eventuate in arrests. As it happens, the figures for murder and manslaughter show a similarity between the two sets of records. In instances where the race of the assailants was known, blacks were responsible for 50.6 percent of all criminal deaths and accounted for 48.8 percent of the murder and manslaughter arrests.

Altogether, 61.7 percent of the people who reported that they had been robbed during the previous year also said that their assailants were black, which is close to the 64.4 percent of black robbery arrests. All these figures support the view that blacks are more likely than whites to commit these kinds of crimes. As will be noted in a moment, whites who engage in larcenies have less need to rely on armed encounters, since they tend to have safer and more lucrative options.

On the other hand, the census reports on rape victimization differ quite markedly from rape arrest records. In all, 19.9 percent of the women who said they had been raped identified their attackers as black. However, among the men arrested for that offense, 34.1 percent were black. This disparity suggests either that assaults by white rapists are less likely to be reported to the police or that if they are, they are less apt to lead to arrests.

The most obvious question is why blacks are responsible for so large a ratio of crimes entailing threats or acts of violence. One explanation is economic: those most drawn to violent crimes tend to be poorer members of society. That blacks account for a high proportion of the nation's poor needs no reiterating here. The contrast is vivid among men between the ages of twenty-five and forty-four, a group most likely to run afoul of the law. The 2000 Census reports that white men in this group have a median income of $37,120, whereas for black men the median is $26,608, or about 30 percent lower. In addition, 81.2 percent of white men of this age have full-time year-round jobs, compared with only 68.6 percent of black men. Nor do these numbers include people who have given up looking for work, or those who are in prison. Clearly, there is a considerable pool of black men who feel they have few opportunities in the legal economy. That could cause them to turn to crime.

Yet despite some initial plausibility, this explanation needs further scrutiny. For one thing, most poor people of all races labor honestly, even for a modest return. By the same token, persons who do choose to break the law come from every tier of the social structure. What can be said, then, is that class positions facilitate—or circumscribe—individuals' options. If poorer prostitutes walk the streets rather than meet customers by appointment, so poorer men who decide to steal find they must resort to open-air robberies. Thieves who work in offices have a wider and less easily detected choice of larcenies, ranging from rigging computers to fixing prices in private dining rooms. If more black felons end up in prison cells, not the least reason is that they lacked office-based opportunities.

RAPE: THE ULTIMATE ASSAULT

In the view of most people, rape is one of mankind's most brutal crimes. That it persists, even flourishes, in our time undercuts such claims as we have to being a civilized society. Men do not rape for sexual pleasure. Rather, rape is a malicious assault, intending physical and psychic harm. And it is clearly a violent crime. Rapists cannot carry out their acts unless they are prepared to beat their victims into submission or threaten them with injury or death. Even if victims submit, they may still be maimed or killed, since sexual conquest does not always satiate the rapist.

Not all men are potential rapists, if by that is meant that they are prepared to use the violence associated with the act. Even so, not all men can be sure just how they might behave in a situation that might awaken passions they never knew they had. On this entangled question, we have little objective information but no shortage of speculation. While most men may protest that they have never considered rape, some analysts will say that what happens in

THREE CRIMES

Murder	Perpetrators	Victims
White	49.4%	54.7%
Black	50.6%	45.3%
	100.0%	100.0%

Perpetrator and Victim Both White	46.5%
Perpetrator and Victim Both Black	42.4%
Black Perpetrator, White Victim	8.2%
White Perpetrator, Black Victim	2.9%
	100.0%

Rape	Perpetrators	Victims
White	80.1%	85.8%
Black	19.9%	14.2%
	100.0%	100.0%

Perpetrator and Victim Both White	79.0%
Perpetrator and Victim Both Black	13.1%
Black Perpetrator, White Victim	6.8%
White Perpetrator, Black Victim	1.1%
	100.0%

Robbery	Perpetrators	Victims
White	38.3%	70.6%
Black	61.7%	29.4%
	100.0%	100.0%

Perpetrator and Victim Both White	37.3%
Perpetrator and Victim Both Black	28.4%
Black Perpetrator, White Victim	33.3%
White Perpetrator, Black Victim	1.0%
	100.0%

Derived from reports where the perpetrators and victims were identified as black or white.

men's fantasies and dreams tells another story. Indeed, studies have found more than a few men admitting to rape fantasies, in which they take women against their will. Some feminist writers have argued that the men who actually commit rape are acting not only on their own, but also on behalf of other men who do not dare to take the step. Note how many men, on hearing reports of rape, wonder whether the victim did something to lure her assailant on.

Rapists hate—and fear—women. They often see them as haughty, castrating creatures who must be put in their place. Many pick their victims pretty much at random: so long as she is a woman, she represents her sex. Others may vent their anger on particular women whom they feel need an indelible punishment. In these cases, the victims are often persons they know: acquaintances or dates or even wives. The rapist's aim is to inflict a grievous wound, a humiliation that will haunt the victim forever.★ (This is why so many rapes involve sodomy.) So rape is also a political act. And beyond politics, it is war: a campaign whose purpose it is to pacify, indeed destroy, a historic enemy.

Several statistics stand out. One is that almost two-thirds of the black men who commit the crime of rape choose black women as their victims. A second is that regardless of the race of the victims, black men commit this crime at a rate five to six times greater than that for white men. These findings suggest that black rapists regard women of their own race as warranting intimidation and humiliation as much as white women. And given the segregated spheres in which the races move, black women are more readily available for black men seeking a victim.

Still, there remains the question of whether black men feel more hostility toward women than do white men. About the

---

★Men are also raped every day, usually within the walls of prisons. But this is not "homosexual" sex in a literal sense. Most of the assailants regard themselves as fully heterosexual, which is how they conducted themselves prior to going to prison and will act after they get out. Still, the aim of prison rape is much the same as when the victims are women. It is an overpowering act, designed to show new convicts who their masters will be.

most we can say is that some lower-class black men have been more candid on this score. Insofar as rap lyrics echo some ghetto attitudes, we hear women referred to as "bitches" and "whores" with a bitterness seldom heard in even cruder white circles. In reply, it can be argued that expletives do not constitute evidence. White manners may mask quite similar enmities. Yet, as was mentioned earlier, more black women are achieving higher status in education and occupations, which can create social divisions and stir tension between the sexes. Men have always sought to bring down women whose ambitions or achievements threaten male esteem.

Yet the fact remains that a high proportion of black rapists take the trouble—and the risk—of assaulting white women. And they do this with the realization that if they are caught, they will be more severely punished. Given the purposes of rape, choosing a white victim compounds defiance with the thrill of danger. Eldridge Cleaver once claimed that violating white women has political intentions as well. Each such act brings further demoralization of the dominant race, exposing its inability to protect its own women from the worst kind of depredation.

Certainly, the conditions black men face in the United States generate far more anger and rage than is ever experienced by white men. To be a man is made doubly difficult, since our age continues to associate "manliness" with worldly success. If black men vent their frustrations on women, it is partly because the women are more available as targets, compared with the real centers of power, which remain so intangible and remote.

VIOLENT CRIMES AND POLICE REACTIONS

Robbery is also a personal encounter, in which the assailant is usually armed and threatens to use deadly force. Unlike rape, the reasons people rob are relatively simple: to obtain money or articles of value. It is also the crime in which blacks are most heavily represented. They account for more than half of all reported robberies and subsequent arrests, which works out to a rate four times greater than that for whites.

Robbery is also the crime where blacks are most likely to pick whites as their victims. One reason, obviously, is that whites can be expected to carry more cash or items of worth. Each year, several hundred thousand white and black Americans find themselves accosted by black thieves. In fact, more blacks than whites are victimized by black robbers. Indeed, black crime rates would be dramatically lower if blacks did not prey so frequently on members of their own race.

For white victims caught in interracial robberies, the loss of cash or valuables is seldom their chief concern. Rather, the racial character of the encounter defines the experience. In the social scheme of things, the tables have been turned. At the moment, a black man has the upper hand. Hence the added dread that your assailant will not be satisfied simply with your money but may take another moment to inflict retribution for the injustices done to his race.

Some white Americans might agree that they owe blacks some form of repayment, although they would prefer not to bestow it in this way. Given the choice, white people would far rather be confronted by a thief of their own race. Indeed, they would be happy to lose considerably more money rather than face the prospect of racial revenge.

Reactions like these show that white Americans in fact acknowledge that the crimes blacks commit are in some part expressions of resistance. Given the disproportionate violations of the nation's laws by black Americans, it may to some degree be because they feel they never consented to the content of those statutes or the ways they are enforced. In the words of Bruce Wright, a black New York City judge, they are simply breaking "a social contract that was not of their making in the first place." Viewed this way, engaging in crime becomes a form of rebellion, not dissimilar to the banditry of earlier eras. Very many blacks who are young and poor feel they have never had a fair chance, nor do they see that prospect changing. In light of the insults and discrimination they have faced throughout their lives, it is not surprising that as many as do vent their resentment in violence. Through crime, blacks are paying whites back, in the most ominous way they can. That they harm themselves as much, if not more, compounds the tragedy.

The dread of black crime whites feel goes beyond actual risks or probabilities, and remains even when crime rates decline. Far more troubling is the realization that white citizens can be held in thrall by a race meant to be subservient. In the antebellum South, an abiding fear among slave owners was that their chattels might rise in revolt. Any night, they could enter the manor house and slay their masters and mistresses in their beds. Hence the recourse to whips and other tortures to break rebellious spirits and show the price of defiance. Historians differ on the frequency of slave uprisings or on how often they were contemplated. Still, it would take only a few sullen glances to stir fears in an owner that his turn could come next.

After the end of slavery, the nation found it expedient to maintain blacks as a subordinate caste. But given their admission to citizenship, new controls had to be devised to keep them in place. One was to give the police a long leash, devising ways to absolve them if they went too far with their powers. The 1991 videotaping of Los Angeles policemen mauling a young man named Rodney King made it clear that they felt such impunity. Even today, in most parts of the country, black men who stir suspicions cannot count on being accorded a presumption of innocence. Despite constitutional safeguards, police and prosecutors and judges still find it relatively easy to ensure that one out of every five black men will spend some part of his life behind bars.

Of course, it will be replied that all of these individuals were found to have broken the law. If they have, it is difficult to argue that they should have been acquitted because of their color. At this point, it may simply be noted that many black Americans, who are not paranoid by nature, often feel they see an extra zeal on the part of police and prosecutors. While the possibility of guilt always exists, might there be an urge to undercut the stature of black men? We certainly know that being prominent provides no protection. Indeed, the opposite may be the case. Witness the trials of Mike Tyson, O.J. Simpson, and Marion Barry, along with what sometimes seems just a few too many indictments of black legislators and judges, as well as the sons of black officials.

Much of what has been said about robbery and rape applies to murder as well. With most homicides, as with other assaults, the assailant and victim are of the same race. In the past, most such slayings involved relatives or acquaintances, which meant they were usually followed by arrests and convictions. Today, many more murders occur during robberies, which means more people are dying at the hands of strangers, so that fewer slayings are being solved. In racial terms, the most striking development has been the sharp rise in black youths killing one another, so that homicide has become this group's leading cause of death.

This self-inflicted genocide, reflecting both bravado and despair, causes a great deal of grief. There is hardly a black teenager who cannot cite a friend or schoolmate who died on a nearby street. Yet it often appears that black Americans express even more concern over cases where persons of their race have been killed by policemen, or a black youth has been slain by a white gang. One reason is a reluctance to talk about black-against-black crimes within white hearing. But another is that deaths at white hands bring home their race's minority status.

Given their proportion of the population, black Americans have a three times greater chance than whites of dying from a police officer's bullet. As it happens, a disproportionately high number of these killings of blacks are by black policemen, which suggests that departments tend to give black officers assignments where they encounter suspects of their own race. (This is especially the case with undercover drug work.) For many years, police forces hired few if any blacks; now there is a tendency to use blacks to control blacks.

Black Americans know as well as anyone that there are felons of their own race, not a few of whom are armed and prepared to use their weapons. Why, then, the readiness to defend even offenders who run afoul of the police rather than side with officers whose job it is to preserve safety and order?

The first answer is that by no means is every black person slain by the police a criminal. Most law enforcement officers are white, and many lack the intuition or experience to distinguish a law-abiding citizen from a dangerous offender. As a result, tragic "mistakes" are often made. Quite enough incidents have made the news to suggest that blacks are more likely than whites to be killed in error. Indeed, in many cases, no weapon was found on the suspect's body; or in some instances with youngsters, it was only a toy gun. Most blacks can recite a litany of names to be memorialized as victims of official white force. Here are just a few from the New York City area: Arthur Miller, Marian Johnson, Elizabeth Mangum, Peter Funches, Jay Parker, Michael Stewart, Eleanor Bumpurs, Nicholas Bartlett, Yvonne Smallwood, Stephen Kelly, Kevin Thorpe, Phillip Pannell, and Amadou Diallo. White citizens would be hard-pressed to cite even a single person of their race who was killed by the police.

And even if the police do not draw their guns, most black Americans can recall encounters where they were treated with discourtesy, hostility, or worse. At issue is a proclivity of police personnel to judge individuals first by their color. Perhaps day-to-day experience has jaundiced so many officers that they see even law-abiding blacks as belonging to the "other side." Compounding these stereotypes is the fact that the typical police officer is a high school graduate from a working-class background, who had never previously set foot in the areas he now patrols. (In many cities, officers commute from the suburbs.) And it would appear that at least a few police officers still move in circles where no censure attaches to using the word "nigger."

SELF-DESTRUCTIVE SPIRALS

As was remarked early in this chapter, all social and ethnic groups, including the very rich, include men and women who show a propensity for larceny. For reasons we only dimly understand, some individuals are more prone than others to steal money or articles of worth. Within the middle and upper classes, such thieves stand less danger of getting caught, since the kinds of crimes they commit may be difficult to detect. (In many cases, victims never realize they have been swindled.) Such crimes tend to be job related, since many white-collar jobs offer opportunities for embezzlement or fraud. There is also plenty of "blue-collar" crime, at factories and warehouses or on building sites, where it is not hard to make away with equipment or materials. Department stores suffer more from thefts by their employees than they do from shoplifters.

So there is no reason to presume that poor people have a greater proclivity for larceny compared with persons of other classes. However, as was also noted, their alternatives are much more limited. Among young black men who choose to steal, even breaking into private homes is less of an option. As earlier figures for arrests showed, black rates for burglary are half those for robbery. If nothing else, their visibility makes it harder for black criminals to move surreptitiously in better-off neighborhoods. This is why so many black people who do decide on crime end up stealing from people on the streets or robbing small shops.

As it happens, the thieves who prowl the streets do not enjoy what they do. Most would prefer safer and more rewarding kinds of theft. Even if only a small fraction of all robberies are solved, the eventual odds of a petty thief getting caught—and much crime committed by blacks is petty theft—are relatively high: after all, one in five black men ultimately spends time behind bars, almost seven times the rate for whites. (And the "white" rate is even lower if Hispanics aren't counted.)

If whites typically faced as many social and visual barriers as blacks, then the racial distribution for open-air crimes would be more proportionate to the population. This is not to say that all whites are law-abiding. In fact, across small-town America, there are white men who have been raised in an atmosphere of firearms and violence, and who are apt to use both. They are not the sort of people one would want to anger on a steamy Saturday night. The prisons of West Virginia, or Oregon and Idaho, have inmate populations that are overwhelmingly white, and most were convicted for crimes that in other states tend to be associated with blacks.

Moreover, while black inmates now outnumber whites in America's penal institutions, this was not always the case. Indeed, during the last half century, there has been a discernible shift in the racial composition of the prison population.

The figures on the next page tell several stories. For one thing, it is noteworthy that so few blacks were behind bars in 1930. This would suggest they were really very law abiding, since most blacks lived in the South, where they could have been imprisoned with relative ease. At the same time, the dramatic drop in the white proportion does not necessarily mean that white people have become more honest. A more accurate explanation is that over the last half century most white Americans have moved upward on the social scale, so that fewer of them remain among the class of people who tend to receive prison terms. In the United States and elsewhere, people who are poor and have sporadic employment end up filling most of the cells. Most of this group used to be white; now the largest number are black.

Given the crimes black Americans commit, the proceeds tend to be small. The typical armed robbery involves relieving someone of a wallet rather than commandeering an armored car. Most who are caught do not usually have enough cash to raise bail; so they languish in jail cells until their trial dates come due. Since the chances of eventual arrest are so high and the takings so low, those who live off crime are on the whole probably no better off than

RACIAL MAKEUP OF PRISON INMATES

	1930	1950	1970	2000
White	76.7%	69.1%	60.5%	36.1%
Black	22.4%	29.7%	35.8%	46.3%
Other*	0.9%	1.2%	3.7%	17.6%
	100.0%	100.0%	100.0%	100.0%

*Mainly Hispanic

their neighbors who take jobs washing dishes or sweeping floors. In fact, their prospects may be worse. Considering the employment market and the scarcity of housing, criminals released from prison stand less chance of remaking their lives than they formerly did. This is one reason black men are so numerous among the homeless. Many go directly from prison cells to the streets. For them, a criminal life is less a livelihood than part of a self-destructive spiral.

PUNISHING CRIMES

So long as we use imprisonment as a punishment, there will be debates over who deserves to be locked away. One reason we put men and women behind bars is to protect society: if not incarcerated, they might continue preying on the rest of us. Also, we may feel that their offenses were so serious that only some years in a cell will impress upon them the gravity of their acts. Nor are these the only reasons. We also imprison people as expressions of outrage and revenge. Or in hopes that correctional programs will prove rehabilitating. Along with the belief that knowing they can be sent to prison will scare most citizens into behaving lawfully.

There is also controversy over what constitutes a "serious" crime. One criterion, certainly, is economic: how much did the person steal? The sums can be quite high. Not so long ago, *Fortune* magazine devoted an article to "corporate crooks." It told of one manager who embezzled $1 million by passing fake invoices through his company's billing system. Another involved a banker who secretly withdrew $4 million from numerous accounts. The latter felon received a sentence of two years. The former's was somewhat sterner: two to six years, depending on his conduct and prospect for parole.

Both of these culprits were white men in white-collar occupations. If their sentences are any gauge, their million-dollar thefts were not deemed as serious as offenses described as "violent" crimes, for which prison terms can run to ten or more years, even though they involved considerably less money.

The justification generally given is that people who engage in robbery are in fact more dangerous than individuals who embezzle large sums. According to this reasoning, if we wish to maintain a civilized society, we should be able to expect a reasonable degree of safety. Violent crimes threaten our lives and health; those who commit them are predators. Moreover, robbery and rape involve more than weapons and actual or threatened force. They are acts of terror, intimidating not only the victims but everyone else who may become prey.

So long as blacks commit more than their share of violent crimes, they will account for more than their share of prison cells. Moreover, American society has shown itself increasingly impatient with alternatives like community service or release on one's own recognizance, not to mention furloughs. And here, too, race intrudes. The feeling persists that a black man who rapes or robs a white person has inflicted more harm than black or white criminals who prey on victims of their own race. It is as if an assault by a black is an act of desecration that threatens the entire white race.

CHAPTER TWELVE

THE POLITICS
OF RACE

THAT A BOOK about race concludes with a chapter on politics
should not cause surprise. Problems associated with race continue
to beset this nation, as they have since its earliest origins. Americans of all persuasions look to the political process, if not always for
solutions then for gradual progress and pragmatic remedies. In this
view, politics is seen as a means for achieving compromise and
coping with social change. So conceived, the process can work to
redistribute resources, redress injustices, and improve the atmosphere in which people live and work. This, at least, has been the
hope.

To the minds of many people, the civil rights movement of the
1960s provided a memorable model. By combining protest and
pressure, plus appeals to majority opinion, many discriminatory
practices were officially ended. Further moves toward racial
equity helped to enlarge the black middle class. Since much
remains to be done in the realm of race, it should be asked what
can still be expected from the political process.

Of course, politics is a mélange of activities occurring in the
streets as well as within conference rooms. It ranges from judicial
decisions and administrative rulings to legislative trade-offs and

moral leadership. And where race is concerned, the process can lead to a confrontation between minority and majority.

Of course, well-organized minorities can make their weight felt. Gun owners have proved that, as have opponents of abortion. Pursuing this theory, it could be argued that since black Americans have an intense interest in racial redress, they should be able to mobilize their numbers with similar effectiveness. On occasion that appeared to happen, especially during the 1960s and 1970s, when the Congress passed some serious civil rights laws. Recourse to the courts also succeeded, not least because judges saw individual plaintiffs as having broad backing in the black community.

Yet the political power of black Americans faces limitations. For one thing, many black Americans are preoccupied with personal matters and are not easily organized. Money plays a vital role in politics, if only to make one's case heard, and blacks have less available cash than many other groups. Moreover, black voters tend to be concentrated in segregated areas, which means they have little sway over politicians in other districts. Indeed, the majority of lawmakers in the United States have few if any black residents in their constituencies. While governors and senators have more varied electorates, in twenty-one of the fifty states, blacks comprise less than 5 percent of the population.

WHO GETS ELECTED?

As hardly needs saying, no person of African ancestry has been elected president, or nominated by either of the parties for that office or the vice presidency. In 1993, soon after Bill Clinton entered the White House, pundits began talking about his possible successor. The most mentioned name at that time was Colin Powell, who had recently retired from the military. In polls, many white voters indicated they would support his candidacy, saying they were impressed by his record of public service, along with his stature and demeanor. However, Powell soon asked that these discussions end, saying he had no taste for electoral politics. So whether all those whites would actually have voted for him was never put to the test.

Since 1966, three black candidates have been elected to prominent statewide office, in all cases defeating white opponents. In 1966, Edward Brooke was elected senator from Massachusetts, a post he held for twelve years. And in 1992, Carol Moseley-Braun became an Illinois senator, but was defeated when she sought reelection. In 1990, Douglas Wilder won the governorship of Virginia, but was unable to run again since the state has a one-term limit.

To place these elections in perspective, we should look at who have been our senators and governors. Between 1966 and 2002, a total of 230 persons served as United States senators. Of these, as has been noted, two were black. Apart from five Asians and one Hispanic, all of the remaining 222 were white. During the same period, 316 men and women have been state governors. Among them have been four Asians, four Hispanics, and 307 whites, while only one was black. All told, Wilder, Brooke, and Moseley-Braun added up to less than one percent of the 546 individuals statewide electorates chose as governor or senator. Put another way, during these thirty-six years, whites have held 96.9 percent of the two offices.

Below the two top spots, in 2001, only eight of the fifty states could point to major posts held by black officials. They ranged from Colorado's lieutenant governor to Georgia's attorney general, plus New York's comptroller and Connecticut's treasurer. In Illinois and Ohio, the position was the essentially powerless secretary of state, while Texas's only black had been elected to the railroad commission. All of the states, including those in the Deep South, still have white electoral majorities. So it is basically their choice whether they wish to be represented by someone of another race. And in 2001, in forty-two states, neither the parties nor white voters showed much interest in elevating black candidates to prominent positions.

Where there is a greater black presence, at least numerically, is in state legislatures. In Alabama, for example, blacks make up 24 percent of the voters, and hold 25 percent of its legislative seats. In Illinois, they equal 14 percent of the voters, and fill 13 percent of the places. And in California, where blacks form about six percent of the electorate, they fill five percent of the legislature. However, it was not simple justice that led to figures like these. Political maps were purposely drawn to pack black voters in what were de facto segregated districts. But an even more important aim was to design another, much larger, set of segregated seats: ones with sufficient white majorities to ensure the election of white candidates. The legal implications of this strategy will be discussed later in this chapter.

PLAYING ON WHITE FEARS

Sometime during the mid-1970s, changes began to be observed in the attitudes of white citizens who had earlier been willing to support measures intended to bring black Americans to parity. Those changes persist today.

At the most visible level, growing numbers of white people had been expressing misgivings about how a lot of black people were conducting themselves. Along with censuring welfare dependency and violent crime, more and more whites have come out against preferential programs and have criticized blacks for acting as if they were victims who are not wholly responsible for their behavior or condition. In the same vein, white Americans are more open about opposing measures for racial redress, largely by denying that they have gained any advantages because they are white. In their view, the behavior of some black citizens is a major explanation for what ails America.

A good way to explore the politics of race is to examine what the two principal parties have made of this major division. The Republican position is more straightforward. The party whose most illustrious leader was Abraham Lincoln has all but explicitly stated that it is willing to have itself regarded as a white party, ready to enlist Americans of that race and defend their interests. Of course, Republican administrations have made sure to appoint a few black officials, either vocal conservatives or taciturn moderates willing to remain in the background. An unwritten plank in the party's platform is that it can win the offices it needs without black votes. And by sending a message that it neither wants nor needs ballots cast by blacks, it feels it can attract even more votes from a much larger pool of white Americans.

The suggestion that the Republicans are essentially a "white" party should not be taken to extremes. Still, most white voters in most elections back the Republican slate. Even when Democrats like Jimmy Carter and Bill Clinton were winning the White House, the majority of whites sided with their Republican opponents. Put another way, if the electorate were entirely white, the GOP would always win the presidency. Of course, the party does not close its doors to black voters. At its 2000 convention, blacks made up 4.1 percent of the delegates; and in that year's election, about eight percent of black voters supported George W. Bush. (At that year's Democratic convention, black delegates made up 20.1 percent of the total; and some 90 percent of black voters backed Albert Gore.)

In its legislative proposals and administrative policies, the view of the Bush administration has been basically that the country has no racial problems that need to be addressed. True, the president is periodically photographed at predominantly black churches and classrooms. But these visits do not bring pledges to do something concrete about segregation and discrimination. Like most Republicans, the president feels that being too specific might unsettle the whites who are his core constituency.

Where the Bush administration has been truly sophisticated is in its executive appointments. If only 830,000 or so black voters supported him, they constitute a pool from whom cabinet-level jobs can be filled. Most visible, of course, have been Colin Powell as secretary of state, and Condoleezza Rice as national security adviser. In the Justice Department, the second-in-command is Larry Thompson, who serves as deputy attorney general. Charles James is in charge of the antitrust division, while Ralph Boyd heads the civil rights division. Rod Paige is often given center stage as secretary of education, and Michael Powell is frequently headlined as head of the Federal Communications Commission. All are loyal Republicans, which they in no way find discordant with having African ancestries.

In the past, Republican presidents were less likely to give blacks important powers. In the twelve years from 1980 to 1992, for example, Ronald Reagan and George Bush named 558 judges to federal courts, and only seventeen—or 3 percent—were black. By way of contrast, during Bill Clinton's eight years as a Democratic president, 378 judges were appointed, and 62 of them—a substantial 16.4 percent—were black. As of October of 2002, seventy-six of George W. Bush's court nominations had been confirmed, and eight—or 10.5 percent—were jurists of African ancestry. Interestingly, when the younger Bush was campaigning, he said that the model for his judicial appointments would be Clarence Thomas, whose conservative ideology places him on the far right of the court. Yet the first eight black judges he named had moderate positions, or kept their convictions to themselves.

A politics permeated by race plays on anxieties of white Americans, intensifying their fears that their identity and interests are under serious attack. This is not to say that most of these people are bigots or reactionaries. It is that they feel their status is in jeopardy, and not always in ways they understand. But what, precisely, is the threat? After all, the United States is not South Africa, where whites are heavily outnumbered and the racial balance of power is undergoing basic change.

VOTING: PARTY AND COLOR LINES

The way people cast their ballots often provides insights into how they think and feel about race. These sentiments surface most graphically in contests in which a black and a white candidate oppose each other. As it happens, in most such contests—but not all—most black voters support the black contender, and most whites rally behind the white. Of course, the colors of the candidates are not the only variables at work. Ideology may play a role, as can party labels and impressions of personality and character. So if a white voter does not cast his or her ballot for a black candidate, it should not be automatically assumed that race was the reason.

At the same time, we know that many citizens feel comfortable when they see persons of their own origin holding public office. This has long been the role of "ethnic politics." Thus white citizens who are recent immigrants feel they are coming closer to acceptance when members of their group obtain honors and recognition. No one was surprised when a lot of Greek-Americans lined up behind Michael Dukakis's 1988 bid for the presidency. So it is hardly unusual that black Americans want to see people of their race in official positions. (Whether the same reasoning can be applied to whites as a generic group will be examined shortly.)

In politics as in other arenas, black behavior has been subjected to extra scrutiny. All eyes focus on blacks who are elected to office, if only to see how they will conduct themselves once power is in their hands. Hence the murmurings among whites that black voters sometimes seem to settle for representatives who have less-than-gleaming credentials. Whites have also been heard to complain that blacks appear unwilling to condemn dubious behavior on the part of "their" politicians. These and similar remarks suggest that blacks need white counseling, as if they were somehow unaware of their own interests. In fact, it makes sense for members of a racial minority to pull together. Blacks have had a long history of being divided and conquered, especially in the white media, and this practice persists. In the view of many black Americans, whites take a special delight in searching for and exploiting differences among blacks.

If black citizens have a chance to vote for someone of their own race, they tend to turn out in larger-than-usual numbers. When David Dinkins first ran for mayor of New York City, 91 percent of the black voters gave him their support. When he sought a second term, he received 95 percent of the ballots cast by blacks. In Douglas Wilder's bid for the governorship of Virginia, 95 percent of black voters rallied behind him. And in 1988, in the thirty states where Jesse Jackson competed for the Democratic presidential nomination, he was the choice of 92 percent of the blacks who voted. Figures like these make it clear that even if some black voters had mixed feelings about some of these candidates, most of them definitely wanted these men to win.

But race was not the only factor. Dinkins and Wilder were both Democrats running against Republicans. For well over half a century, the overwhelming majority of black voters have been loyal Democrats. So loyal, in fact, that they have generally turned out to support white Democrats at much the same rate as they do for candidates of their own race.

A similar willingness to back their party's standard-bearers is less in evidence among white Democrats. New York City has always been a Democratic stronghold. When David Dinkins ran for mayor, however, 71 percent of the white voters—most of them regular Democrats—gave their votes to his Republican opponent. Perhaps it was to be expected that many voters of Italian origin chose to back a candidate named Rudolph Giuliani. But so did 63 percent of Jewish New Yorkers. Indeed, no segment of the white electorate gave more than 36 percent of its votes to Dinkins. And when he ran for reelection, his share of the white vote declined to 23 percent. (This was at least an improvement over Chicago's 1983 balloting, when only 12 percent of the white voters supported Harold Washington.)

CROSSOVER POLITICIANS

As was noted earlier, no one regards it as strange if blacks—or Jews or Mormons or Greek-Americans—want to see people of their origin in prominent positions. However, it is not as easy to claim that white Americans added together—after all, there are almost two hundred million of them—constitute an "ethnic group," whose members share common interests and attributes. So when whites vote for fellow whites, as they generally do, their reasons are not strictly analogous to those that impel blacks to vote for blacks.

Of course, white voters who support the white candidate in an interracial contest will argue that they have done so for other than racial reasons.

Yet for many whites, the prospect of a "black administration" can generate alarm. These fears rise to the surface when, in the course of a campaign, they hear—or think they hear—blacks claiming, "It's our turn." These words are interpreted to mean that since whites have hitherto run things, blacks now want that power. Behind these imaginings is the dread that blacks will treat whites as whites have treated blacks. Louis Farrakhan once put it just that way: "You fear we'll do to you what you did to us." Thus white homeowners might worry about who would be behind the desk when they went to a city office to object to a tax assessment. Here the apprehensions of white Americans and South Africans share some common ground.

Is this saying that even middle-aged gentlemen like Douglas Wilder and David Dinkins rouse such anxieties? The answer is they can. This is what happens when voters choose to look not at black candidates as individuals but, rather, to focus on a bid for racial power that the candidates are seen to represent.

But this is not always the case. In several cities and—thus far—one state with predominantly white populations, black candidates have defeated white opponents. Indeed, in some of these instances, a majority of the white voters actually supported the black candidate over his white rival. The first such election took place in Los Angeles in 1973, when Tom Bradley was elected to his first term as mayor mainly with white votes. More recently, New Haven and Seattle, as well as Minneapolis and Kansas City, have seen black mayoral candidates defeat white opponents by gaining the support of a majority of whites. And in the 1990s, virtually all-white districts in Connecticut and Oklahoma elected black candidates to Congress. The table on the next page shows that Southern and Northern cities, ranging from Charlotte, North Carolina, to Rockford, Illinois, have chosen black mayors even though their populations are preponderantly white.

Perhaps white voters in these areas do not share the fears of whites elsewhere. In fact, the overriding factor is how the image of a black person in public life is filtered through white opinion. This perception depends partly on the candidate's actual attributes and views. The more crucial characteristics, however, are those that whites decide to impute to blacks who are running for office. In Minneapolis and Seattle, cities with comparatively few black residents, the black candidates were more apt to be seen as persons in their own right, rather than as representing a racial claim to power. This was also clearly the case with Edward Brooke, where blacks numbered less than five percent of that state's population.

Thus far, black candidates who gain white support have come from middle-class backgrounds and display a middle-class demeanor. While these candidates are undeniably black, to many whites they seem less "racial" or less threatening. Even if they allude to injustices their people have suffered, they do so without the bitterness and rancor that tends to unsettle whites. In some cases, they make a point of dissociating themselves from figures who speak with a sharper voice. Thus David Dinkins explicitly repudiated Louis Farrakhan, while Douglas Wilder let Jesse Jackson know that he did not want him sojourning in Virginia during his gubernatorial campaign.

These individuals have been called "crossover" politicians,

BLACK POPULATIONS OF CITIES
THAT HAVE ELECTED BLACK MAYORS

Detroit	81.6%
Birmingham, Alabama	73.5%
New Orleans	67.3%
Baltimore	64.3%
Atlanta	61.4%
Memphis	61.4%
Washington, D.C.	60.0%
Newark	53.5%
St. Louis	51.2%
Cleveland	51.0%
Beaumont, Texas	45.8%
Philadelphia	43.2%
Cincinnati	42.9%
Rochester, New York	38.5%
Chicago	36.8%
Tallahassee	34.2%
Charlotte, North Carolina	32.7%
Kansas City, Missouri	31.2%
New York City	26.6%
Dallas	25.9%
Houston	25.3%
Columbus, Ohio	24.5%
Minneapolis	18.0%
Rockford, Illinois	17.4%
Cambridge, Massachusetts	11.9%
Los Angeles	11.2%
Denver	11.1%
Seattle	8.4%
San Francisco	7.8%

since they make a frank appeal for white votes. Quite obviously, they tread a fine line. While they cannot ignore their home base, they have to hope it will remain loyal since they must spend the bulk of their time courting white support. Indeed, as has been seen, the thrust of their campaigns must be to allay white anxieties. Thus they portray themselves as if they had no racial connections and certainly did not aspire to represent "black power." They even evaluate the risks in taking time off to talk at an all-black meeting. With television cameras turning up everywhere, cheering crowds of black supporters might induce tremors in white viewers.

RACIAL GERRYMANDERING

For at least a generation, the principal branches of government have sought to increase the number of black Americans elected to public offices. If Republicans have joined with Democrats in this effort, different motives impel the two parties. The federal Voting Rights Act, enacted in 1965, was intended to oversee the electoral process in Southern states and localities, due to that region's history of preventing black citizens from voting. Under one provision, the Civil Rights Division of the Justice Department was mandated to intervene if the number of people voting became suspiciously low. While physical threats and biased tests are no longer usual, a new set of concerns about voting rights has arisen. Now the issue is not whether black people can register and vote, but what results they achieve when they do cast their ballots.

A 1982 amendment to the Voting Rights Act provides that the Justice Department may take action if it suspects that members of any racial group

> have less opportunity than other members of the electorate to participate in the political process and to elect representatives of their choice.

This proviso, like any other legal wording, deserves a close reading. If black citizens no longer face barriers when they seek to vote, then how might they still have "less opportunity" than whites when it comes to their ability "to participate in the political process"? And what obstacles might prevent them from being able to "to elect representatives of their choice"?

So long as all electoral districts have populations of approximately equal size, all voters and their votes would seem to have the same weight and worth. Of course, district lines can be drawn so that the ballots cast by one party's supporters will end up electing more of its candidates to office. Here we have the venerable art of gerrymandering, which has been given new life as computers fine-tune constituency lines. Those doing the designing can also ensure that a large number of the other party's ballots will be "wasted." This can be effected by concentrating its voters within certain districts, so as to give the people who win there needlessly large majorities. If gerrymandering has traditionally been aimed at giving one or another party an electoral edge, the reference in the Voting Rights Act to "representatives of their choice" has an additional meaning where race is involved.

Many black Americans still complain that almost all of the people governing them are white. Not only has every president of the United States been white, but at this writing so is every governor and senator. Moreover, most black citizens live in districts with white majorities, almost all of which send white representatives to Congress.

It is the view of at least some black citizens that they lack "representatives of their choice," because in all too many cases they find themselves being governed by white officials. Indeed, there are still many black Americans who have yet to be represented by a person of their race at any governmental level. Of course, there is the reply that white officeholders can be attentive to the needs of their black constituents. Even so, an increasing number of black voters feel that their interests really need the empathy that comes from having lived a black life. As it happens, most whites also prefer being represented by someone of their own race. Indeed, as has been seen, they often make these feelings clear by turning against black candidates nominated by the party they ordinarily support.

Due to the way districts have usually been designed, it can be argued that black voters have fewer opportunities than whites to cast ballots that will give them "representatives of their choice." Until recently, those who enjoyed this option have tended to live in large inner-city areas, where they have been clustered in one or more "black districts." White politicians have been happy to oblige on this score, not least because those seats serve to devalue black votes by giving black winners wastefully large majorities.

So the right to cast a vote is not enough. The ballot cast should also be one that has a fair chance of achieving a result desired by the person who cast it. Responding to this sentiment, several states have created additional districts with black majorities. Most of these, however, are not situated within large cities but, rather, extend across much of the state. A typical House of Representatives constituency has to hold almost six hundred thousand people. While several black-majority seats can be carved out within New York or Chicago, this is less easily achieved in states like North Carolina and Alabama, whose black populations are more widely dispersed.

So in Louisiana, for example, a congressional district was drawn that stretched for 300 miles along the northern and western edges of the state, collecting a majority of black voters from Shreveport to Baton Rouge. The same aim was attained for a North Carolina seat, which ran for 160 miles along a highway from Durham to Charlotte, with side roads included to take in black neighborhoods in Winston-Salem and Gastonia. Another less-remarked-upon consequence of the rearrangement is that the other 397 districts represented in the House contain fewer black voters, which means that those districts' representatives feel less obliged to pay attention to black interests.

Not all whites were happy with these exercises in mapmaking. A group in North Carolina sued to invalidate the "highway" district, claiming that it violated their constitutional right to participate in a "color-blind" electoral process. In June of 1993, by a narrow five-to-four vote, the Supreme Court declared that what it called "racial gerrymandering" could not be permitted. Writing for the majority in *Shaw* v. *Reno,* Justice Sandra Day O'Connor allowed that while districts might be devised for one party's political advantage, to base them on race would be unconstitutional:

> Racial classifications of any sort pose the risk of lasting harm to our society. They reinforce the belief, held by too many for too much of our history, that individuals should be judged by the color of their skin. . . . Racial gerrymandering, even for remedial purposes, may balkanize us into competing racial factions.

The North Carolina seat and any others having a racial purpose, she and four of her colleagues concluded, show "an uncomfortable resemblance to political apartheid."

What the Supreme Court seemed to be saying was that districts designed to have black majorities are "racial" and thus damage our society. However, constituencies with white majorities were somehow seen as nonracial, or neutral, and therefore do not inflict any harm. It was also implied that black citizens can be just as well represented by whites, although nothing was said about the long record of whites' unwillingness to be spoken for by black officeholders. Indeed, the demand for specifically black seats arose because in most white districts—which is what they should be called—white voters have been disinclined to support black candidates. Had more whites shown such a willingness, "highway" districts would never have been found necessary.

If the decision in *Shaw* v. *Reno* prevails, then as many as a dozen seats held by black representatives may have to be dismantled, with their voters sent back to districts in which they will again be in the minority.

In 2001, the Supreme Court returned to North Carolina, where it was again asked to rule on an elongated district in a case called *Hunt* v. *Cromartie.* Here, too, one side argued that the seat was intentionally designed to have a large black population so as to elect a black candidate. Were that so, it would have been created for a strictly racial purpose, which was declared invalid in *Shaw* v. *Reno.* However, this time a five-member majority decided that the district was permissible. In their view, race was not the primary consideration. Rather, they argued, "politics drove the legislature's districting decision." The aim was partisan: a Democratic state legislature sought to add another Democrat to the congressional delegation. So they fashioned "a district containing more heavily African-American precincts for political, not racial reasons." This time, Sandra Day O'Connor was among the five who approved this seat, despite her worries about "apartheid" in the *Shaw* case eight years earlier.

An important question arises: why all this concern, both in drawing legislative districts and creating affirmative action programs, to say that note cannot be taken of people's races? The reasoning rests in a new interpretation of what is generally called the "equal protection clause" of the Fourteenth Amendment. This phrase, ratified in 1868, was intended to protect black Americans who had recently been freed from slavery. They were now to be full citizens, and the clause banned any discrimination that might be imposed upon them because of their race. In this sense, all laws were to be "color-blind." Whether a person was white or black or brown or yellow was not to figure in how he or she was treated under legal authority. This was the original, and quite benign, purpose of the Fourteenth Amendment: to erase the vestiges of slavery that might keep black Americans in a subordinate status. So "color-blind" meant that race was not to be mentioned or used in making decisions.

Now, as has been seen, some people want to use the Fourteenth Amendment to protect certain white Americans, who claim that they are suffering from discrimination because of their race. In a way, this is a curious twist. The white persons who say they are being harmed are not poor, nor are they shut out by society. On the contrary, they belong to the race that still makes up the majority and continues to be dominant in power and positions. These same people object if their whiteness is a liability when they apply to college, or when legislative districts are formed. Of course, the reason they complain is that they may lose some of their dominance if other races are given extra help. In reply, it has been argued that black Americans still start further behind, and therefore need such assistance. But people who are ahead are disinclined to give up their advantages. That attitude essentially explains why so many white people are taking their cases to the courts.

"CAN'T WE JUST GET ALONG?"

Some months after the initial publication of this book, the city of Los Angeles was hit by a wave of violence unlike any the United States had seen for a quarter of a century. Some sixty persons lost their lives, hundreds of businesses were looted and burned, and a belated police intervention resulted in thousands of arrests. While no one forecast that such an outbreak would occur, when it actually happened, few people were surprised. Even those who wanted to believe that race relations had been improving—after all, Los Angeles had long had a black mayor—realized that resentments were not far from the surface. More than that, the rioting made vivid many of the causes and conditions that sustain racial tensions in our time. It was also a political event. Not in the sense of parties and elections, but as a graphic display of power, uncovering tensions and feelings that could not be vented through customary channels.

As no one needs reminding, the upheaval came after a suburban jury acquitted four police officers who had been charged with using unjustified force when arresting Rodney King. The blatant beating of King, a videotape of which was seen on television

by millions, seemed to typify how all too many police officers feel
and act toward black citizens. That the officers even lined up, eager
to land another blow, reminded all black Americans that they
could well be the one lying on the ground. And the exoneration of
the officers, by jurors who lived far from the inner city, was taken
as mandating the police to do whatever they feel is needed to keep
blacks under control. Americans were telling the police to keep
inner-city "problems" from crossing the county line. In Los
Angeles, race was seen as more crucial than class. After all, it was
not misbehaving whites who worried suburban householders.

What happened in Los Angeles has been viewed in various
ways. Some have called it an uprising, a rebellion, an act of resistance to injustice and oppression. Others have seen it as a sponta-
neous outburst, an expression of pent-up anger and rage. Still
others have emphasized the massive looting, asking how theft can
be endowed with political motives.

The short answer is that all these factors were at work. Los
Angeles's South-Central section is part of inner-city America, in
which many thousands of black men, women, and children know
a poverty and a despair unmatched elsewhere in the advanced
world. Seen as subordinate citizens, they know they are scorned
by mainstream society, and few see hope for a change in their for-
tunes. Indeed, there had been similar rioting in Los Angeles and
elsewhere a quarter of a century earlier. Yet despite exhortations to
action and political promises, the festering conditions remained in
place. To burn down the shops you will need the next day may not
seem to make sense. But one cannot always expect peaceful
protests from people who have been rebuffed and betrayed by the
American dream.

Discontent like that which surfaced in Los Angeles will not easily be assuaged. Several dozen other cities could at some point
become scenes of similar disorder without planning or fore-
warning. Yet at the time of the Los Angeles riots, the most widespread worry among white Americans was that such carnage
might come closer to their homes. When this did not happen, they

turned to other concerns, choosing to forget about neighborhoods they would never enter and people they would never know. Nor was this difficult to do. It was only a matter of months before individuals living elsewhere had persuaded themselves that they bore no responsibility for the conditions that ignited the flames.

Is anyone responsible for the fact that a growing group of Americans, the majority of them black, feels imprisoned from birth behind forty-foot walls? They know they are regarded as superfluous, as excess human beings for whom the society has no need or use. Their belief that there is no way to escape those walls leads to desperation and despair. This explains why the Kerner Commission used the term "ghetto" to explain similar outbursts of a generation earlier:

> What white Americans have never fully understood—but what the Negro can never forget—is that white society is deeply implicated in the ghetto. White institutions created it, white institutions maintain it, and white society condones it.

By this time, we know the response. Most white Americans will protest that they have never done anything to oppress or exclude anyone of African ancestry. If blacks live behind a wall—and whites question even this assertion—they reply that they did not sanction or build it or even supply a single brick.

PRISONERS OF RACE

As hardly needs detailing, black political power is most visible in cities that have large poor populations and a declining economic base. Black mayors, black police chiefs, and black agency heads find themselves confronted with problems seldom faced by their white predecessors. Despite promises of becoming showcases of self-help, all too many cities have drifted into decay and dependency. While Detroit and Atlanta and Baltimore have plenty of decent and hardworking citizens, what they can contribute is overwhelmed by those around them who seem unable to make it on their own.

With economic investment going to the suburbs—or to distant states or overseas—fewer and fewer central cities can cover their costs through local taxes. Federal administrations have taken the view that they reap little benefit by propping up declining cities. State legislators, who come largely from small towns and suburbs, cannot be counted on to sympathize with a terrain they seldom visit and do not care to know. Admittedly, many white communities are poor, due to loss of industries or population or because they were never very productive. But since their misfortunes are not placed in a racial context, they often end up with proportionately more aid than do urban dwellers.

Politics worked well in the early struggles for civil rights: the right to vote, fair treatment in the courts, and entry to hotels and restaurants and other public accommodations. But after those victories, those concerned with racial redress began to talk of more radical measures. Debates over affirmative action, of qualifications versus quotas, deflect attention from more chronic disparities; in fact, that may be their purpose. At issue is whether the country can or will commit itself to so raise black Americans that they will stand on a social and economic parity with members of other races.

In a not-so-distant past, much was said about the need for "massive" measures to remedy ills resulting from poverty and racial inequities. Today such proposals are barely heard. The chief reason is that few white Americans feel any obligation to make any sacrifices on behalf of the nation's principal minority. They see themselves as already overtaxed, feel the fault is not theirs, and have become persuaded that public programs cannot achieve a cure. Instead, calls are heard for a tougher posture toward what is seen as the misbehavior of many blacks. The Republican party has regained its ascendancy by stressing these sentiments, easily undercutting the Democrats' bid for white votes.

So it is not a lack of leadership or a failure of will that has made common action so remote. The reasons rest with a past that has shaped our present and a present that makes use of that past. Race has made America its prisoner since the first chattels were landed on these shores. So the cause of disharmony runs deeper than the condition of the parties or the capacities of government. A nation that has done so much to stress racial divisions should not be surprised if the result is not compassion and fellow feeling but withdrawal and recriminations.

A VISITOR'S PREDICTIONS

As was noted in the Preface to this book, Gunnar Myrdal saw America beset by a social and moral paradox. Of all the world's nations, the United States speaks eloquently of universal justice and equal opportunity. Yet its treatment of its principal minority belies those basic commitments. But it may have been that Myrdal misread America's ideals. Alexis de Tocqueville, an earlier visitor, heard the same declarations, about equity and equality. However, he soon concluded that they were never intended to apply to members of the black race. White Americans, he observed, "scarcely acknowledge the common features of humanity in this stranger whom slavery has brought among them." Nor, Tocqueville added, would this racism disappear once slavery ended. In fact, he predicted, "the abolition of slavery will, in the common course of things, increase the repugnance of the white population for the blacks." The analysis in *Democracy in America,* reproduced on the next page, revealed racial enmities as so ingrained that Tocqueville predicted they would plague the future as they had haunted the past. His observations, set down a century and a half ago, might have been written today.

White Americans, Tocqueville noted, could countenance slavery only by persuading themselves that human beings of African origin were inherently "inferior to the other races of mankind"

ALEXIS DE TOCQUEVILLE
ON THE RACES IN AMERICA

The most formidable of all the ills that threaten the future of the Union arises from the presence of a black population upon its territory.

The whites and the blacks are placed in the situation of two foreign communities. These two races are fastened to each other without intermingling; and they are unable to separate entirely or to combine.

The Europeans chose their slaves from a race differing from their own, which many of them considered as inferior to the other races of mankind. Nor is this all: they scarcely acknowledge the common features of humanity in this stranger whom slavery has brought among them.

Although the law may abolish slavery, God alone can obliterate the traces of its existence. You may set the Negro free, but you cannot make him otherwise than an alien to those of European origin.

White Americans first violated every right of humanity by their treatment of the Negro. But with his liberty, he will acquire a degree of instruction that will enable him to appreciate his misfortunes and to discern a remedy for them.

If the Negroes are to be raised to the level of freemen, they will soon revolt at being deprived of almost all their civil rights. And as they cannot become the equals of the whites, they will speedily show themselves as enemies.

If I were called upon to predict the future, I should say that the abolition of slavery will, in the common course of things, increase the repugnance of the white population for the blacks.

The danger of a conflict between the white and the black inhabitants perpetually haunts the imagination of the Americans, like a painful dream.

and hence suited for bondage. This view, so firmly entrenched, would persist after emancipation. "You may set the Negro free," he told his American readers, "but you cannot make him otherwise than an alien to those of European origin." So citizenship for black Americans would always be shadowed by their past; they would ever remain outsiders to the nation's other inhabitants.

Sooner or later, Tocqueville said, black Americans would "revolt at being deprived of almost all their civil rights." And by this he meant not just legal entitlements but a lack of social and economic parity. Hence the visitor's final forecast, which haunts all phases of current life, from party politics to violent crime: "The danger of a conflict between the white and the black inhabitants perpetually haunts the imagination of the Americans, like a painful dream."

Alexis de Tocqueville knew that relations between the races— or their lack—are not formed in isolation. If race figures so centrally in the life of the United States, it has much to do with the kind of country America is and has been from its start. A combination of forces has served to heighten racial awareness and exacerbate tensions.

America is hardly the only nation to perpetuate racial prejudice and ethnic bigotry. Nor is it the worst by most objective measures. Even today, in such varied places as Northern Ireland and Sri Lanka and Rwanda, people are marked for slaughter because of tribal animosities and religious rivalries. Throughout Europe, the arrival of immigrants of African descent has generated new tensions, many of them strikingly similar to those long known in the United States.

Still, the United States considers itself more socially advanced than Sri Lanka and Rwanda, which means it sets a higher standard for human life and racial harmony. Most Americans are not especially surprised when they hear of groups murdering one another in Third World countries. Even compared with Europe, the United States has always prided itself on emphasizing equal treatment and social mobility. Given these aims and ideals, the United States carries a greater obligation to achieve amity and equity in relations between the races. The fact that it remains so far from its own goals justifies its subjection to scrutiny and its vulnerability to censure.

If America is short on excuses, it has no lack of explanations, most of them centering on its special history and circumstances. As was noted, to expect tolerance and fellow feeling from white Americans is to ask a great deal, considering the competitive pressures pervading their lives.

Hence the weight Americans have chosen to give to race, in particular to the artifact of "whiteness," which sets a floor on how far people of that complexion can fall. No matter how degraded their lives, white people are still allowed to believe that they possess the blood, the genes, the patrimony of superiority. No matter what happens, they can never become "black." White Americans of all classes have found it comforting to preserve blacks as a subordinate caste: a presence that despite all its pain and problems still provides whites with some solace in a stressful world.

A MORAL ISSUE

In the end, there remains the question of responsibility. The American tradition has said that all individuals are expected to make it on their own. Both the earliest settlers and current immigrants have known they had to enter the competition and create lives for themselves. Demands for special dispensations have never stirred much sympathy or support. (Even the Freedmen's Bureau, set up after the Civil War, had a brief and controversial history.) So most white Americans feel it is time for blacks to put their lives together and make what they can of themselves. They should muster the will to stay in school and gain the skills needed in today's economy. They can avoid having children they cannot support, just as they can steer clear of pursuits that end in self-destructive spirals.

Just to cite a single example: black youths have taken to carrying guns and firing them at one another, making homicide the most frequent cause of death among young men of their race. In part, these deaths are ways of settling scores within the drug industry, much as bootleggers dealt with competitors during Prohibition. More frightening are killings that result from random arguments or perceived disrespect. Not to mention scattered shots from rooftops or cars, which end up hitting children on the street. These would certainly seem to be acts for which the perpetrators should be held strictly responsible. How can the blame for such mayhem be laid at the door of white racism?

Yet it may also be asked *why* so many young men are engaging in what amounts to a self-inflicted genocide. While in one sense these are "free" acts, performed of personal volition, when they become so widespread, they must also be seen as expressing a despair that suffuses much of their race. These are young men who do not know whether they will live another year, and many have given up caring. If they are prepared to waste the lives of others, they will hardly be surprised if their turn comes next. No other American race is wounding itself so fatally. Nor can it be said that black Americans chose this path for themselves.

So in allocating responsibility, the response should be clear. It is white America that has made being black so disconsolate an estate. Legal slavery may be in the past, but segregation and subordination have been allowed to persist. Even today, America imposes a stigma on every black child at birth.

Of course, life can be unfair. We cannot vouchsafe that every infant will be born with sight or hearing or the full use of his or her limbs. However, not all disabilities derive from nature; many are contrived by society. Some have argued that black Americans deserve reparations for their centuries of bondage and subjection. That is what the argument about affirmative action is essentially about. Others claim that ratifying their status as victims will only perpetuate condescension and subordination. Moreover, it insults the many black Americans who have surmounted the most daunting of obstacles and made decent lives for themselves.

A huge racial chasm remains, and there are few signs that the coming century will see it closed. Almost one hundred and forty years after the ending of slavery, white America continues to ask of its black citizens an extra patience and perseverance that whites have never required of themselves. So the question for white Americans is essentially moral: is it right to impose on members of an entire race a lesser start in life and then to expect from them a measure of resolution that has never been asked of your own race?

STATISTICAL SOURCES

STATISTICAL REPORTS

(Figures are from websites as well as printed reports)

America's Families and Living Arrangements (Bureau of the Census, 2001). Source for tables on pages 89 and 96.

Births: Final Data for 2001 (National Center for Health Statistics, 2002). Source for tables on pages 92 and 105.

Capital Punishment Statistics (Bureau of Justice Statistics, 2002).

Cohabitation, Marriage, Divorce, and Remarriage (National Center for Health Statistics, 2002).

College-Bound Seniors: A Profile of SAT Program Test Takers (College Board, 2002). Source for tables on pages 164, 165, and 167.

Crime in the United States: Uniform Crime Reports (Federal Bureau of Investigation, 2001). Source for table on page 211.

Criminal Victimization 2000 (Bureau of Justice Statistics, 2001). Source for table on page 215.

Deaths: Final Data for 1999 (National Center for Health Statistics, September 2001).

Degrees and Other Awards Conferred; 1999–2000 (National Center for Education Statistics, December 2001). Source for table on page 136.

Digest of Education Statistics (National Center for Education Statistics, 2001). Source for tables on pages 136 and 205.

Educational Attainment in the United States (Bureau of the Census, 2000).

Employment and Earnings (Bureau of Labor Statistics, 2002). Source for tables on pages 120,130,132, and 136.

Fertility, Family Planning, and Women's Health (National Center for Health Statistics, 1997).

Fertility of American Women (Bureau of the Census, 2001).

First Marriage Dissolution, Divorce, and Remarriage (National Center for Health Statistics, 2001).

Hispanic or Latino by Race: 2000. Summary File 1, Table P8 (Bureau of the Census, 2001). Source for table on page 7.

How They Voted: A Portrait of American Politics (*New York Times,* November 12, 2000).

Living Arrangements of Children (Bureau of the Census, 2001). Source for tables on pages 89 and 96.

Money Income in the United States: 2000 (Bureau of the Census, 2001). Source for tables on pages 111, 112, 114, and 119.

Nonmarital Childbearing in the United States, 1940–1999 (National Center for Health Statistics, 2000). Source for tables on pages 92 and 103.

Poverty in the United States: 2000 (Bureau of the Census, September 2001). Source for table on page 117.

Prisoners in 2001 (Bureau of Justice Statistics, 2002). Source for table on page 224.

Profile of General Demographic Characteristics: 2000 (Bureau of the Census, 2001). Source for table on page 21.

Schools, Colleges, and Libraries. Internet database with racial breakdowns for individual institutions (National Center for Education Statistics, 2002). Source for tables on pages 162, 178, 183, and 184.

Statistical Abstract of the United States (Bureau of the Census, 2001). Source for tables on pages 119 and 120.

Teenage Births in the United States, 1991–2000 (National Center for Health Statistics, 2002).

Trends in Pregnancies and Pregnancy Rates by Outcome (National Center for Health Statistics, 2000).

EARLIER REPORTS

Detailed Characteristics 1970 (Bureau of the Census, February 1973). Source for tables on pages 21 and 132.

Detailed Occupations for the Civilian Labor Force 1980 (Bureau of the Census, 1983).

Family Composition 1970 (Bureau of the Census, 1973). Source for table on page 89.

Marital Status 1970 (Bureau of the Census, 1972). Source for table on page 96.

Race of Prisoners Admitted to State and Federal Institutions, 1926–1986 (Bureau of Justice Statistics, 1991). Source for table on page 224.

Vital Statistics of the United States: Natality 1970 (National Center for Health Statistics, 1975). Source for table on page 92.

QUOTED AND
CITED SOURCES

vii " 'Two nations' ": Benjamin Disraeli, *Sybil; or, The Two Nations* (1845).

vii " 'Our nation is moving . . .' ": *Report of the National Advisory Commission on Civil Disorders* (Dutton, 1968).

viii " 'The most formidable . . .' ": *Democracy in America,* translated by Henry Reeve and edited by Phillips Bradley (Vintage Books, 1956).

ix "among these are authors . . .": J. Anthony Lukas, *Common Ground* (Knopf, 1985); Elijah Anderson, *Streetwise: Race, Class, and Change in an Urban Community* (University of Chicago Press, 1990); Nicholas Lemann, *The Promised Land* (Knopf, 1991); Alex Kotlowitz, *There Are No Children Here* (Doubleday, 1991).

x Gunnar Myrdal, *An American Dilemma: The Negro Problem and Modern Democracy* (Harper and Brothers, 1944).

x Murray's best-known work is *Losing Ground: American Social Policy, 1950–1980* (Basic Books, 1984), and Wilson's is *The Truly Disadvantaged: The Inner City, the Underclass, and Public Policy* (University of Chicago Press, 1987). An interchange between Ravitch and Asante can be found in *The American Scholar,* Spring 1991.

33 " 'Nobody wishes more than I . . .' ": Letter to Benjamin Banneker, August 30, 1791, in *Thomas Jefferson: Writings,* edited by Merrill D. Peterson (Library of America, 1984).

35 William Shockley's views were confined to speeches before lay audiences. For Arthur Jensen, see "How Much Can We Boost IQ and Scholastic Achievement?" *Harvard Educational Review,* February 1969.

37 "a black chef . . . ,": *New York* magazine website (September 20, 2002).

37 "ideological positions.": See Nicholas Pastore, *The Nature-Nurture Controversy* (Kings Crown Press, 1949).

38 " 'ice people' . . . 'sun people' ": These phrases were devised by Leonard Jeffries, a professor of political science at the City University of New York. They are quoted in Arthur M. Schlesinger, Jr., *The Disuniting of America: Reflections on a Multicultural Society* (Whittle, 1991).

39 "cannot be called racists . . .": Coleman Young quoted in Ze'ev Crafets, *Devil's Night and Other Tales of Detroit* (Random House, 1990).

255

40   James Baldwin, *The Fire Next Time* (Dial Press, 1963).

43   "Ralph Ellison wrote . . .": Ellison in *Time,* April 6, 1970.

44   " 'two thoughts . . .' ": W. E. B. Du Bois, *The Souls of Black Folk* (1903), in *W. E. B. Du Bois: Writings,* edited by Nathan Huggins (Library of America, 1986).

45   " 'We're a different people.' ": August Wilson quoted in *New York Times,* April 15, 1990.

45   " 'At no moment . . .' ": Toni Morrison quoted in *New York Times,* January 15, 1986.

47   "usually about 85 percent . . .": See, for example, the survey reported in *New York Times,* April 1, 1987.

48   "Atrium Village": *New York Times,* July 24, 1987.

50   "reaches 10 percent . . .": Gerald Jaynes and Robin Williams, eds., *A Common Destiny: Blacks and American Society* (National Academy Press, 1989).

52   Ralph Ellison, *Invisible Man* (Random House, 1952).

56   " 'African-American . . .' ": *Political Trendletter* (Joint Center for Political and Economic Studies, March 1991).

57   "African names.": Communication from Professor Richard Allen, University of Michigan, September 2, 1989. Also see his article in the *American Political Science Review,* June 1989.

58   "from the Caribbean . . .": See Thomas Sowell, "The Fallacy of Racial Politics," *Harpers,* June 1984.

60   "Bangladesh.": Colin McCord and Harold Freeman, "Excess Mortality in Harlem," *New England Journal of Medicine,* January 18, 1990.

67   "support racial integration . . .": Howard Schuman, Charlotte Steeh, and Lawrence Bobo, *Racial Attitudes in America* (Harvard University Press, 1985).

78   "In exit polls where . . .": Larry Hugnick and John Zeglarski, "Polls During the Past Decade in Biracial Election Contests," paper delivered at the American Association for Public Opinion Research, May 1990.

79   " 'the nigger . . .' ": James Baldwin, *The Fire Next Time* (Dial Press, 1963).

79   " 'sex and race . . .' ": Gunnar Myrdal, *An American Dilemma: The Negro Problem and Modern Democracy* (Harper and Brothers, 1944).

88   "remained remarkably stable.": Herbert Gutman, *The Black Family in Slavery and Freedom: 1750–1925* (Random House, 1977).

90   " 'men's liberation.' ": Stanley Lebergott, *The American Economy: Income, Wealth, and Want* (Princeton University Press, 1976).

94   " 'absence of a father . . .' ": Andrew Cherlin, *Marriage, Divorce, Remarriage* (Harvard University Press, 1981).

94   " 'lack of a male income.' ": Also Cherlin, as above.

98   Table on Pregnancy Rates: E. F. Jones et al., "Teenage Pregnancy in Developed Countries, *Family Planning Perspectives,* March–April 1985.

100   "Equilla, Zanquisha, and Lakeisha . . .": Cathy Jackson, "Names Can Hurt," *Essence,* April 1989.

103   "end in abortions . . .": *An Overview of Abortion in the United States* (Alan Guttmacher Institute, 2002).

105   "overrun by conquerors or colonizers . . .": For an analysis of groups whose homes were subjected to conquest or colonization, see John Ogbu, "Minority Status and Literacy in Comparative Perspective," *Daedulus,* Spring 1990.

106   "a harsh analysis . . .": *The Negro Family: The Case for National Action* (U.S. Department of Labor, 1965).

113   "earnings of male attorneys . . .": Unpublished figures derived from the Public Use Microdata Sample of the 1990 census.

116   "a white underclass.": See, for example, James Howard Kunstler, "Schuylerville Stands Still," *New York Times Magazine,* April 25, 1990. For some urban counterparts, see Jay MacLeod, *Ain't No Making It* (Westview Press, 1987).

125   "headed by Oprah Winfrey . . .": "100 Top Celebrities," *Forbes* (June 20, 2002).

126   "black businesses are local . . .": See the analysis by the Joint Center for Political and Economic Studies published in *Focus,* October 1990.

127   "printed a list . . .": "50 Top Black Executives in Corporate America," *Ebony* (January 1992).

128   "three major corporations.": "The New Black Power," *Newsweek* (January 28, 2002).

128   "outside this country.": "How They Got There," *Forbes* (May 18, 1998).

140   "by no means new.": Much of the background material cited here, including the quotations from Lyndon Johnson and court decisions, relies on Melvin Urofsky's *A Conflict of Rights: The Supreme Court and Affirmative Action* (Scribner, 1991).

143   " 'find his proper element . . .' ": "Report on Manufactures," in *The Reports of Alexander Hamilton* (Harper and Row, 1964).

146   "being productive scholars . . .": Ernest Boyer, *College: The Undergraduate Experience in America* (Harper and Row, 1986).

146   " 'archaic rules . . .' ": Jesse Jackson quoted in *New York Times,* May 10, 1990.

147   "not an easy test . . .": See Lawrence Fuchs, *The American Kaleidoscope* (Wesleyan University Press, 1990).

156   "At Princeton . . .": *Journal of Blacks in Higher Education* (Winter 1997–1998).

157   "Harvard officials . . .": *Chronicle of Higher Education,* May 27, 1991.

157   "permissible goal . . .": *Bakke v. Board of Regents* 438 US 265 (1973).

158   "In 1981, only 3.8 percent . . .": *Freshman Admissions at Berkeley* (University

of California Academic Senate, 1989). Other 1980s figures for the University of California are from this report.

158 "Under the Texas system . . .": *How Affirmative Action Worked at the University of Texas School of Law* (University of Texas website, June 25, 2001).

159 " 'may not use race . . .' ": *Hopwood* v. *Texas* 861 F. Supp. (W. D. Texas, 1994); 78 F. 3d (5th Cir., 1996).

160 "on a 150-point scale . . .": "Judge Affirms Affirmative Action in Michigan Admissions Policy,": Associated Press, December 13, 2000.

160 " 'a racially diverse . . .' ": *Gratz* v. *Bollinger* 122 F. Supp 2nd (ED Mich Dec 2000); *Grutter* v. *Bollinger* 2002 Fed App. 0170P (6th Circ.).

163 " 'right for Harvard . . .' ": David Karen, "Who Gets into Harvard," Ph.D. thesis, Department of Sociology, Harvard University, 1985.

164 Table on Average SAT Scores: All aggregate SAT scores cited in this chapter, as well as personal information about the students taking the tests, come from unpublished reports provided by the College Board.

166 " 'no significant relation . . .' ": *Annual Report, 1966–1967* (Educational Testing Service). David McClelland, "Testing for Competence Rather than for 'Intelligence,' " *American Psychologist,* January 1973.

168 "in the business world.": See Daniel Goleman, "Successful Executives Rely on Their Own Kind of Intelligence," *New York Times,* July 31, 1984.

169 "a wider 'modern' consciousness . . .": The term "modern" is used by Jim Sleeper in *The Closest of Strangers* (Norton, 1990).

170 "children of immigrants.": *Philadelphia Inquirer,* May 10, 1988.

170 " 'telephone test . . .' ": See "The Next Wave," *New York,* May 12, 1980.

171 "California's medical school . . .": "Affirmative Action and Other Special Consideration Admissions," *Journal of the American Medical Association* (October 8, 1997).

174 " 'abandoned by the institution . . .' ": Jacqueline Fleming, *Black in College* (Jossey-Bass, 1984).

179 "the 115 schools . . .": *2002 NCAA Graduation Rates Report* (Indianapolis, Indiana: September 26, 2002).

185 "black students and faculty members.": See Adam Nossiter, "Separatism Down South," *Nation,* June 18, 1990.

190 "in the eighteen states . . .": Gary Orfield, *Schools More Separate: Consequences of a Decade of Resegregation* (The Civil Rights Project, Harvard University, 2001).

190 "retarded, disabled . . .": See Lori Granger and Bill Granger, *The Magic Feather* (Dutton, 1986).

192 " 'segregated once they are inside . . .' ": *New York Times,* February 18, 1990.

194 " 'attended desegregated schools . . .' ": Gerald Jaynes and Robin Williams, eds., *A Common Destiny: Blacks and American Society* (National Academy Press, 1989).

194   " 'Thrusting the black child . . .'": Harold B. Gerard, in Phyllis Katz and Dalmas Taylor, eds., *Eliminating Racism* (Plenum, 1988).

194   "optimal achievement . . .": Rita Mahard and Robert Crain, in Christine Rossell and Willis Hawley, eds., *The Consequences of School Desegregation* (Temple University Press, 1983).

195   "high school dropout rates . . .": *New York Times,* May 1, 1990.

196   " 'intellectual and educational oppression . . .'": *A Curriculum of Inclusion* (New York State Department of Education, 1989).

198   " 'Shakespeare or Emily Dickinson . . .'": *Visions of a Better Way* (Joint Center for Political Studies, 1989).

199   " 'apparently irrelevant topics . . .'": *New York Times,* June 24, 1988.

199   " 'telling . . . Eddie Murphy to shut up.'": Janice Hale-Benson quoted in *New York Times,* November 4, 1990.

200   "only 7.1 percent . . .": *New York Times,* August 27, 1990.

200   "Pre-Columbian sculptures . . . Lewis Howard Latimer . . .": Pat Brown of Indianapolis school system quoted in *New York Times,* October 10, 1990.

201   "cesarean sections . . .": Larry Obadele Williams of the Atlanta school system, in *Southern Education Foundation News,* December 1990.

201   "Vaccination . . . Carbon steel . . .": *African-American Baseline Essays* (Portland, Oregon, Public Schools, 1987).

201   " 'mental genocide.'": Leonard Jeffries, quoted in Andrew Sullivan, "Racism 101," *New Republic,* November 26, 1990.

203   " 'in private rather than public . . .'": Richard Alba, *Ethnic Identity: The Transformation of White America* (Yale University Press, 1990).

204   " 'men are disproportionately at risk . . .'": *Minorities in Higher Education,* Seventh Annual Status Report (American Council on Education, 1988).

208   "a nursing home chain . . ." and other citations: *Corporate Crime Reporter* (American Communications and Publishing, January–September, 2002).

210   "according to a study . . .": *Cellblocks or Classrooms?* (Justice Policy Institute, 2002).

217   "has political intentions . . .": Eldridge Cleaver, *Soul on Ice* (McGraw-Hill, 1967).

218   " 'a social contract . . .'": Bruce Wright, *Black Robes, White Justice* (Lyle Stuart, 1987).

225   " 'corporate crooks . . .'": *Fortune,* April 25, 1988.

232   "from 1980 to 1992 . . .": A. Leon Higginbotham, "The Case of the Missing Black Judges," *New York Times,* July 29, 1992.

232   "a Democratic president . . .": Kevin Murphy, "Clinton Doubled Black Judges," *Milwaukee Sentinel,* March 25, 2001.

232   "jurists of African ancestry . . .": *Judicial Selection Project* (Alliance for Justice, September 2002).

234 "Dinkins . . . 91 percent . . .": *New York Times,* November 9, 1989.

234 "Wilder's . . . 95 percent . . .": Joint Center for Political Studies, *Focus,* November–December 1989.

234 "Jackson . . . 92 percent . . .": *New York Times,* June 13, 1988.

235 " 'what you did to us . . .' ": Louis Farrakhan quoted in *New York Times,* March 29, 1990.

237 Table on black mayors: *Thirtieth Anniversary Count of Black Elected Officials* (Joint Center for Political and Economic Studies, 2002).

238 " 'representatives of their choice.' ": For a full analysis of the Voting Rights Act, see Abigail Thernstrom, *Whose Votes Count? Affirmative Action and Minority Voting Rights* (Harvard University Press, 1987).

241 " 'Racial classifications . . .' ": *Shaw* v. *Reno,* 509 US 630 (1993).

242 "an elongated district . . .": *Cromartie* v. *Hunt,* 119 S. Ct. 1545 (1999).

245 " 'implicated in the ghetto.' ": *Report of the National Advisory Commission on Civil Disorders* (Dutton, 1968).

247 "Alexis de Tocqueville . . .": *Democracy in America,* translated by Henry Reeve and edited by Phillips Bradley (Vintage Books, 1956).

ACKNOWLEDGMENTS

Two Nations owes its initial inspiration to Edward T. Chase, my editor at Scribner. It was he who suggested that a book like this needed to be written and I should take on that task. During the five years required for its completion, he offered every kind of encouragement an author wants and needs. I also benefited from the expert assistance of Scribner senior editor Bill Goldstein, as well as copy editor Estelle Laurence and designer Erich Hobbing. Lorrie Millman provided additional—and timely—help in shaping the manuscript and organizing the index. Amanda Patten, Mindy Werner, and Jason Warshof provided valuable editorial assistance for this updated edition.

Parts of this book first appeared, in somewhat different forms, as review/essays in *The New York Review of Books.* I am grateful to that publication for permission to reprint this material. And I owe particular thanks to Robert Silvers and Barbara Epstein for their steadfast attention and incisive suggestions.

Members of the reference staffs at the New York Public Library and the Queens College Library were invariably helpful in tracking down government documents. Margaret Padin-Bailo, Beverly Wright, and Marie Morales of the New York office of the Census Bureau went out of their way to provide me with updated figures.

My agent, Robin Straus, assisted at every stage, from the original outline to those penultimate months when this book finally began to take shape. Her enthusiasm and support are reflected on every page of *Two Nations*.

INDEX

culture (*cont.*)
  housing options for blacks and, 49
  multicultural identity and, 14
  racial differences in opinions and, 4
  segregation and, 62

Declaration of Independence, 31–32, 61
Democracy in America (Tocqueville),
  247–49
Democratic party, 231, 234, 246
Detroit, 25, 245–46
Dinkins, David, 234, 235, 236
discouraged workers, 121–22
discrimination, 57
  affirmative action and, 140, 150–52
  SAT scores and, 168
diversity, and education, 157–61
divorce
  black Americans and, 59, 90, 97
  white Americans and, 107
domestic service, 133–34
Dominicans, 7
Dre, Dr., 125
Du Bois, W.E.B., 44
Dukakis, Michael, 233

Ebony (magazine), 127
education, 155–72. *See also* colleges and
  universities
  Asian-Americans and, 12–13
  black teachers needed in, 199–200
  choices of blacks in, 50, 57
  community control of schools and,
  74–75
  curriculum expansion for variety of
  cultures in, 195–97
  emphasis on African history and culture and, 200–202
  employment and level of, 119–20
  equal opportunity and, 155
  Eurocentric orientation of curriculum
  in, 195–96
  focus on white achievements in, 53–55
  gender gap in, 135, 136, 204–5
  housing options of blacks and, 50
  income levels and, 111–12
  integration and, 173–74, 190, 193–95
  interracial comparisons for, 95, 136,
  145–46
  learning style differences and, 198–200
  marriage and, 95
  segregated schooling and, 173–87,
  190–91

special education classes and, 190–91
  tracking in, 191–92
  transmission-of-values hypothesis in,
  193–95
  white conservatives on, 66–67
Eisenhower, Dwight D., 140
Ejabat, Mory, 129
elections, 83
  candidates for state legislatures and,
  229–30
  crossover candidates and, 235–38
  voter registration drives and, 81
  voting along party and color lines in,
  233–34
  white voters and black candidates in,
  78, 228–29
Ellison, Ralph, 43, 52, 54
employment, 125–53. *See also* income
  affirmative action and, 139–53
  black men and, 118–19, 120
  black-owned enterprises and, 126–27
  black representation in occupations
  and, 129–33
  blacks in corporations and, 127–28
  business and blacks and, 137–39
  choices of blacks in, 46, 57, 58–59
  crime and lack of, 213, 224
  discouraged workers in, 121–22
  domestic service and, 133–34
  educational level and, 119–20
  fathers and families and, 88–89, 94–95
  gender gap in, 135–36
  legal and illegal immigrants and,
  58–59, 120–21, 153
  mothers in single-parent families and,
  94–95
  small business sector and, 126–27
  white conservatives on, 66–67
England, immigration from, 9, 10, 53, 54
English language, 9
entrepreneurship, and blacks, 126–27
Equal Employment Opportunity Commission, 140, 141
equal opportunity
  affirmative action compared with,
  155–56
  education and, 155
  racial differences in opinions on, 4
equal rights, 31–32
ethnic identity, 203. *See also* racial identity
ethnicity, and Hispanic groups, 7
eugenics, 35
Eurocentric orientation, 195–96